THEOLOGY
AND CHURCH
IN
TIMES OF CHANGE

Edited by
EDWARD LeROY LONG, JR.
and
ROBERT T. HANDY

THE WESTMINSTER PRESS

Philadelphia

Scripture quotations from the Revised Standard Version of the Bible are copyright, 1946 and 1952, by the Division of Christian Education of the National Council of Churches, and are used by permission.

ISBN 0–664–20881–9

LIBRARY OF CONGRESS CATALOG CARD No. 78–96699

BOOK DESIGN BY
DOROTHY ALDEN SMITH

Published by The Westminster Press ®
Philadelphia, Pennsylvania

PRINTED IN THE UNITED STATES OF AMERICA

CONTENTS

PART THREE

The Person and Thought of John Coleman Bennett

ESSAYS IN HONOR OF
JOHN COLEMAN BENNETT

❖ ❖ ❖ *Henry Pitney Van Dusen is President Emeritus and Lamont Professor of Christian Theology Emeritus of Union Theological Seminary. Following his graduation from Princeton, he completed the B.D. at Union and earned the Ph.D at Edinburgh. He served as a member of the Union faculty from 1926 until his retirement in 1963; he was Dean of Students in the 1930's and was elected president of the seminary in 1945. He has played prominent roles in the missionary and ecumenical life of the Christian churches, and has served on the boards of trustees of many educational institutions. His many interests have been reflected in the wide range of his publications as contributor, editor, and author. Among his some twenty books are* Spirit, Son and Father: Christian Faith in the Light of the Holy Spirit (1958), *and* Dag Hammarskjöld: The Statesman and His Faith (1967). *With John T. McNeill and John Baillie, he has been editor of* The Library of Christian Classics.

PREFACE

❖ ❖ ❖ *Henry Pitney Van Dusen*

FRIENDS AND ADMIRERS of John Coleman Bennett—they are legion—and especially the hundreds of his former students and colleagues will rejoice that he is being honored on his retirement from the presidency of Union Seminary. As they turn the pages of this volume, they will be even more gratified by the appropriateness and uniformly high quality of this tribute. Those of us who are privileged to share in it, whether by full-length essays or in these few introductory pages, would wish to join in gratitude to the editors, Robert T. Handy and Edward LeRoy Long, Jr., for their masterly conception, enlistment of contributors, and able editorship in our behalf.

My close friendship and rare colleagueship with John Bennett has been continuous across forty-three years. Those who knew the diffident and modest young man who entered Union Seminary in the autumn of 1926, after two years of theological study at Mansfield College, Oxford, following graduation from Williams College, could never have foreseen the mature man of exceptional force as well as the distinguished scholar and leader of today. To be sure, some basic and persistent characteristics were already foreshadowed—intellectual preeminence, outgoing if shy friendliness, and, above all, bold and determined dedication to unconventional reform. At Williams he had declined to have any part in the fraternity system decades before it was abolished. If "balance" has rightly been identified by Daniel Day Williams as the controlling principle of his thought, undeviating "consistency" is perhaps the most outstanding mark of his life practice.

This volume, concerned with theology, inevitably stresses John Bennett's contributions to theological interpretation. Not until an index is prepared will it be discovered how many times his name dots these pages, not through deliberate intent, but because only thus can the wide-ranging themes of successive chapters be adequately set forth. However, this natural stress is somewhat at the expense of another facet of his life which, in the end of the day, may be more significant and may loom more prominently when a definitive biography is prepared, may it be many years hence. That is: concrete achievement in action. For, with all his devotion to learning and teaching, John Bennett has been, all along the way, in the best sense an "activist." Indeed, at the core of his being, he is a "reformer." I suspect that history will so categorize him.

Take Dr. Bennett's role in ecumenical Christianity. In his touchingly personal profile of the man, Reinhold Niebuhr has focused upon John Bennett's contributions to the thought of the Oxford Conference (1937) and the Amsterdam Assembly (1948). However, he first emerged upon the ecumenical scene as secretary of the Oxford Section on "Church, Community, and State in Relation to the Economic Order." He appeared in the same capacity at Amsterdam. And at the Second Assembly of the World Council of Churches at Evanston in 1954, he was vice-chairman of Section III on "Social Questions"; he had been co-chairman of the Preparatory Commission. From its first beginnings, he was a key figure—one is tempted to say *the* chief leader—in the World Council of Churches Department of Church and Society. His crowning achievement in this area may well have been in the projection, preparations, and then participation in the World Conference on Church and Society in 1966— probably the most creative and formative ecumenical meeting other than World Council Assemblies. Again, at the Uppsala World Council Assembly in 1968 he continued in his well-established role. John Bennett is today the senior American churchman in unbroken leadership within the ecumenical movement.

Dr. Bennett is best known and usually regarded as a "social theologian." No wonder; most of his writings and activities have been in that area. His successive professorial appointments on the Union Seminary faculty have been so named, presently as Reinhold Niebuhr Professor of Social Ethics. But he began as a teacher in Systematic Theology and the Philosophy of Religion; and his chairs at Auburn Seminary and the Pacific School of Religion were in Christian Theology. Dr. Daniel Day Williams has performed an invaluable service in interpreting him as a Christian theologian. I confess that, familiar as I supposed I was with every aspect of John Bennett's teaching and writing, I had not appreciated the range, balance, and inclusiveness of his thought until I read Dr. Williams' essay prepared for this volume.

What the church needs most today is precisely the "balanced" catholic and evangelical liberalism of which John Bennett is our ablest and most persuasive exponent. In the leisure and perspective of retirement, it is my hope that he will devote his major energies to the further elucidation and elaboration of the rounded and complete Christian theology which Dr. Williams has so illuminatingly and convincingly set forth. Dr. Bennett himself would shudder at the suggestion of a Bennett School of Theological Thought; his ingrained and unfailing modesty as well as his basic principles would disavow such an idea. Nevertheless, I must repeat: what American Christianity, indeed world Christianity, awaits as a cure of its aberrations and delivery from its morasses is John Coleman Bennett's determinative influence upon its theology. May this volume contribute to that much-to-be-desired end.

Scholar, Theologian, Teacher, Administrator, Prophet, Reformer, Theological Educator, Writer—these are among the titles by which John Bennett might be characterized. I suggest there is another, far more fundamental, far more inclusive, far more appropriate— *Christian statesman*. I shall venture the forecast that it is as Christian statesman that John Bennett's life and achievements will be recorded in the annals of the history of this tortured, confused, and despairing age.

PART ONE

The Life and Thought
of the People of God

❖ ❖ ❖ *Robert McAfee Brown has won a major place in the contemporary theological world not only through his many writings on a wide range of significant topics but also by his forceful participation in church, ecumenical, and public affairs. He was educated at Amherst College; Union Theological Seminary; Mansfield College in Oxford; and received his Ph.D. from Columbia University in 1951. He has served in the Navy chaplaincy, in the pastorate, and in teaching posts at Amherst, Macalester College, Union Theological Seminary, and Stanford University, where he is now Professor of Religion in Humanities Special Programs. Among his many books are* The Spirit of Protestantism (1961), Observer in Rome (1964), *which is an account of his experiences as a Protestant observer at the Second Vatican Council, and* The Ecumenical Revolution (*revised and expanded edition, 1969*). *He is joint author, with Abraham J. Heschel and Michael Novak, of* Vietnam: Crisis of Conscience (1967).*

In the following essay Professor Brown devotes his attention to the burning question of how theological method must change in order to speak with relevance and power to a world in turmoil.

1

THEOLOGY AND THE GOSPEL:
REFLECTIONS
ON
THEOLOGICAL METHOD

✧ ✧ ✧ *Robert McAfee Brown*

THE FUNDAMENTAL WORD in the theme of this chapter is not "theology" but "gospel." "Gospel," as all but the most unlettered know, comes from the Greek *euangelion,* and means "good news." It describes what is constitutive about the Christian faith. The gospel itself is not a word but a deed—something happened; and theology is only the attempt to reflect upon the meaning of the deed —*what* happened, and what does it mean for us? Thus theology is always subordinate to gospel, since thinking about the meaning of good news can occur only after there has been some good news to think about. It is the perennial temptation of theology to seek to replace that about which it is reporting, as though (to borrow an image from Kierkegaard) one could expect a love letter to be intrinsically more important to its possessor than the actual presence of the beloved.

The word "gospel," interestingly enough, has not become outdated even in the most *avant garde* theological circles today. The outstanding proponent of the "death of God" theology, for example, describes his position as "the gospel of Christian atheism,"[1] and with the new stress on Christian hope as the theological wave of the future, the descriptive term "gospel," or "good news," is even more appropriate.[2] A man of another era, G. K. Chesterton, could even speak of "the good news of original sin." In the current stress on the ethical involvement of Christians in the world, many are reconstructing an updated version of what was once called the "social gospel," always being careful to point out that the new version avoids the limitations of its predecessor—an interesting example of the enduring character of *hubris* within the theological enterprise.

So the contention that the Christian faith is fundamentally gospel, "good news," is widely accepted. Even those whose faith compels them to leave institutional Christianity presumably believe that such faith is a liberation, and hence good news of a significant sort, since liberation is always preferable to bondage.[3]

It is when we attempt to describe the content of this good news, or gospel, that the difficulties begin. I shall shortly suggest that any "reflections on theological method" (to give the subtitle its due) have to seek new ways both of raising the question about the gospel and of finding ways to answer the question once it has been legitimately posed. But even here, there may be a broader base on which to launch an investigation than might be assumed in this period of theological disarray. Historically, of course, the gospel has always centered on a series of claims made about a first-century Jew, Jeshua bar-Joseph, who so spoke and acted that those whom he confronted felt themselves confronted by God himself, incarnate in this very human life, in a way that both judged and redeemed those who knew him. The Biblical language is straightforward: "The Word became flesh and dwelt among us"; "God was in Christ reconciling the world to himself"; "He who has seen me has seen the Father."

In the creedal controversies of the third and fourth centuries an attempt was made to systematize such affirmation. It is important to recall that the first great problem in Christian theology was to safeguard the *humanity* of him by whom the revelation came in its fullness. Even so, if subsequent centuries have erred in what they have said about the central actor in this drama, it has been to err on the side of downgrading the humanity rather than the divinity of Jesus of Nazareth, whom men call the Christ. Today, surely, this possible imbalance is being redressed, and the emphasis is upon assuring, whatever else is assured, that Jesus of Nazareth was fully one with us, that he was "in every respect . . . tempted as we are," that he is discovered first and foremost as the "man for others," and that it is, not by abstract speculation about his person, but by existential involvement in his work, that men will truly come to know him. Even those who most loudly proclaim the "death of God" have held, sometimes nostalgically and wistfully, sometimes tenaciously, to the impact of Jesus of Nazareth upon them and for them.[4]

Theology, of course, is not just Christology, but its starting point and inspiration have surely been Christological from the beginning. So there is also more to start with at this pole of our subject than might at first seem apparent.

I. A Backward Look for Perspective

The attempt of theology to reflect upon the primal data of the Christian revelation has gone through some interesting permutations and gyrations during the lifetime of the man whom these essays attempt to honor. The early part of John Bennett's theological career coincided with the height of theological liberalism, of which he was indeed an exemplary product. This position took with utmost seriousness its self-won emancipation from Biblical fundamentalism, the new horizons toward truth offered by scientific investigation, the willingness to see truth in as wide a variety of ways as possible, the recognition that reason had much to contribute to the life of faith, and the ongoing attempt to relate the gospel to the social and secular affairs of men. Liberalism has probably suffered an exceptionally bad press in the wake of its successor, neo-orthodoxy, which stressed a return to Biblical faith and imagery, a recognition that the foolishness of God was likely to be wiser than the wisdom of men even if it had to be expressed in paradox, a critique of secular (and religious) optimisms, and a considerably chastened estimate, in the light of two world wars, of what could be hoped for, let alone achieved, on the human scene. In this movement too, John Bennett has been a participating critic, and his transitional essay on the doctrine of man is a model of how old movements can contribute to new.[5]

But methodologies change quickly, and neo-orthodoxy, which was largely a Protestant phenomenon, shortly began to be displaced by what could be called "ecumenical theology," a movement in which John Bennett has played an ongoing role. First developed as the member churches of what became the World Council of Churches began to think of work together, ecumenical theology represented the beginning of a breakthrough from continental and Anglo-Saxon domination that gradually reached in more worldwide directions.[6] But this brand of ecumenism itself very soon turned out to be too parochial, for even as it was developing, the Roman Catholic Church, after centuries of its own style of parochialism, began to be an active participant on the ecumenical scene, and with the completion of the Second Vatican Council (1962–1965) it was clear that no Protestant, Orthodox, or Catholic thinker could any longer theologize without taking full account of what was being done in the other Christian confessional bodies. In this task, likewise, John Bennett has been at the forefront.

It would be pleasant to report that this is where theology now stands, and that the task is simply to weave together creatively the strands of the major traditions that have thus confronted one another. But such a response would be far too simple. For to anyone with eyes to see, it is clear that much contemporary ecumenical theological discussion is no more than a tiny group of people talking to one another, while the rest of the world simply couldn't care less. Two things, at least, have brought this about: (*a*) many persons *within* the church have found themselves unpersuaded by the formulations of the past and are searching in radically new directions, and (*b*) most persons *outside* the church have moved from hostility to indifference. We live in an age of massive disaffection with the Christian faith, and it is the first task of theological method to ponder the consequences of this situation with utmost seriousness. To great numbers of mankind, the stifling of a yawn would be about as close as they could come to responding to either gospel or theology.

Let us trace this path once more in a slightly different sequence. The theological odyssey of most of the writers in this volume, colleagues and students of John Bennett, has probably been rather similar. Most of us, too, were children of theological liberalism, well nourished by it during our college days. We went through exciting and threatening times of theological maturation at the feet not only of John Bennett but also of Reinhold Niebuhr, Paul Tillich, Richard Niebuhr, and others, through whom we also appropriated (with varying degres of enthusiasm) Barth, Brunner, Bultmann, and other giants from the Continent. Many of us, not discerning men of similar caliber in our own theological generation, conceived our task as that of "translating" the theological giants who had been our mentors into the idiom of our own generation.

We could not have been more mistaken. For however much we continue to draw upon such teachers (William Hamilton has characterized Harvey Cox's *The Secular City* as "pop Barth"), our primary task has become more basic. It is to discover a new mode of communication with a new generation asking new questions, indeed to discover for ourselves a way of thinking through problems which we once thought we had worked out and "solved" but which we discover to be once again immensely perplexing and threatening, and for which old modes and methodologies simply do not work. This does not mean that we may not ultimately end up closer to our forefathers than might now seem likely, but it does mean that we must get there by new questions, by new routes, and (provisionally at least) by new forms to our answers.

If one is to characterize this new situation to which we are called upon to speak, perhaps the most useful description is to call it the radical rediscovery of the secular. To many, such words have become no more than fad or fetish, and they must be rescued from such abuse. Some indeed will respond that the characterization is already out of date.[7] But what I am trying to suggest, without waving flags or brandishing slogans, is that this widespread affirmation of the secular, far from being a passing mood of the moment, is a fundamental relocation of our understanding of the human enterprise, and that theology has an obligation to respond to it with considerable sympathy and alacrity. I am talking about a deep-seated kind of human orientation, based on the fact that we have now *consciously* entered into the technological era in which machines can do many things we used to think only men could do and can do them more efficiently; in which the emancipation of modern man from an obsessive hope of heaven or fear of hell enables him to affirm his present world as a world of incredible possibilities; in which the old authorities to which theology used to point (Scripture, papacy, tradition, the binding nature of the Christian conscience) are questioned if not discarded by increasing numbers of thinking people. Men have faith, to be sure, but it is a radically this-worldly faith, faith in man, faith in the future, faith in technology, faith in intelligence. In the face of all this it will no longer do simply to sound our doomsday warnings about human pride and pretension; for with all his problems modern man has a lot going for him and can certainly make a strong case that he has achieved this not only without benefit of clergy but in the face of centuries of clerical opposition, and that on both counts he sees no reason to invoke clerical help in the future.

There is a sense, of course, in which none of this ought to be the least bit surprising to us. For surely no theology that has had at its center such doctrines as those of creation and incarnation ought to be surprised when men take seriously the goodness of the earth (as any doctrine of creation should persuade them to do) and seek to enhance the human situation (as any doctrine of incarnation should persuade them to do). Indeed, there are those such as Freidrich Gogarten and Arend van Leeuwen who have argued that modern secularization is nothing but an inevitable outgrowth of a Biblical faith that knows what it is about.[8]

Nevertheless, what we have today is not simply more of the same, but a new atmosphere rooted not only in Biblical faith but in Enlightenment and Renaissance faith as well, where in the very midst of the frightening abyss that our technological power opens before us, of which neo-orthodoxy properly made us all aware, there are also incredible new human possibilities that simply were not present before. It is now within our grasp, for example, to achieve a world in which no one is without food and shelter, and in which all are educated. That we do not achieve these ends, and probably will not in the foreseeable future, is an ongoing tribute to the tenacity of human pride and selfishness, but the point for the moment is that mankind has never before had such possibilities technically within reach. To this extent, at least, it is an entirely new situation, unlike any that man has faced before.

II. A Forward Look for Direction

In the face of such a new set of circumstances, what can we say about the shape of a theological method able to learn from, cope with, and speak to such facts? I suggest half a dozen ingredients for such a stance.

a. *We must be willing to let the questions be framed for us.* We can no longer presume to tell the world that we know its own mind even better than it does itself and that it should accept our diagnosis of its ailments and possibilities. Bonhoeffer spoke a persuasive word when he reminded us that it is no part of our task to pound people over the head with the reality of sin so that we can then preach the releasing word of grace.[9] In more pedestrian terms the point is made in a Thurber cartoon in which a woman has just succeeded in touching with her toe a hat held by a male companion several feet above her head. A look of ecstasy is upon her face at this magnificent achievement. A Thurber man, watching the scene, is muttering, "Unhappy woman!"

The "in" way to make the point these days is to say that "the world must write the agenda for the church." Initially this sounded to me like the worst kind of "accommodation theology," but I shortly became persuaded that it enshrined a real truth for our generation, however much it may latterly have approached the nature of a cliché. For it means that the church (and theology) are called upon to participate in a life of servanthood, to respond to and to be present at every basic point of human need. Binding up the wounds of the injured and feeding the hungry, whatever their contemporary political counterparts may imply for the church, can thus not be looked upon as the mere busywork of a social service agency but as ways of incarnating the fundamental character of Christian *diakonia*, which means not to be ministered unto but to minister.

Where, then, are the points of human need? We will discover them not so much by meditating in our seminaries or classrooms or pastors' studies as we will by listening to the cries of our contemporaries, even more by participating in the common human venture with more than a grudgingly minimal openness. For example, a theology truly concerned with the gospel will listen with intentness and penitence to the cry of "black power." What is being said in this cry? What are we learning through it of human exploitation? What are we learning about the white man's sins? What is it telling us about the church's blindness in past and present? We will do our "devotional reading" less from Thomas à Kempis than from the report of the Presidential Commission on Civil Disorders. Our "retreats" will be less to the countryside than to the inner city. If we read *A Diary of Private Prayer*, we will also read *The Diary of Che Guevara*. Along with *Christianity and Crisis* we will also consult *The New Republic* or *The Village Voice*. Next to Niebuhr's *Nature and Destiny of Man* will be Marcuse's *One-Dimensional Man*. We will listen not only to leaders of the church but to leaders of the S.D.S. When we seek to deepen dialogue, it will be not only with Vatican Council fathers such as Cardinal Suenens but with French Marxists such as Roger Garaudy. It will be out of such exposure and involvement that the problems and possibilities of a new theology will be forged.

One reason it seems possible for theology to adopt this new posture is that most of us who are called theologians are less insulated from "the world" than we may once have been. For most of us it is no longer the case that "we" are set apart from "the world." We are a part of that world. Its questions have become our questions. When we listen to what the world is asking we are hearing our own voices and consciences. In a way that may be quite different from the original meaning of the imagery, we are once again citizens of two cities—the city of faith and the city of doubt, the church and the university, the church and the suburb, the church and the inner city.

b. *We must recognize that the questions will come from the sciences as well as the humanities.* In recent years theology has engaged in a significant interplay with history, political science, urban sociology, philosophy, and literature.[10] All this has been to the good. We have had new concerns focused for us and new questions posed. But in a way quite different from the earlier "science and religion" controversies, the physical sciences may now be the disciplines that are going to pose the new questions and problems for us. For while those in the humanities continue to reflect upon the meaning of the human venture, the scientists are also struggling existentially with the great decisions that dictate the future of the human venture.[11]

What is life, and how does one determine when it has ceased? Doctors have to struggle with the question in deciding when an organ can be removed from one individual and transplanted to another.

What criteria determine the worth of one human life over against another? Translation: who gets the artificial kidney when there are ten potential recipients and only one machine?

Is man more than a complicated bit of electrical circuitry? Is he worth as much as a good machine? The cybernetic revolution is confronting increasing numbers of people with the disturbing information that they are worth less to society than a computer that can not only do the job they used to do but can do it ten times more accurately in one millionth of the time.

Is man's value measured by what he contributes to society? The old ethic (much too loosely called "the Protestant work ethic") answered "yes." But today, due to the extraordinary efficiency of the above-mentioned machines, many persons can no longer contribute significantly to society and can only receive from society. What does this say about the nature of the *humanum?*

Have a few people the right to determine the future of the race?

Some biologists are close to achieving this by their ability to manipulate the genetic code. Some research scientists are already able to do this, if so requested, by means of the deadly germ warfare products they have manufactured. Some physicists can place the whole human venture in jeopardy by the chain reactions they may set loose in atomic experiments, let alone the genetic damage they may cause to future generations by atomic fallout.

These are only a sampling of the hard, tough problems with which most theologians quite rightly feel ill-equipped to cope. And it will be only by listening and by extending the scope of our listening to include the scientists that theologians will be able to understand, and cope with, the world of today and tomorrow.[12]

c. *We must acknowledge that the theological thrust will be less directed to inner church concerns and more directed to outer world concerns.* Part of a rediscovery of the secular is a rediscovery that God does not first of all love the church, but the world. In Christ he was not reconciling the church to himself, but the world. The church can no longer be understood as a rather special arena in which God operates; rather, it must be understood as that portion of the world which is already aware of God's work in the world, which looks for the signs of his presence and seeks both to draw attention to those signs and to employ men in working with God in those places where his love and concern have become manifest. The church, then, is for the sake of the world, rather than vice versa. And to whatever degree theology concerns itself with the church (as it will surely continue to do) such concern must be a functional one, designed to equip the church more adequately to fulfill its mission in and for the world. Truth is in order to goodness, as our forefathers said long ago. Inner concern will be for the sake of outer concern. But the task of outer concern must now claim a certain priority so that inner concern will not be too all-absorbing or too irrelevant.

This kind of direction can be illustrated by what has been happening within the World Council of Churches.[13] The original ecumenical impetus in our century came from the World Missionary Conference of 1910, in Edinburgh. The conference was designed to help missionary societies develop a common strategy for reaching out to the unconverted world. As the World Council of Churches gradually developed, it emerged as the confluence of two streams, both flowing from Edinburgh. One stream was Faith and Order

24   THE LIFE AND THOUGHT OF THE PEOPLE OF GOD

(dealing mainly with internal matters of theology and doctrine); the other Life and Work (dealing mainly with external matters of "church and world").[14] Both emphases were present in the World Council from the start, but it is surely fair to say that in the early years more stress was placed upon the former emphasis than upon the latter. This was probably as it should be, for the churches had hundreds of years of suspicion and downright animosity to overcome in their dealings with one another, and ecumenism was thus a concern for restoring unity in the divided Christian family.

But in recent years the emphasis appears to have been changing. Increasing attention has been given to the themes of Life and Work, and three events can be cited in support of this contention. The first of these was the Geneva Conference of July, 1966, on "Christians in the Technical and Social Revolutions of Our Time," which discussed the following themes: "Economic Development in a World Perspective," "The Nature and Function of the State in a Revolutionary Age," "Structures of International Cooperation—Living Together in Peace in a Pluralistic Society," and "Man and Community in Changing Societies."[15] The ecumenical flavor of the conference is indicated by the fact that a number of Roman Catholic observers and guests played significant roles in its deliberations.

The second event was the Beirut Conference of April, 1968, dealing with the theme "World Development: The Challenge to the Churches." This conference had an even stronger ecumenical flavor, since it was jointly sponsored by the World Council of Churches and the Pontifical Commission for Justice and Peace. This conference dealt specifically with many of the concerns voiced at the Geneva conference and recommended that official joint structures for implementing world development be established by the World Council of Churches and the Roman Catholic Church.[16]

The third event was the Fourth Assembly of the World Council of Churches, held at Uppsala in July, 1968. This assembly not only gave official implementation to the proposals of the Beirut conference, but its overall emphases symbolized the decision to move from inner ecclesiastical concerns to outer world concerns. Of the six discussion sections, five were dealing quite distinctly with the theme of "The Church and the World," while the remaining section, dealing with "The Holy Spirit and the Catholicity of the Church," gave ample evidence that, as the report put it, "The churches need a new openness to the world in its aspirations, its achievements, its restlessness and its despair." The reports of the sections dealing with "World Economic and Social Development" (specifically implementing the concerns of Geneva and Beirut) and "Towards Justice and Peace in International Affairs" were particularly significant examples of an attempt to turn ecumenical attention to the immediacy of issues such as underdeveloped nations, racism, trade policies, selective conscientious objection, and human rights.[17]

d. *We must recognize that theology will clarify and fulfill its task as much by doing as by thinking.* Victories won by exploiting a distinction between "thought" and "action" are usually too cheaply won. Thought is seldom thought in a vacuum, and action usually presupposes a set of basic assumptions in terms of which one acts. But the interrelationship of the two has a new urgency on the contemporary theological scene. For as theologians face the new questions of our age, it will no longer be possible for them to retire to their studies to figure out the answers. Significant answers, I suggest, will come only in an existential, acted response to the questions. Theologians and churchmen, confronted with new questions demanding decisions, will no longer have the luxury of time to ponder all angles, check out the church fathers, see what Aquinas and Luther thought, and even having done so, find that thought relevant. It will be only out of the further anguish of personal wrestling with the new questions, sometimes wrongly at first, that insight may begin to emerge. The theologian cannot be mainly a thinker; he must also be an actor, a participant.

Martin Buber has some hard but important words for us in this situation. "The intellect," he writes, "can be redeemed from its last lapse into sin, from the desecration of the word, only if the word is backed and vouched for with the whole of one's life."[18]

Nothing could be more threatening. But I think the only way the theologian will be able to speak authentically in the world today will be as he, in the contemporary expression, puts his body where his words are. Indeed, it may be only as he puts his body somewhere that he can actually discover what his words should be, and that the deed itself may be his definitive theological expression.[19]

An illustration of these uncomfortable truths in our days comes from the concern of the American churches with the war in Vietnam, and it is a tribute to the man to whom this *Festschrift* is offered that he has been at the forefront of the struggle and that he has been an inspiration for many more timid than he. In World

War II, the moral issues seemed relatively clear to most churchmen: Nazism represented something so evil, and so inhuman, that resistance to it was not only justified, so many theologians felt, but required by the Christian conscience. The great evil that the Allies had to do in defeating Nazism was justified by the even greater evil that would have resulted for mankind had Nazism not been defeated by whatever means were required.

But such considerations do not seem valid for most of the same people in relation to Vietnam.[20] They have considered the war morally intolerable, politically wrong, economically disastrous, and humanly brutalizing. They have been (until recently) in the minority in so thinking. Their judgments have forced them to disagree with the judgment of publicly elected officials and have forced upon them the disturbing discovery that there were no vehicles within the ordinary democratic processes through which their intensely held convictions could be adequately voiced. They also found, as men well beyond draft age, that the burden of fighting an immoral war was not being borne by them but by young men who likewise felt the war to be immoral, but to whom the only options given by their government were (1) to fight against conscience, (2) to leave the country, or (3) to go to jail.

In the resultant situation in which many Christian consciences found no vehicle of expression through lawful procedures, the whole issue of illegal activity—of deliberately breaking the law, of risking years in jail, of denouncing the decisions of duly elected authorities, was raised in a new and poignant manner. Parallels from the German Church's opposition to Hitler were of some help in developing convictions, but not of full utility, since even at their worst American administrations can hardly be accused of being totalitarian.

The point of the above discussion is not to make a moral indictment of contemporary American administrations (although I believe history will render such a verdict) but to suggest that in taking seriously the injunction "We must obey God rather than men" (Acts 5:29), it was little help merely to theorize about the issues and develop axioms to govern conduct. It was only by actual involvement that one could truly discover the moral poignancy of the issues, and through engagement and encounter discover viable means of dealing with them. Proclaiming a theology of civil disobedience, for example, had little meaning until those proclaiming it were themselves ready to engage in civil disobedience for the sake of the gospel.

I suggest that those theologians who have been, to whatever degree, "radicalized" by the necessity to oppose American foreign policy in Southeast Asia, have come to their theological understanding of this position not only by reading books and speeches but by active involvement in marches, demonstrations, draft card turn-ins, court appearances on behalf of noncooperators, and whatever else has served to remind them existentially that human lives are at stake and that the one who stands with another human being is best equipped to speak about the theological dimension of that human being's situation.

Whatever theology emerges, therefore, about the relationship of conscience and the state will emerge as much from the active involvement of those who theologize about it as from their intellectual grasp of earlier ways of dealing with the problem.

e. *We must anticipate that theological method in the future will probably become more inductive than deductive.* We have lived through a theological generation that has emphasized the priority of revelation. It has insisted that we start from the Word instead of the world, that Jesus Christ is not only the Omega but also the Alpha, and that our human response is always precisely a response and not the initiating factor. Such an approach is being challenged today, and it may be that the old scholastic distinction between the *ordo essendi* and the *ordo cognoscendi,* between the order of being and the order of knowing, may be of use in the discussion. Certainly God is the first fact and not the last, but we do not always know him first as the first fact. We may not know him for a long time, if at all, but we may, whether we know it or not, be working our way toward him, even if finally at the end of the day, having found him, we make the discovery that he actually found us long before, and that our whole quest was no more than the grace-impelled pilgrimage on which he guided our feet all the while.

I firmly believe in the prevenience of grace and in the *pensée* of Pascal, where Jesus says, "Console thyself, thou wouldst not seek Me, if thou hadst not found Me,"[21] but I have more recently come to believe that such an exhortation can be an extremely inept apologetic device, particularly when employed prematurely. This is surely a conclusion to which the Christian comes, but it is not a conclusion one Christian can thrust upon another.

All this is by way of making the point that in the existential experience of our generation, the *ordo cognoscendi* is likely to develop a set of starting points for the theological venture that is almost exactly the reverse of those articulated by our immediate predecessors.

To illustrate: we may well move, for example, *from ethics to theology,* and not vice versa. In the past, ethics has usually been seen as the outgrowth of theology. The first commandment is, after all, to love God, and having attempted that, one does discover that one must love the neighbor, because the neighbor is likewise God's creation and loved by him. But for our generation it may well be that, as Horst Symanowski has pointed out, the real issue is not the discovery of the gracious God but the discovery of a gracious neighbor. All of us find many people these days who do not believe in God and yet who love their neighbors intensely, with a love that puts the love of conventional Christians to shame. And it may be only from the observed phenomenon of love of neighbor that we can begin to ask the question about what it would mean to love God. Why, indeed, is the neighbor worth loving? Should the neighbor continue to be loved if he refuses to love in return, even unto seventy times seven? Can one indefinitely continue to love the unlovable? In loving the neighbor, is one, in fact, saying something about his understanding of the ultimate ordering of things, namely, that the universe is so ordered that love is what the universe should elicit and even demand? When we begin to ask these and other questions, all of which flow naturally from the reality of neighbor love, we have already come remarkably close to the question of what it might mean to love God.

To broaden the point, our theological methodology may well move *from man to God* and not vice versa. Older theology began with the doctrine of God, and then moved on to man, who could be understood only as created in God's image, destined by God for eternal fellowship with him. But today in a world where many deny the existence of God, all must still affirm the existence of man, however discordantly they may do so. And although many treat man as a means to an end, many others treat him as an end who is exceedingly precious. It will not do to score too many quick victories by pointing out that the estimate of man's worth is part of the spiritual capital of a Christian heritage that is not yet fully expended, but it should be possible to pose the question of how long men will continue to treat one another as possessing infinite worth after they have come to the conclusion that men do not in fact have that worth but are only, as Dostoevsky pointed out, fertilizer for the future. *Is man fully explicable only as a child of dust, or as a rather complicated bit of circuitry, who can be manipulated and exploited as the planners see fit?* If so, then let us be done with the Christian myth and move on into the nightmare. But if not, then let us ask again what it means to say that man has a "nature" and the promise of a "destiny." However we start with man, we are soon at the point where what has been meant traditionally by "God" begins to intrude into our thinking.[22]

We may well move from *Jesus the man* to *Jesus the revelation of God,* and not vice versa. As indicated earlier, the major impact of historical theology has surely been on the uniqueness of the revelatory activity of God in Christ. But our day is witnessing a new stress on Jesus as the "man for others," as the one in whom first of all we see fully and definitively what it means to be a human being. This is not a bad place to start. For if within the secular order we can find a point at which the possibilities of a true humanity are acted out for us, then we are more likely to be able to discover what our own humanity might become. If there is anything we need in our confused world today, it is some sense of the true measure of what it means to be a man. And if in true man we discover something about the ultimate mystery of human existence, and that the one who was true man found himself willing to cry out, "Abba, Father," we may learn something about a new order of possibilities for ourselves.

In so doing, we would be doing nothing other than did those who knew Jesus in the flesh. These did not discover him as a divine theophany, but as a first-century Jew, a carpenter's son, who had something compelling about him which elicited their response of loyalty and trust. Only much later, apparently not until near the end, did it occur to one of them to say, "You are the *Christos,* the one for whom we have been waiting."

f. *We must be aware of the dangers of "reductionism."* Readers who have followed this far may feel that reductionism has already taken over and destroyed what they understand to be "the faith once delivered to the saints." Have not so many things been chipped away that nothing remains save a kind of this-worldly ethic? I do not believe that this has happened, but I agree that it is always in danger of happening and that we must remember the old warning, "Our worst enemies are the accommodating theologians," the theologians who scale the gospel down to "what Jones can be persuaded to swallow," and for whom the word "God" is finally only the word "man" writ large.

When Bultmann says that theology is anthropology, we would of course have to resist if by that he meant that God is no more, that man has displaced him, and so on. But if by it he means, as I think he means, that any theological statement is of necessity also an anthropological statement, and that it is saying something about the ultimate dimensions of human existence, then I do not see how we can fault the assertion. For what the above pages have tried to do is precisely to indicate that our concern for the secular, for the *humanum,* is an attempt to think about and look at those realities theologically, i.e., in terms of the impingement upon them of *theos,* of God. Our *logos,* or discourse, about *theos*—our *theo-logy*—is trying to place man and the world in a context of ultimate meaning, of the divine purpose. It is not an attempt to reduce Christianity to an ethic, but rather to see the context in which a Christian ethic must operate. It is not saying that God is dead, though it is implying that many of our concepts of God have long since been dead and deserve a decent burial. It is not saying that grace is unreal, but rather that new modes for describing grace may be needed. Leslie Dewart, surely not one to be accused of holding on to timeworn notions, has stated, "What is absolutely fundamental to the Christian experience is that which is conceptualized in the doctrine of *grace.*"[23]

During the writing of these final pages, I shared in a funeral that was an occasion of joy as we sang and prayed and rejoiced about the fullness of a human life and the shared assurance that was expressed in the words

> Let goods and kindred go,
> This mortal life also;
> The body they may kill:
> God's truth abideth still,
>   His Kingdom is forever.

And this surely is the heart of the gospel, of the good news that beyond all that we can do or say or think is the fact that we are judged, threatened, upheld, sustained, renewed, and refashioned by a force or power we must ultimately describe as personal and gracious, and that beyond all our deserving, something has been done for us about which our final response can only be one of gratitude.

We may need new words, new methodologies, new analogies, and even the newest words will falter, the newest methodologies will fail, and the newest analogies will limp—but we still feel the need both to abase ourselves and to lift up our hearts, and on rare occasions to feel strangely renewed and strengthened.

We can never catch the Light in our net of words. But we will never be able to cease trying. And therein lies both the pain and the glory.

NOTES

1. Thomas Altizer, *The Gospel of Christian Atheism* (The Westminster Press, 1966).

2. Cf. Jürgen Moltmann, *The Theology of Hope,* tr. by James W. Leitch (Harper & Row, Publishers, Inc., 1967); Maryellen Muckenhirn (ed.), *The Future as the Presence of Shared Hope* (Sheed & Ward, Inc., 1968); and Symposium on "Hope," *Cross Currents,* Vol. XVIII, No. 3 (Summer, 1968).

3. Cf. the significance of Paul van Buren's title, *The Secular Meaning of the Gospel* (The Macmillan Company, 1963).

4. Cf. *inter alia* William Hamilton, *The New Essence of Christianity* (Association Press, 1961).

5. John C. Bennett, "The Christian Conception of Man," David E. Roberts and Henry P. Van Dusen (eds.), *Liberal Theology: An Appraisal; Essays in Honor of Eugene William Lyman* (Charles Scribner's Sons, 1942), pp. 191–204.

6. A good example of this "ecumenical consensus" as it existed a few years ago is in Walter Marshall Horton, *Christian Theology: An Ecumenical Approach* (Harper & Brothers, 1955, 1958).

7. The perceptive editors of the *New Theology* series suggest in *New Theology No. 4* that we may already be moving "beyond the secular" to a new concern for "religion," a theme further developed in *New Theology No. 5* by much emphasis on the theology of hope and resulting in affirmations about an open future. Cf. Martin Marty and D. G. Peerman (eds.), *New Theology No. 4* (The Macmillan Company, 1967) and *New Theology No. 5* (The Macmillan Company, 1968).

8. Cf. Friedrich Gogarten, *Verhängniss und Hoffnung der Neuzeit* (Stuttgart: Friedrich Vorwerk Verlag, 1953); Arend van Leeuwen, *Christianity in World History* (Charles Scribner's Sons, 1965) and *Prophecy in a Technocratic Era* (Charles Scribner's Sons, 1968).

9. Dietrich Bonhoeffer, *Letters and Papers from Prison* (rev. ed., The Macmillan Company, 1967), esp. the letters of 25 May 1944 and 8 June 1944.

10. Cf. *inter alia,* Herbert Butterfield, *Christianity and History* (London: G. Bell & Sons, Ltd., 1949); Alan F. Geyer, *Piety and Politics* (John Knox Press, 1963); Harvey Cox, *The Secular City* (The Macmillan Company, 1965); John Macquarrie, *God-Talk* (Harper & Row, Publishers, Inc., 1967); Nathan A. Scott, *The Broken Center* (Yale University Press, 1966).

11. Cf. *inter alia,* Ian G. Barbour (ed.), *Science and Religion* (Harper & Row, Publishers, Inc., 1968).

12. Theologians on the forefront of this venture have drawn heavily on the philosophical insights of Alfred North Whitehead and Pierre Teilhard de Chardin.

13. I have developed this material more fully in my book *The Ecumenical Revolution* (Doubleday & Company, Inc., 1967).

14. A third stream, flowing from the missionary concern that first inspired the Edinburgh Conference, was embodied in the International Missionary Council, organized in 1921, which finally merged with the World Council of Churches at the New Delhi World Assembly in 1961.

15. Cf. World Conference on Church and Society, Geneva, 1966, *Christians in the Technical and Social Revolutions of Our Time,* Official Report, with a description of the conference by M. M. Thomas and Paul Abrecht (Geneva: World Council of Churches, 1967).

16. *World Development: Challenge to the Churches,* Official Report of the Exploratory Committee on Society, Development and Peace (Geneva: World Council of Churches, 1968).

17. *The Uppsala Report,* ed. by Norman Goodall (Geneva: World Council of Churches, 1968).

18. Martin Buber, *Israel and the World* (Schocken Books, Inc., 1963), p. 235.

19. These paragraphs obviously owe much of their inspiration to the life and death of Dietrich Bonhoeffer. Bonhoeffer's theology forced him into an increasing confrontation with Nazism, but Nazism had its impact upon Bonhoeffer's theology in return. And Bonhoeffer's present theological impact is surely in part to be explained by the fact that as the final confrontation drew near, the man's life was the measure of his mind.

20. The following themes are developed in more detail in Robert McAfee Brown, Abraham J. Heschel, and Michael Novak, *Vietnam: Crisis of Conscience* (Association Press; Herder & Herder, Inc.; Behrman House, 1967).

21. Blaise Pascal, *Pensées,* #552, "The Mystery of Jesus" (Modern Library, 1941), p. 177; cf. also #534, p. 179.

22. This is something very different from anthropomorphism, attempting to make God in man's image. It is insisting only that a full enough analysis of a doctrine of man will have implications for a new approach to a doctrine of God.

23. Leslie Dewart, *The Future of Belief: Theism in a World Come of Age* (Herder & Herder, Inc., 1966), p. 207.

❖ ❖ ❖ *Few Roman Catholic priests or scholars have had a greater influence in the councils of their church or a more genuine acceptance in ecumenical circles than Father Bernard Häring, C.Ss.R. He was the first Roman Catholic occupant of the Harry Emerson Fosdick Visiting Professorship at Union Theological Seminary, a position to which he came under the presidency of Dr. Bennett. Educated in the Humanistisches Gymnasium, the Rottenfel, and Gars am Inn seminaries, and the University of Tübingen in Germany, he holds the S.T.D. from the latter and two honorary doctorates from American universities. He has held numerous teaching positions on the Continent and in America while away from his regular position as Professor of Systematic Moral Theology at the Academia Alfonsiana, Lateran University, Rome. He has written extensively on moral theology. His best-known three-volume work, published in several languages, is* Das Gesetz Christi (The Law of Christ). *Recent works include* Toward a Christian Moral Theology (1966) *and* Shalom: Rejoice in Peace; Sacrament of Reconciliation (1967).

Years of concern about the theological aspects of ecumenism are focused in this essay, which analyzes the changes in spirit and content that must occur in the theology of both Roman and Protestant churches if a profound common understanding of the gospel is to bring them together.

2

DEOSSIFICATION
OF THEOLOGICAL OBSTACLES
IN VIEW OF ECUMENISM

✧ ✧ ✧ *Bernard Häring, C.Ss.R.*

THE IMPORTANCE of the *Sitz im Leben* for a right understanding of the Biblical message is made evident by the recent development of Biblical studies. Listening to the word of God in the Bible, we are not confronted with something similar to Platonic "eternal ideas." What we are hearing is a divine message in human language: a message that is meaningful for men of all times but which they can understand only to the extent that they first understand what it meant to the people of the concrete historic situation to whom it was directly delivered.

Fundamentalism, although it intends to be faithful to the truth of the Bible, often fails to grasp the real issues of its divine message. As a result of this ahistoric understanding of revelation, the gap between religion and life becomes even deeper and wider the more our culture, new possibilities, hopes, anguishes, concrete life experiences, and tasks differ from the context in which the persons and communities of the Bible received the message.

This applies even more to the theological systems and formulations that we have inherited from the polemical disputes of the Reformation and the Counter-Reformation. Those who cling to the frozen forms left over from those controversies can neither grasp the specific religious values that were at stake nor liberate themselves from the prejudices of either side. A one-sided theology of controversy—an aggressive confessionalism or any kind of scholasticism that has insisted on seeing everything through the eyes of the sixteenth-century Reformers, the Council of Trent, or Thomas Aquinas

—has, to a great extent, caused an alienation of theology and religion from the existential questions and experiences of modern men. A theology built on confessionalism not only has been a scandal to the whole world because it was in opposition to the fundamental testament of the Lord "that they may be one"; it also has been one of the chief causes of ossification of theology and consequently of preaching.

The new spirit of today's ecumenism and the common experience of our difficulties in reaching men of our time through our traditional approach oblige theologians to work for the deossification of all those attitudes and formulas which cannot proclaim to sincere men of our age the faith in the God of history and the gospel of the Word Incarnate.

A number of Protestant theologians who did not want to continue the fight against past expressions and attitudes have in the past decades done much to understand Catholic doctrine and theology in its proper context. By studying the historical context of earlier approaches, they have tried to evaluate, as positively as possible, the dynamism of present Catholic theology. On the other side, many Catholic theologians have made competent efforts to evaluate the theology of Luther, Calvin, and Zwingli in their own existential context and concerns.[1]

The following reflections approach the problem of deossification of our theological quarrels in view of ecumenism and pluralism, and in awareness of the new tasks imposed on theology by the fact of secularization in so much of today's world.

I. Pluralism and Complementarity in Theology

Men of our age are very sensitive in matters of variety, diversity, and pluralism. They easily recognize that pluralism of itself enriches genuine human unity, and that diversity can threaten unity only if it is degenerating and/or if violent efforts are made to eliminate legitimate claims for pluralism.

Many factors besides the modern sensitivity about pluralism have sharpened the understanding of theological pluralism. Biblical studies have shown that even in the inspired books of Holy Scripture a cultural and theological pluralism shines through. This does not diminish the unity of God's revelation but demonstrates that salvation truth is always greater and deeper than man's perception and possibility of expression.

Historical studies of theology become more fruitful in the light of modern sociology and comparative culture. The interdependence between the total cultural context and religious and theological expressions has fostered a broader understanding. Sociology and philosophy of language have made us aware that the total meaning of a word or thesis cannot be grasped without attention to the vital context. All this has helped to destroy the "absolutism" of theological systems: not at all in the sense of agnosticism or of total relativism but in the sense of a fuller awareness that our relationship to truth—particularly to revealed truth—can by no means be one of monopoly but has to be one of humility and mutual sharing.

Pluralism in theology is not to be understood in the sense of a political or diplomatic ideology of ecumenism. It is, rather, a part of an ecumenical repentance that opens new horizons. Vatican II clearly revealed a manifold pluralism within the Roman Catholic Church itself without threatening its unity. The Decree on Ecumenism of Vatican II frames the problem of pluralism in an ecumenical perspective. In his opening discourse Pope John indicated the way for reflection on theological diversity. "The deposit of faith is one thing; the way it is expressed is another. For the truths preserved in our sacred doctrine can retain the same substance and meaning under different forms and expressions."[2]

This statement is echoed by the programmatic declaration: "While preserving unity in essentials, let all members of the Church, according to the office entrusted to each, preserve a proper freedom in various forms of spiritual life and discipline, in the variety of liturgical rites, and even in the theological elaborations of revealed truth."[3] From this conviction follows the confidence that ecumenical dialogue can enrich our understanding of faith. "When comparing doctrines, Catholic theologians should remember that in Catholic teaching there exists an order or 'hierarchy' of truths, since they vary in their relationship to the foundation of the Christian faith. Thus the way will be opened [in ecumenical dialogue] for this kind of fraternal rivalry to invite all to a deeper realization and clearer expression of the unfathomable riches of Christ."[4]

This "hierarchy" of truths will vary particularly in accordance with a more sapiential or a more existential approach to the reflection on revealed truth.[5] "The heritage handed down by the apostles was received in different forms and ways, so that from the very beginnings of the Church it has had a varied development in various places, thanks to a similar variety of natural gifts and conditions of life."[6] Pluralism here is seen in the light of God's gifts, in the light of the Lord of history. And it is remarked that only because of external causes, and above all because of "mutual failures in understanding and charity, all these circumstances set the stage for separation."[7]

Reconciliation between the various traditions is considered a necessity "in order faithfully to preserve the fullness of Christian tradition."[8] Although in the context this refers primarily to the various liturgical traditions, the same idea is then expressed regarding the theological understanding of faith. "In the investigation of revealed truth, East and West have used different methods and approaches in understanding and proclaiming divine things. It is hardly surprising, then, if sometimes one tradition has come nearer than the other to an apt appreciation of certain aspects of a revealed mystery, or has expressed them in a clearer manner. As a result, these various theological formulations are often to be considered as complementary rather than conflicting. . . . This sacred Synod declares that this entire heritage of spirituality and liturgy, of discipline and theology, in their various traditions, belongs to the full catholic and apostolic Church."[9]

It is true that this text speaks directly only about the Orthodox churches, but there can be no doubt that Vatican II approached the relationship to the special spiritual and theological heritage of the Protestant churches in the same spirit. The difference is only that the churches of the sixteenth-century Reformation cannot, like the Orthodox churches, make claims about the most ancient traditions. But the final theological reason for appreciation of all the good in the churches separated from the Catholic Church is not antiquity but the praise of the Lord who gives all good gifts. In this spirit it is said about the churches of the Reformation, "The faith by which they believe in Christ bears fruit in praise and thanksgiving for the benefits received from the hands of God."[10]

II. Ecumenical Theology in a Secular Age

If theology wants to be a service to the understanding of faith and a help to the proclamation of the good news for men of today, theologians of all churches have to be very much aware of the process of secularization in all its complexity and pluralism.

I cannot attempt here to give a full description of what I understand to be secularization, but I want to indicate some of the aspects that influence the ecumenical effort and oblige theologians of all churches to liberate their ecclesiastical approaches and formulations from narrowness. I shall urge attention especially to those aspects which oblige both Protestants and Catholics to rethink what they have said and have formulated about "faith alone," "Scripture alone," and "grace alone." We have to ask ourselves whether or not we must relinquish some of our perspectives in order to be at the same time more faithful to God who reveals himself and better able to talk to men of today about the Lord of history.

First among the many features of secularization that force us to rethink our approaches is the tremendous impact of the secular world upon the man of today. He is enthralled by the events, insights, new powers, and new responsibilities that are happening in the secular realm of life. Those concerns that characterize the secular world—the whole reality beyond and outside the ecclesiastical world and beyond the events and images of the Bible—impress him more and more. If he does not find God there in all these new experiences, the God of the Bible alone will seem to him too small to be God.

Man sees the reality of life in the light of the modern sciences—social sciences, psychology, comparative culture, anthropology, mathematics, cybernetics, and so on. If theology is something extraneous to all this and speaks about "salvation through faith alone" in such a way that all the exciting and dangerous reality of the secular life is excluded from talk about salvation and faith, then modern man feels that theologians assign to God a very narrow precinct.

The second feature is that if theology speaks in the old "sacred" language of confessional theology (theology of controversy), the citizen of the new secular world will rebel and assert his own better competence about all this. Or if he does not lose faith completely, he will respond with compassion toward the alienated theologian and preacher.

The third point is that in view of the new experiences of the depth of being and the immense dimensions of the world's history which modern sciences have brought to men, the realization of man's tremendous power and weakness can bring about a new openness to religious questions. Like the prophetic preaching and the efforts of theologians of the Old Testament to find God in man's history, achievements, and failures, the new horizons of being, opportunities, and risks can in a very different way be a "grace" that leads to a more vital understanding of faith in God.

At the same time—and this is the next point—we see new forms of idolatry. The great secular city, and especially its dynamic open future, offers itself to many as the divinity. The open future and man's planning for it take the place of God whether it is actually called God or receives man's total interest, dedication, or fear under other names. Here I follow the line of thought of Friedrich Gogarten, that unless we adore the true God and have faith in him who is infinitely greater than the secular city and our own human thoughts about him, there will be no genuine secularity. There will be only a new idol—the so-called "secular" city, man's own achievements—or a new demon—man's own threat and anguish of quasi-religious dimensions.

The fifth point is that the preaching of the prophets and, above all, of Christ and his apostles did "desacralize" a whole sphere of life and destroyed many taboos. It entrusted to man full responsibility for the world around him, a responsibility for his fellowmen not to be hampered by unreal distinctions between holy and unholy things, holy and unholy foods, and so on.

The desacralization that we find in the prophetic parts of the Bible has its counterpart now in a new vast phenomenon of desacralization which becomes particularly visible in countries predominantly Catholic. Thus Catholicism receives a new image insofar as it survives this movement—and seemingly it does survive to a great extent. There is less emphasis on "sacred things"—blessings, holy places, images, relics. Only a few traditionalists still believe in a "sacred language" (Latin). Liturgy and sacrament are no longer spoken about in such terms as "use of sacred things" but in a more personalistic idiom such as: "Christ still proclaims the Gospel," or "The assembly of the people of God listens and praises God." I am convinced that the more authentic Catholic tradition and basic doctrine is expressed more clearly in this way, but many problems posed by this desacralization are not yet resolved.

The process of desacralization also affects the Protestant world, although in a different way. Is the true sense of the sacred endangered by all this, or are there still "sacred cows" of old formulas and approaches preventing access to the Holy God in this age of secularization?

The sixth factor to be noted is the coincidence of secularization with today's wide sharing in modern culture. The churches and theologies are confronted with more critical men, the "crowd" of highly educated and critical people. Many secrets that in past times provided an occasion or invitation for the quest of faith, many things that were awe-inspiring, are now plain and clear before the critical mind. There is no longer a place for a paternalistic clergy or a paternalistic theology.

Finally, to some extent secularization implies a process of the demythologizing of church authority. There is a sharp awareness of past sacralizations of styles of authority which cannot be identified with the gospel. The critical mind of modern man, equipped with better historical knowledge about the varying styles of authority in interdependence with structures of social and cultural life, imposes a sharp distinction between real competence and office. There is greater awareness of the distinction between the truly prophetic voices in the church and regular officers and administrators in the institutional church. There is also a growing attitude of suspicion toward "institutionalized charisms," especially if those in authority all too easily command in the name of a divine mandate. Martin Luther King, Jr., comes to mind as one who exercised a greater moral influence in the church than many men of high rank in the Protestant churches and many Catholic bishops. Karl Rahner and Hans Küng are more read than almost all the pastoral letters of bishops and cardinals. Individual laymen or groups of laymen can exercise a great moral authority if they are competent and dedicated active members of the church.

The divine mandate that is the ground of church authority is a reason for men of our age to look with more discernment to the deeds and words of those in authority. Does all this mean a decay of authority in the church? Or can the result of this process of demythologizing be a better understanding of the ministry of the Word and of the Sacrament, and a greater spiritual power of humility in those who are called to be leaders or coordinators in the community of faith?

III. "Salvation by Faith Alone" and a Christian Ethics in a Secular Age

In all times one of the most fundamental questions of theology has been this: What is the relation between faith and morality?

This question has its particular accent not only in the ecumenical dialogue but also in view of the new emphasis on social involvement of the Christians of all churches.

Vatican II praises the Protestant churches for their social commitment and indicates how this is related to faith. "This active faith has produced many organizations for the relief of spiritual and bodily distress, the education of youth, the advancement of humane social conditions, and the promotion of peace throughout the world."[11] Is faith only an internal force that motivates men to do these works or does faith also indicate the way? Does it help us to understand God's will?

"Salvation by faith alone" as a thesis of Martin Luther is intimately related to his *sola scriptura*. Do we, by divine revelation as it is presented to us, know what we should do now in our time? Many secular men of today would assert with Erich Fromm that "ethical norms are based on our knowledge of the nature of man and not on revelation."[12]

James M. Gustafson, who is very much aware of the new problems raised by ecumenism as well as by secularism, has done a masterly study of how, according to representative Protestant and Catholic thinkers, faith does influence and shape morality. He puts the question concretely in this form: "What claims for the significance of Christ for the moral life do theologians explicitly make or apparently assume?"[13] This is an apt approach to our problem. The intention of my reflections here is in much the same vein. The goal, however, is not so much a study of what has been said but what, in my conviction, should be our way of faithfulness to the revealed truth and, as far as possible, to the particular traditions of our churches in openness to the present needs of men.

Salvation by faith alone was no doubt, one of the most fundamental concerns of Martin Luther. He and his followers were deeply convinced that they faithfully followed the Bible, especially the words of Paul. The Council of Trent expressed and emphasized in its own way that according to the Apostle of the Gentiles "man is justified by faith through grace"; that is, in the sense that " 'faith is the beginning, foundation and root of all justice; without it it is impossible to please God' (Heb. 11:6) and impossible to receive a share in the communion of His children. We say that justification is given by grace since nothing that may precede justification, neither faith nor work, can be deserved. As the same Apostle says,

'If it is by grace, then it does not rest on deeds done, or grace would
cease to be grace' " (Rom. 11:6).[14]

a. *From Paul to Luther.* In the ecumenical dialogue the first
thing is to meet each other on the basis of the Bible. But since ecumenism is itself the pastoral concern for proclamation of the
salvation message to men of our time, more is required than the
understanding of the Bible in its proper context. Joined with it must
be an effort to understand also the context of the polemical formulations of the message in the time of the Reformation and the Counter-
Reformation and the context in which theology exercises its ministry
today. The final concern of theology, as I understand it, is the faithful stewardship of the deposit of faith in order to make it fruitful
for the here and now.

The doctrine of Paul on salvation through faith alone was polem-
ically formulated and emphasized against the wrong concept of
justice held by the Pharisees, Judeo-Christian nomists, and later in
confrontation with the Hellenistic trust in human wisdom. Paul's
theology cannot be fully appreciated without attention to his own
experience as the persecutor of Christ's disciples. Since Saul, as a
docile student of the school of the Pharisees, gave prime importance
to the law and to human achievements in, and according to, the law
and believed in the monopoly of Israel and its sacred traditions, he
had locked his heart and mind from the gospel of Christ. He
judged Christ and the community of his disciples according to his
ideal of absolute allegiance to the law and the sacred traditions.
Thus the law and traditions had blinded him to the mighty self-
manifestation of God in Christ, the humble servant of God. Alone
the undeserved grace of Christ healed the persecutor's blindness and
granted him faith in Christ. Solely through faith his eyes were
opened when Christ graciously manifested himself. Thus Paul knew
that salvation is alone in Christ through faith, and not in "sacred
traditions."

From this Paul's other great insight followed: that Christ has
torn down all the barriers between Jews and Gentiles. Faith and
the unity of all of mankind in Christ became a synthesis in his
religious experience and theology. His own conversion and his mission to the Gentiles were most intimately connected.

With this perspective it was for Paul a vital concern that morality
and law should not be presented as the first thing: Christ is not a
servant to morality or to any sacred tradition or law. The saving

reality is not law and custom but Christ alone, faith alone in Him. Paul's teaching is expressed identically with the words "Christ alone" and "faith alone." In faith Christ reveals himself mercifully, thus manifesting the saving justice and mercy of the Father; in faith the human person experiences the liberating power of Christ; in faith the person surrenders himself to Christ. Law—or "morality" as Paul had experienced it before his conversion—was not a way to salvation but rather an obstacle to grace and to the unity of mankind in faith. All this, of course, is a matter of perspective and not of any details of law and morality. The problem was, If you look to Christ in the perspective of a law that has made itself somehow independent, overshadowing Christ, what is your faith in Christ? The position of Paul is clear: the decisive conversion is to Christ. Then faith in him gives also the right perspective to morality, to a life with Christ and for Christ, to the building up of the one body of Christ.

With the same vigor Paul took issue with the great temptation of the Hellenistic culture, the "wisdom of this world," which made itself independent, as did "justice by law" in the theology of the Pharisees and the Christian nomists. Those Christians who organized the opposition against Paul's gospel accepted Christ, but chiefly as a servant of the law and of the sacred traditions. Similarly the Hellenistic pride in wisdom would have accepted Christ if he had been presented only as another splendid example of man-made wisdom. Paul was fighting for the uniqueness and glory of Christ. In this perspective appears also the characteristic uniqueness of Christian morality: faith in Christ that unites man with Christ's redeeming love and thus bears fruit in charity and unity.

b. *Martin Luther.* A situation somewhat similar to Paul's confronted Luther. A monastic asceticism that overemphasized external and secondary things, a tendency to inculcate legal prescriptions without proportion to their relevance to faith in Christ and love of neighbor, the dealings in indulgences that promised salvation all too easily and for external performances, superficial forms of popular devotions and of official liturgy, ritualism that obscured the faith as total dependence on Christ: all these were the *Sitz im Leben* for Luther's own passionate understanding of the theology of Paul about faith and freedom from law.

He had also to contend with the pride of human wisdom which Paul had confronted in the Greek philosophers. In the humanism of the Renaissance there was too much trust in human wisdom, to the detriment of faith. Furthermore Luther was scandalized by a part of the scholastic theology that, by its undue reliance upon human concepts and by a systematization alien to the Bible, had dimmed awe and respect before the ineffable mystery of the gospel.

Both scholasticism—as Luther knew it—and the humanistic thinking of the time obscured the existential element in faith by giving prime attention to the intellectual element. Faith seemed to be reduced either to human insights or to adherence to a certain set of theses and formulations proposed by ecclesiastical authority. Against this background we can understand why he called human reason or reasoning a "whore." According to the prophetic language of the Bible, the man who puts his trust and faith more in human wisdom—albeit the wisdom of theologians and bishops—than in the life-giving word of Christ commits adultery.

c. *The Catholic Response.* Confessional differences were often oversimplified in the theology of controversy. Matching Luther's *sola fides, sola gratia, sola scriptura* was the Catholic *et et*: reason as well as faith, works as well as faith and grace, tradition as well as Scripture. Such a way of thinking by no means does justice to the authentic Catholic doctrine of the past and of today if this "as well as" is understood as an unproblematic juxtaposition. At least the Council of Trent did not allow such a dualism.

Morality ("works") is not something besides grace; right reasoning in matters of salvation is not something besides faith, although it must be distinguished from the full meaning and reality of faith; human merits have relevance in the perspective of salvation only insofar as they are produced by God's unmerited gifts.[15] In remuneration God is crowning his own grace. Faith arises from grace alone; but faith is a dynamic reality. It cannot be conceived without its dynamism bearing fruit in love for the life of the world. What does not bear fruit will be cut down. But faith can bear fruit for everlasting life only to the extent that God's gracious love guides man and is freely and gratefully accepted by man. It is common doctrine of the Christian churches that law, morality, works, man's wisdom, and intellectual endeavor mean something for eternal life only in the light of Christ, through the grace of the Holy Spirit given in view of Christ. A redeemed freedom is possible only under the influence of redeeming grace in faith. In this sense a Catholic can grant to the Lutheran doctrine of "faith alone" not only an acceptable but even an eminent meaning and content.

But in Luther's doctrine there are overtones and polemical accents which do not simply and fully reflect Paul's experience and doctrine. Luther's upbringing in a particular kind of Catholic theology, and the monastic training to which he was exposed, were to a great extent individualistic. Whereas Paul's chief concern was to tear down all the barriers between Jews and Gentiles, Luther's starting point was one of personal anguish, How can I find a merciful God? Luther read the letter to the Romans against the background of his individual experience and did not fully grasp its historic context of salvation history. He elaborated one great perspective of liberating faith, which certainly is necessary if understood in complementarity with the perspective prevailing in the Catholic Church. But neither he nor the great number of his followers of the past centuries saw the necessary polarity and complementarity as long as a polemical attitude determined theology. The same is true for most of the post-Trindentine Catholic theologians, in spite of the good efforts of the Council of Trent to give attention to the chief concern of Luther.

d. *The New Situation.* Paul and Martin Luther must be understood in their own historical context and life experience. Only to the extent that we succeed in this understanding can we distinguish the abiding values from the particular accents and formulations which responded to that actual context. The situation of today is quite different from that of Paul's day and even more so from the time of the Reformation.

The Christian churches, and especially their theologies which were developed with polemical overtones, all stand accused of the alienation of religion from life; from decisive historical developments, and from social commitments. This reproach is made not only to Catholic theologians who have been satisfied to protect "the purity of faith" by clinging to past systematizations and by repeating —in Latin or in vernacular—ever the same formulations. The Lutheran preacher who knows just the appropriate word of the Bible for all situations, or who repeats Luther's polemical *sola fides, sola scriptura,* can empty his church as effectively as the Catholic priest who reads the gospel in Latin and the Catholic moralist who resolves all the new moral problems with instruments of the natural law doctrine formulated by old Roman lawyers and philosophers concerned for the exercise of political power over submitted tribes.

The gap between religion and life can be widened not only by a religion that gives more attention to indulgences, sacred vestments, relics, and images of saints than to burning social issues but also by one that practices an unproblematic repetition of old controversies about works, merits, and reason as opposed to "faith alone." This is the conviction of Protestant theologians as well as of their Catholic colleagues.

A great part of Protestant theology, especially in the United States and in Germany, has liberated itself from an individualistic and pietistic bias. Outstanding theologians have developed, in genuine fidelity to the best of their heritage, a theology of responsibility to the world, of social reconciliation, and of worldwide brotherhood. Great men such as Richard and Reinhold Niebuhr, Paul Tillich, Dietrich Bonhoeffer, and John Bennett stand alongside many others. Without betraying the religious inspiration inherited from the Reformation of the sixteenth century, they speak a new language and turn their attention to new problems in solidarity with the world of today.

Constant efforts are necessary to avoid these extremes: tendencies such as that of the "social gospel," of the *Kulturchristentum,* of the enthusiastic adorers or admirers of the secular city who want to make Christianity relevant by reducing its doctrine to this-worldly dimensions and, on the other side, a new temptation toward a polemical theology concerned for the affirmation of the otherworldliness of salvation to the detriment of the incarnational element of Christian faith.

e. *"Faith Alone" in the Perspective of a Holy Worldliness.* Teilhard de Chardin is not the "fifth gospel," but I look upon him as a great pioneer in the effort to deossify theology. In him we find an astonishing synthesis of allegiance to the church and of courage to rethink theological approaches in view of the modern scientific age. He looks to the whole history of the universe and of mankind in the light of the point Omega: Christ in whom God manifests the fullness of his loving design for man. There is no separation of the natural sphere from salvation history: all is one creation and one design.

What Teilhard has said in modern terms was always the doctrine of the church: Christ is not only the Savior of souls but the Lord and Redeemer of the world, the One who opens the seals of the book of history (cf. Rev. 5:1–10). In the light of the mystery of Christ we see the oneness of revelation throughout all the works of God, throughout all of history.

Teilhard's vision of faith is dynamic. It includes a presence of all that is past, and total openness to all that is in the future. It is a theology of hope. He does not overlook the mystery of sin. Perhaps his optimism did not everywhere and always fully evaluate the reality of sin in the world, but I do not think that the imbalance is greater than in the pessimism of Augustine and Luther. In any event, the optimism of Teilhard de Chardin is not based on man's own achievements. He sees everything in the light of God's holy design: everything is "sacred" insofar as it is a manifestation of God's majesty and love, an invitation to praise him, an appeal to serve him through fraternal love.

The self-manifestation of God as the one Father and Creator of all men, the incarnation and redemptive death of the only begotten Son of God, is a rallying call: all men are called to be sons and daughters of God and thus to be brothers and sisters before God. Faith is the response to this manifestation of God, the humble, grateful, and joyous acceptance of the salvation truth offered to man in Christ. This acceptance and response is wholly determined by the divine message, by the undeserved gifts of God. In faith there is the complete expression of man: everything in man except his sin is revelation of the gracious love of God. In its total openness and its total surrender, with intellect, heart, and will, faith in Christ gathers all the energies of man.

Empirically, however, we cannot overlook the weakness of faith in many believers and the danger of misunderstanding faith in a narrow way, either from the bare viewpoint of intellect or will, or as mere liberation from anguish, an event only between God and the individual soul. The all-embracing character of faith as response to the all-embracing nature of revelation unfolds itself in man only in the process of continuous conversion. Nevertheless the dynamism toward wholeness belongs to the very essence of faith. This can never be overstressed in theology.

The totality of faith urges us also to listen and respond to all the ways in which God manifests himself and his design. One does injustice to the uniqueness of revelation in Christ not only by a syncretism wherein Christ seems to be one religious genius among others but also by isolating the revelation in Christ from the totality of the history and the world.

The "Yes" to Christ includes a "Yes" to a holy worldliness. Christ did not destroy the Law and the Prophets but brought everything to completion. Thus our "Yes" to Christ is also an affirmation of God's revelation given to Abraham, Isaac, Jacob, Moses, and the prophets, although we are aware of the imperfection of many of the ideas of the patriarchs, the sages, and the prophets of Israel.

Why should we exclude from this perspective the truly religious men and women outside Israel? The Old Testament opens toward the sages of the Orient who did not belong to the tribes of Israel, and sees even in humble people—even in the donkey of Balaam— an instrument of God's revelation. The Letter to the Hebrews praises Christ's hidden presence and the saving power of faith in Abel, Enoch, Noah, and even in the Canaanite prostitute Rahab (Heb., ch. 11). We do not exceed the theological courage of the Letter to the Hebrews if we praise God's dynamic presence in men like Confucius and his disciples or in those modern scientists who, far from absolutizing their own knowledge, remain constantly open to newer insights and broader horizons which can be inserted into all efforts to know man better in order to serve him better.

Whatever is good, true, and noble in the different religions and in the honest endeavor of men to build brotherhood can have its origins only in the one God, the Father of our Lord Jesus Christ. It cannot be severed from the dynamism of the whole work of God which is directed toward the point Omega, Christ. If any of these seeds of wisdom and goodness leads men to salvation, it is because of that graciousness of God which has revealed itself fully in Christ: the work of the Holy Spirit, who has made Jesus Christ the source of life for all men.

We adore God in truth and in the Spirit if, confronted with all the saving deeds of God in the men of all ages, we praise "salvation by faith alone." We do this neither in the sense of a bare intellectualism which makes faith a matter of formulas and concepts nor in the sense of a self-centered yearning for the salvation of one's own soul, but in the one great perspective of God's own work. All things become for us a "word," a message, a gift, a gracious appeal, pointing to that openness and searching for the good and the truth in all fields of life. In this attitude we find at least an *analogia fidei*.

Speaking on this "analogy of faith," I think I am not too far from the thought of the later Karl Barth if I include in it not only the direct and immediate religious assent of man to the revelation of

God's Fatherhood but also all the humble service to the community of man wherein God's Fatherhood is implicitly acknowledged through that dedication to universal brotherhood without which faith would be sterilized in its very roots.

By going so far I do not mean to imply that works can save men without faith. I agree with Luther's conviction that proud trust in man's own achievements is one of the greatest obstacles to salvation by faith. Rather, I mean that fundamental attitude of openness to the "Thou" and the "We" which has its origin in God's own love, and which incorporates the existential qualities of faith: openness, acceptance, gratitude, dedication. Thus a broader concept of revelation—with Christ ever at its center—leads to a broader concept of faith—but always with that dynamism toward fullness in Christ. It is not up to men to judge why the initial openness in individual persons and communities did not lead to the explicit and total adherence to Christ which is, nevertheless, the innate finality of revelation and faith.

IV. Religious and Nonreligious Predicaments

Catholic theology was more inclined than a part of the Protestant tradition to include the whole reality of creation and history in the vision of faith, but it can be doubted whether it was always done in a way that manifested the saving quality of faith and its existential character. What does it matter for the saving faith whether the sun turns around the earth or the earth around the sun? What does the dispute about an annihilation of a physical or metaphysical substance of bread add to the faith in the saving event of the Eucharist?

Much more could be said. This essay can illustrate only selected theological issues where the totality of divine revelation and religious perspective has been inadequately treated, that is, without the proper degree of attention to salvation, truth, and existential faith.

Catholic apologetic theology—which should be a dialogue with all men—gave greatest attention to the proofs for God's existence. The concept of causality thereby received a focal attention. Max Scheler criticized this approach from a religious viewpoint.[16] He held that the whole predicament of "causality" or Prime Cause and secondary causes is alien to the understanding of faith, whatever may be the metaphysical value of such proofs about the existence of an absolute Prime Cause. The failure, he said, is not only the accentuation of the concept of "proof" but also the very coldness of the category of "causality." (This says nothing against the philosophical reflection in terms of causality, as long as the philosopher is fully aware that by this kind of predicament and system of thought he does not approach the truly religious phenomenon of faith. Such respectful awareness may even be a sign of openness to faith itself.)

But the decisive key for a religious understanding of the created universe is God's own will to manifest his majesty and graciousness, and correspondingly, man's openness in awe, gratitude, and adoration. The vital element is a truly religious attitude and a vocabulary that expresses an "analogy of faith" transcending the bare philosophical categories of man's capacity to "prove" something. A relationship conceived on the bare basis of causality is not an "analogy of faith."

Moreover, in the context of the actual situation of man it must also be seen that, in view of the depersonalizing tendencies of the managerial world of causalities, man finds himself as a person only in the I-Thou-We relationships.[17] The personalist is therefore frightened by the idea of a Prime Cause which sets up a world governed by bare causalities, handing it over to man to be managed according to innate second causalities. Such an approach, presented as a way that should lead to faith, lacks both the warmth of the Biblical presentation of the revelation in and through the created universe and man, the image and likeness of God, and the appeal of the final self-manifestation of God in Christ, his only Son, as revealed in the New Testament.

The Biblical vision and vocabulary is both religious and personalistic: God *speaks*, and thus *calls* the world into being. He *makes visible* the splendor of his mighty love and justice; he is *present* in his work-word in a dynamic way, thus calling for reverence, gratitude, holy fear, and joy. In the New Testament, Christ, the final word of God to man, identifies himself with all men; he becomes our brother. The attitude of the created person which is adequate to this religious understanding of all things and events is one of humility, courage in the search for ever better understanding of this message and appeal, readiness to respond with all one's being to God wherever and in whatever way God may speak to him, and avoidance of pride and self-centered trust in man's own capacity. The religious horizon opens with the very openness of the human person for the "Thou" which transcends the claims of the "I." This may be the beginning of "secular" language about God in the sense of Dietrich Bonhoeffer's thinking.

There are good reasons to think that Rudolf Otto,[18] in his scientific research about the essence of all religions, was influenced by the fundamental principle of "salvation through faith alone" as it was taught by Martin Luther and the best of the Lutheran tradition. He tried to find out what is common in religiosity in spite of the great diversity of religions. Of course, in his comparative study of religions he could not find elsewhere the personalistic understanding which characterizes the Christian religion, but after all he was convinced that in the religious experience there is everywhere the fundamental category of "revelation." The religious sentiment or feeling is, in its own intentionality, determined by the "sacred" which dynamically inspires humble fear (awe) and grateful rejoicing together, in a harmonious contrast and polarity (*Kontrastharmonie*). His key word, *"intentionale Fühlen,"* is not at all a kind of sentimentalism that would lock man in his own feelings. On the contrary, its intentional direction is determined by the openness to the sacred whereby man is thoroughly aware or convinced that it is not he who produces the sacred but the sacred reality that makes the meaning and intention of the religious experience.

Otto spoke about *Fühlen* (feeling) and *irrationale* in order to emphasize that in religious experience rational categories are thoroughly transcended. *Fühlen* makes the human person completely open to the sacred. Its very intention is the opposite of all the products of man's own rationality or sentimentality. Wherever man thinks with pride that he is grasping the "sacred" by his own intellectual endeavor, with rational formulas and concepts, there is no longer the sacred; there is no authentic religious experience. Does this not, in a modern way, reflect Martin Luther's attacks against the "whore ratio"? The problematic and the language of Rudolf Otto differed from that of Luther, but the fundamental concern is identical.

In a surprisingly new vocabulary Otto also gave great attention to the relationship between faith and morality. He distinguished *sakrales Ethos* (the very ethos of the religious act) and *sanktioniertes Ethos* (morality that receives religious sanction). What he called

sakrales Ethos corresponds to the quality of faith as existential receptivity to the sacred, as trust in and surrender to the sphere of
the sacred. What we call morality within the sphere of a community
of believers is called by him "the sanctioned ethos." Customs and
value systems arising from tradition and from the cultural and social
conditions of life receive sanction through the experience of the
sacred and through the community of faith.

Rudolf Otto was fully aware of the danger of a dichotomy between the ethos as response to the sacred and the ethos which only
receives sanction. I suspect there is, however, some influence of the
Lutheran "two realms," where the realm of religious experiences
does not manifest all its dynamism in the ethos of worldly activity
and relationships between men. The ethos of professional, cultural,
and civil life is understood too statically in Luther's theology—which
is not surprising in a static society.

Protestant and Catholic Biblical scholars have demonstrated that
in the world of the Bible there is a growing synthesis between the
religious ethos and morality—that in the ethos that allows man to
say "Our Father" there is already expressed a brotherhood of an
unheard-of density and religious quality. A comparative study of different religious experiences and religious systematizations does prove
a wide gap between the ethos in the sphere of the sacred and the
ethos of the temporal, but modern man senses strongly that it is
just this gap that discloses the weakness of religion (of faith: the
sakrales Ethos of Rudolf Otto).

The theology of the "social gospel" and of the *Kulturchristentum*
asserted that only the ethos of commitment to the secular reality
of social and cultural life is the essence of Christianity. This was
right as a critical reaction, but wrong as a conclusion. In this view
"faith" in the gospel is reduced to a kind of religious sanction for
the social involvement. The humanist finds, then, that religion is
not at all necessary. It appears to him as a waste of energy and
time since it is finally his own personality and his knowledge of
man, and not revelation, that determines the existential character
of his ethos and the content of his moral code. He sees no need
to seek sanction for his morality in a religious realm.

The ethicist of the "post-Christian era" develops those forms of
ethical systems and predicaments which were more or less exter-
nally added to a relatively closed religious sphere. We must admit
that not only in non-Christian religiosity but also within the Chris-

tian communities—and particularly within the polemical and apologetic theological systems of the Christian churches—there existed on many levels and many subjects an inorganic juxtaposition of religion and ethics or an undue confusion of both.[19]

Official Catholic doctrine, as it was formulated by the Council of Trent, affirmed an organic unity between faith and morality, with the necessary emphasis on the truth that faith, and not man's own moral endeavor, is the root and source of the whole of salvation. But practically, the Roman type of moral theology[20] did not at all reflect the dogmatic principles about the role of faith and grace. It was a morality of law, of precept, of virtues and merits which seemed to receive only external sanction by religious motivation. The emphasis on "faith alone" becomes real only to the extent that we can show convincingly that this doctrine does not create a gap between faith and life (morality) but rather leads to an authentic and organic synthesis.

V. "FAITH ALONE" AND AN ETHICS BASED ON OBEDIENCE OF FAITH

The theology of Karl Barth has moved through various stages toward a synthesis between faith and morality. First he was fighting against any kind of reduction of Christianity to mere cultural or moral achievements. He also condemned the *analogia entis* of Catholic theology (as he then understood it) as Antichrist. To him it seemed essentially an anthropocentric outlook, pride of human reasoning, and therefore a "whore" in the sense of Martin Luther. But the first stage is not Karl Barth's last word. He moved to an understanding of the whole human reality in the light of faith, to the *analogia fidei*. He treated morality not only in the light of redemption but also in the light of the dogma of creation.[21] His view of revelation includes the dynamic presence of God in all His work, which has always the character of word-message. He sees both sides: that on the one hand it is God who speaks through his work and gifts and assists man to grasp the message, and that on the other hand the *analogia fidei* supposes receptivity, docility, acceptance, and submission by the human person. All this finds its value only in the view of Christ.

The chief bridge between faith and morality, in the thought of Karl Barth, seems to be the "obedience of faith" reflecting itself in

total submission: the will to obey God's purpose in all things. There
is, however, no legalism in Barth's concept of obedience. He is not
inclined to absolutize unduly any argument taken from insights
into the meaning of the created universe and man's being. He believes in docility toward the Holy Spirit, but the accent on obedience
and submission is strong. Does his prevailing concern for God's
sovereignty psychologically leave space for spontaneity, initiative,
creativity?[22] I think that the way the later Karl Barth understands
all this does leave space. It cannot be seen, however, as man's
creativity side by side with God's initiative and freedom but only as
man's sharing in God's creativity and spontaneity in gratitude and
complete self-surrender.

Indeed, Karl Barth understands obedience above all as trusting
gratitude which liberates man from anguish and self-centeredness,
from the slavery of egotism. But I think that there may be here a
language problem for modern man. After the horrifying experience
of that kind of "obedience" by which so many Christians made possible the tyranny of Hitler, it might be necessary to express the
same religious truth with other words. The accents and vocabulary
have to vary according to the receptivity and needs of man in order
to convey the same message. Dietrich Bonhoeffer was one of the first
who realized this fully.

The effort to bridge faith and morality with the key concept of
obedience has a quite different meaning in Protestant and in Catholic perspectives. A large sector of traditional Catholic moral theology
has connected morality with faith primarily by a concept of *obedience in faith* which focused above all on obedience toward those
who have a divine mandate to teach not only the articles of faith
but also the moral principles and their application to the various
areas of life.

It is true that those who taught this also referred to prudence as
a category for the actual opportunity and possibility, but there was
not enough space for creative initiative. Although it was somewhere
said (by them) that those in authority have to be docile to God's
revelation and mindful of the needs of people, practically, the multitude of man-made laws and ossified formulas did not really educate
toward a vision of faith that bears fruit in love for the life of the
world. The prevalent approach of Catholic theology did manifest rightly—although sometimes too legalistically—that salvation
through faith also necessarily means community of faith, solidarity,

and obedience to the rallying call of God. There was not, however, enough emphasis on maturity or on the initiative and freedom of the sons and daughters of God under the perfect law of freedom.

VI. SALVATION THROUGH FAITH ALONE AND AN ETHICS OF RESPONSIBILITY

Numerous Protestant and Catholic theologians who are concerned about overcoming the gap between religion and life see the unity of faith and morality in the attitude which is characteristic of faith: a listening and response with heart, mind, and will. This attitude leads to an ethics of "responsibility" in complete openness to all the ways in which God manifests his design with the courage to take the human risk necessary in order to shape and reshape the reality in whatever way is fitting to a historical being and a disciple of Christ. In H. Richard Niebuhr's work this approach is classically represented.[23] My own approach is very similar.[24]

An ethics of responsibility tries to attest faithfulness to God, who manifests himself in Jesus Christ but who is not only the God of the Bible but the Lord of history. It is a concern for the dialogue with modern man and, last but not least, a matter of ecumenical dialogue which wants to manifest, by its whole perspective and vocabulary, that faith alone can shed the full light on human insights and provide the energies for a truly Christian morality.

Morality is not something besides faith, not an ethos that receives external sanction through faith. It is the fruit of faithful listening on the part of the believer and a response that wants to be an integral part of the attitude of faith. On the other hand, concern for a dialogue with all cultures should warn us not to absolutize too quickly any specific ethos or specific moral precepts. Faith is richer than just one form of ethos. But the two transform each other according to the perspective of revelation.

Because faith is characterized by a tremendous dynamism toward wholeness and at the same time by an awareness of the incapacity of the believer ever to grasp the fullness of all its implications, its "Yes" means a radical, total openness to all the ways and modes of God's self-manifestation along with a commitment to humble, persistent searching. "For our knowledge and our prophecy are partial. . . . Now we see only puzzling reflections in a mirror." (I Cor. 13:9–12.) In faith we search for wholeness without ever reaching it perfectly on this earth.

In that wholeness toward which faith urges us there shines forth the meaning of our whole existence. The world, the neighbor, the community, the self, are a constitutive part of faith. God manifests his own love in all that he creates and restores in his word. He reveals himself gradually and dynamically in the book of history. Christ is the key, but the book goes on being written and has to be deciphered. All the events are gift, message, and appeal, revealing themselves existentially and truly only to those persons and communities which commit themselves not only to reading the book but also to taking an active, responsible role in writing it in response to God's gifts. The process of listening and of shaping the self and the world around us are to be seen in their organic—although always fragile and threatened—wholeness.

Like Karl Marx, many modern men are disturbed by the religious pietist who by "faith alone" is concerned only for "God and my soul," either neglecting all the rest of the world and events or else looking on them only as means for his salvation. People who oppose this type of religion and faith are not areligious. At least some of the modern men who turned away from the churches are yearning for the wholeness of man and the wholeness of religion in the spirit of the prophets. Will we be able, like the prophets, to manifest that faith enkindles a passionate love for man and his world and that genuine love of men and commitment for the world of man is a testimony of our yearning for God? The Christian ethics of responsibility dedicates itself to fostering this testimony.

Faith was often misunderstood as an individualistic flight from responsibility and commitment. But in its true sense "faith alone" means wholeness of vision and commitment, total acceptance of God's whole message and the fullness of his love, which gathers persons together in a commitment of their energies in solidarity for freedom, peace, unity, and justice to the glory of God's name. Wherever truth and love shine forth in a grateful committed response in responsibility, there faith meets God for all who yearn for the experience of genuine love and justice and peace.

God has manifested himself finally in his Son made man, made our brother. We cannot truly find in faith the God-man Jesus Christ without joining him in his passionate love for man and in his readiness to bear the burden of his brethren. There is no genuine acceptance of the encompassing manifestation of God's design without acceptance of our own situation with its limited but concrete responsibilities, without acceptance of our neighbor, and without a response-in-action to this message and appeal. But since this synthesis always informs our vocation, we live by faith in God's mercy.

Faith is reconciliation going on. Our acceptance of God's reconciling action makes it the rule of our own reconciling responsibility.[25] Thus our involvement in the secular city becomes not an earthly messianism or a triumphalistic theocracy but the humble service of those who are reconciled by grace.

An ethics of responsibility, as I see it, does not try to replace the article of "faith alone" by the new principle "love alone," since love would become in that case a kind of sphinx, an abstract principle open to all kinds of arbitrary interpretations. But an ethics of responsibility can focus thoroughly on love in the sense that all works of God, all the signs of his majesty and power are, in the final analysis, a manifestation of him who is love and who wants men as active sharers of his love. Thus a Christian ethics of response and responsibility is both an ethics of faith and an ethics of *agape*, and therefore an adherence to the "law of grace."

A concept of faith broadened to include response and active responsibility on all levels depends upon a concept of revelation broadened to include the whole of accessible knowledge about man and world. There is a sense of profound continuity in this which must, however, include total openness to the new—and sometimes shocking—reality of man and sciences about man and his responsibility to make the world inhabitable for the new human beings.[26] Of course we cannot confuse the data of modern science with a religious reality, but the man of faith is not confronted only with the Bible. What the secular scientists have found, he tries constantly to integrate into his committed approach of faith and responsibility.

The attitude of living faith includes vigilance and watchfulness to the *kairos*, the here and now in which is God's dynamic presence, his gifts and his appeal, drawing our attention to the needs of our neighbor. Without this watchfulness and readiness, faith does not come to its full stature regarding the present hour of decision. But it must also be underlined that genuine discernment of the opportunity of the moment can be gained only in that spirit of faith and solidarity with the community of faith that inserts us into the heritage of the past and the hopes of the future.

Faith is not another ideology; it is our insertion into the history of salvation, which means undeserved sharing but also active participation in gratitude. We Christians celebrate the "mystery of faith" in praise of all the past marvelous deeds of God—in the sense of the Hebrew word *dabar* (word and deed, deed and word) and in trusting and watchful expectation of what God will do unto the "day of the Lord." Thus the present moment becomes a crossroad, a gift of the salvation history.

Here is a total perspective, with complete commitment to the present moment and openness for the total future: for the future generations and for our final hope. So I understand the *indicative* of the good news and of grace not in a harrowing existentialism but in that personal, communal, and existential involvement which, by opening new horizons, conveys to us constantly a new dynamic *imperative*. In this way the radical obedience of faith is firm and at the same time open to all horizons.[27]

Through faith in Christ we are becoming gradually aware of our sinfulness and therefore also aware that our vision of faith and our understanding of reality is constantly handicapped and threatened by our egotism, our narrowness, and our contagion through the poisoned environment. Through faith, and especially through the mystery of faith celebrated in community, we realize ever more keenly that there is no way out of the pernicious solidarity of sin and the collectivism of prejudice and group egotism unless our "Yes" to Christ means a total commitment to the redemptive community of faith. This redemptive perspective of faith and of a Christian ethics of responsibility is often partially or wholly overlooked. The result is a naïve ethics of involvement in the secular city without the necessary attention to the community of faith and love offered us by Christ and his church.

It must be remembered that the church itself is also constantly in need of redemption and reform. It should be a community of people who are fully believing in all the dimensions of redemption and reconciliation and are at the same time a community of continuous conversion.

VII. Natural Law Ethics in the Light of "Faith Alone"

At least the discussion about Pope Paul's encyclical *Humanae vitae* (about birth regulation) has shown to everyone that there does not exist only one theory about natural law in Catholic theology. Even if the pope expresses his doctrine within the framework of one specific outlook on natural law, this does not at all mean a definition of that outlook or an unavoidable trend toward ossification of that theory.

It is not my intention to develop in these few pages my own outlook about a dynamic, history-related, personalistic natural law theory.[28] But if one confesses "faith alone," he has to explain his understanding of the relationship between faith and human reason and human experiences in such a crucial matter of ecumenical discussion as the ethics of natural law within a truly Christian ethics. Personally I do not cling to the term "natural law," but I use it because what I am speaking about is generally known by that name.[29]

The realm of natural law, as I understand it, is the capacity of the human person in community to share both moral experiences and the effort to decipher their meaning in a search for the best possible way to live a human life. I do not believe in innate platonic ideas, nor in a system of concepts given once and forever. But I do believe in the oneness of God's design for man and in man's capacity to reciprocate love and to gather the richness of human experiences. It is not a matter of an isolated individual or of bare abstract thinking, although there are individual persons who can enrich the moral experience and knowledge of the human community.

Natural law is never a final acquisition, nor the fruit of one person's effort. There is a wealth of wisdom that comes from the past and from the actual capacity of sharing. All the elements of natural law that indicate continuity are permeated by the historicity of human nature. Not only the individual person but all of humanity is on pilgrimage, called to look for the next step in a process of growth, conversion, and risk—always threatened by decay.

Man can find ethical truth—and truth generally—only in a historic context: fully aware of the present reality but also alert to the context of the experiences of the past and the indications for the future. It belongs to man's nature to be constantly in quest of new insights which are to be integrated into his heritage.

Natural law theory can—partially or totally—become a "whore" in the sense against which Martin Luther warned, if it is misused as an instrument of domination over persons, groups, or nations. In the Roman Empire natural law theory originated chiefly within a perspective of policy and power, although precious elements of concern for man's dignity and consideration for human diversity were also integrated. The Greek natural law theory, too, although it

tended toward a more genuine cosmopolitanism, was interwoven
with political concern and its egotisms, and was infected by the pride
of human wisdom. But there was also, at least in some thinkers, an
awareness of a dynamic presence of God.

Within the church, natural law doctrine was sometimes too rational, not sufficiently grounded on experience, not sufficiently aware
of the historic, dynamic nature of human beings and human thought,
not sufficiently aware of the existential element. The great thinkers,
however— men such as Augustine, Bonaventure, Thomas Aquinas
—knew that man can approach the great problems of ethical knowledge only by a certain *connaturalitas* (connaturality with the good),
to the extent that he commits himself to the good. Because of
man's sinfulness, the connaturality with the good is diminished and
disturbed.

My chief concern here is an integrated approach to natural law
theories. We must be aware that there exists no "pure" human
nature, no mere "natural" order of things, although there is a distinction of those truths which are more or less accessible to man's
experience and reflection without that totally unmerited revelation
which we find in the history of salvation reaching its climax in
Christ. Many insights that are an integral part of the Bible can be
found also in ethical cultures which were in no contact with Israel
or with the church of Christ, e.g., in the deep humane natural law
ethics of Confucianism.[30]

A theological approach to natural law ethics is somehow indicated
by the letter to the Romans. The point of chief attention is God's
own work through which "all that may be known of God by men
lies plain before their eyes; indeed God has disclosed it to them.
His invisible attributes, that is to say his everlasting power and deity,
have been visible to the eye of reason ever since the world began, in
the things he has made. There is therefore no possible defence for
their conduct; knowing God they have refused to honor him as God
or to render him thanks" (Rom. 1: 19–21).

From this it is clear that Paul is not speaking of a particular
philosophy about man's nature that would be linked to salvation. It
is in a perspective of revelation and salvation that he sees man and
his capacity to know and adore God, to render thanks in prayer and
by his conduct. It is a perspective of God's dynamic presence and
pedagogy, working not only from outside or merely on an intellectual
level but from man's innermost being, to make known his loving

will. "When Gentiles who do not possess the law carry out its precepts by the light of nature, then although they have no law, they are their own law, for they display the effect of the law inscribed on their hearts. Their conscience is called as witness." (Rom. 2: 14–15.)

Paul sees Christ present to Israel in the desert as the rock that gives the saving water. In this line of thought we can say that man's ethical knowledge and the appeal that arises from his innermost being has saving qualities only because it is God's message, gift, appeal: a grace that brings men into contact with the point Omega, Christ, and is bestowed on them in view of Christ. It is also clear that in Paul's theology man's relationship to truth and to the good is constantly threatened by error and sin; it cannot lead to salvation through man's own effort alone. Wherever men do not render thanks to God "their misguided minds are plunged in darkness" (Rom. 1:21).

This does not necessarily mean that all those who have not yet come to an explicit faith and to religious adoration are excluded from the reality of God's revelation and gracious presence. We can look at natural law from two different angles. One is seen by those who live in the full light of faith. In that light the perspective is the whole reality of the continuous creation and of history, of men's shared experiences, reflections, insights, and innate dynamism toward the good. They try to judge everything in the light of the gospel, and gradually they integrate it into the one reality of adoring faith with its dynamic to bear fruit in love for the life of the world. Of course the process of discerning everything in the light of faith can be more or less imperfect and slow, but their decisive approach is that of faith, as soon as God, who has revealed himself in Christ, has become the center of their life.

In the letter to the Romans, Paul looks at the matter from another angle: that of those who did not come into contact either with Christ or with the revelation of the Old Testament. According to that letter and The Letter to the Hebrews, it seems that the following thesis can be presented as at least possible:

Among men whom the explicit message of Christ or of the Old Testament has not yet reached, in all those searching sincerely for what is good, just, honest, and true, and dedicating themselves to what they understand to be the absolute demand of love and justice, there can already be operating "salvation through faith." Their

search and their commitment find a focal point in God, the Father
of our Lord Jesus Christ; their openness and commitment may,
through the grace of the Holy Spirit, have the structure and saving
power of faith.

This thesis does not exclude, but explicitly includes, the need of
redemption through Christ. If then, in this context, we speak of
"natural" law, of man's natural grasp of what is good and just, we
do not set it in opposition to the "supernatural," for we are not
using categories that imply two different orders, a natural and a
supernatural one. The same concern that the distinction between
"natural" and "supernatural" wanted to express, I try to express by
the emphatic assertion that if there is salvation, it is never through
man's own achievements but through "grace alone." By himself man
cannot find God and his salvation. They are found only through
God's design to reveal his love—and thus himself—in this way to
those persons who respond as men of goodwill. This is possible only
through his gracious presence.

Our whole approach to natural law is based on the doctrine of
the oneness of the economy and order of salvation: a thesis that is
commonly taught in the Roman Catholic Church but not given
equal attention in all times and places. In order to underline the undeserved graciousness of revelation and redemption in Christ, we
do distinguish, on the one side, those truths which are accessible to
man by his experiences, reflection, and shared insights, and, on the
other side, the mysteries of faith that transcend man's reason absolutely. But in the concreteness of a theology of the history of salvation we have to explain everything in a way that reveals clearly the
one—and the only one—order of salvation which extends to all
men. It is the fullness of revelation and redemption in Christ that
sheds its light and saving power on everything that is open to God's
self-manifestation and his loving concern for men.

The very conviction that salvation comes through faith alone
obliges the faithful to be receptive to all new insights and experiences
of mankind that help him to understand better man's destiny, dignity, and needs. The receptivity to God's design and the loving commitment to God's saving work, which characterize faith in Christ,
are the best guarantees for bringing home the whole wealth of the
past and present history of the church and also of the different cultures and religions. Faith warns us against pride and self-centeredness, but it does not allow us to ignore or to despise anything that

God manifests in the secular city, whether it be the fruit of Christian believers or of other men.

Each epoch has to make a new effort to express, in terms of man's particular experiences and changing language, the fundamental truths of salvation through faith, through grace. It is not easy to harmonize the specific religious interest of faith in Christ with a total openness for the joys, sorrows, hopes, and anguishes of all men of all times. Do we as individuals have the necessary discernment along with openness? How do the faithful, as persons in community, reach that synthesis and gain liberation from collective prejudices?

These questions find different responses within the church. An oversimplified solution within Catholic theology was to seek unity between faith and the insights of "natural law" almost exclusively through the teaching of the Magisterium. The argument runs this way: Christ has entrusted to the apostles and their successors, and in a particular way to Peter and his successors, the deposit of faith. But since God manifests his design and holy will not only through the deposit of faith that comes to us through the apostolic community but also through that law which he has written in the hearts of men and which reason can gradually grasp, the order of salvation demands that the Magisterium has also a competence in matters of natural law. Some schools of Catholic theologians would conclude: therefore, since faith teaches us to obey the God-given authority in matters of faith and morals, members of the church act in obedience of faith whenever they follow the norms taught by the Magisterium, whether these norms are taken from the deposit of faith or from principles of natural law.

Careful Catholic theology, however, makes several important distinctions here:

1. Absolute certainty of faith, and therefore an obedience that has the quality of faith, can be given only where we are confronted with the deposit of faith. The promise of the assistance of the Holy Spirit to the Magisterium does not include infallibility in matters not belonging to the deposit of faith. In this sense Vatican II teaches that "this infallibility with which the divine Redeemer willed his Church to be endowed in defining doctrine of faith and morals extends as far as extends the deposit of divine revelation, which must be religiously guarded and faithfully expounded."[31] This text surely does not favor the opinion of those Catholic theologians and bishops

who say that the pope could speak with infallibility on matters of natural law which are not a part of the divine revelation given in Christ. They are free to think this way, but they cannot assert that it is an infallible doctrine of the church.

The official speaker of the Doctrinal Commission of the First Vatican Council, Bishop Gasser, declared to the Plenary Session that it was the explicit intention of the Doctrinal Commission not to include in the definition of infallibility those theological matters not belonging directly to the deposit of faith.[32] The Council of Trent, too, while speaking on the indefectibility of the church, included only the doctrine of Christ "which through the apostles came to us."[33] The uniqueness of faith therefore obliges a Catholic not to speak strictly about "obedience of faith" when it is only a matter of natural law doctrine and not at the same time a doctrine taught by Christ and contained in the apostolic tradition.

2. The whole people of God has the duty to be docile to the Lord of history and therefore to be open to all experiences and insights of moral relevance. God does not oblige the faithful to anything that has relevance for salvation without bestowing his gracious help upon them. The church cannot be bereft of the assistance of the Holy Spirit when it is an important matter bearing fruit in love for the life of the world, but members of the church can be partially lacking in docility toward the Holy Spirit. One is indeed not docile to the Spirit if one is not open and docile toward the insights and experiences of other people.

3. Neither the whole visible church with all its members nor the Magisterium has a monopoly in matters of moral experience and insight based on knowledge of man. The Magisterium is faithful to the divine mandate and docile to the Holy Spirit to the extent that it is ready to use all available means to come to an ever more adequate knowledge. The divine mandate does not dispense from the necessity to earn competence regarding knowledge and to be aware of its limits.

4. The task of the Magisterium is not to teach doctrines of natural law unknown to men by experience and reflection but rather to help the faithful to discern, and to integrate into a perspective of faith and redeemed love, what humanity does already know by way of experience and reflection.

5. The Magisterium can and must teach with authority about assertions made in the name of reason if these assertions contradict

the doctrine of salvation which the church received from Christ. In this case the arguments must be taken from the deposit of faith; then it is not just a matter of "natural law."

6. Since natural law means, by definition, "what is visible to the eye of reason," the Magisterium cannot dispensate itself from the task of giving convincing arguments based on human experience and shared insights. Therefore, in cases where neither positively nor by way of contradiction a truth of the deposit of faith shines forth, the official teaching on natural law must be thoroughly based on listening and learning, on gathering all the possible contributions of people before the integrating effort is made. The teaching of the Magisterium gains moral authority and effectiveness if the limits of certainty or the tentative character of an approach is clearly and humbly indicated by the Magisterium itself. God's authority or the divine mandate should not be invoked where convincing arguments are lacking.

7. The mission of theologians and of the Magisterium is not fulfilled by repeating and inculcating an unchangeable scheme of formulas and concepts. Theirs is always a task of fidelity to the living God of history and service to living men. Here the faithful householder will "produce from his store both the new and the old" (Matt. 13:52).

NOTES

1. Hans Küng, *Rechtfertigung: Die Lehre Karl Barths und eine katholische Besinnung* (Vierte Auflage mitherausgegeben vom Johann Adam Mohler-Institute; Paderborn, Einsiedeln: Johannes Verlag, 1957). English trans.: *Justification: The Doctrine of Karl Barth and a Catholic Reflection* (Thomas Nelson & Sons, 1964). Hans Küng, *Structures of the Church* (Thomas Nelson & Sons, 1964). I find very helpful O. H. Pesch, O.P., *Theologie der Rechtfertigung bei Martin Luther und Thomas von Aquin: Versuch eines systematisch-theologischen Dialogs* (Mainz: Matthias-Grünewald-Verlag, 1967). O. H. Pesch, "Luthers theologisches Denken—eine katholische Möglichkeit," in *Die neue Ordnung* XXIII (1959), 1–19. Cf. A. Hasler, *Luther in der katholischen Dogmatik: Darstellung seiner Rechtfertigungslehre* (Munich: Hueber, 1968).

2. *Acta Apostolicae Sedis*, Vol. 54 (1962), p. 792.

3. Vatican II: Decree on Ecumenism, *Unitatis redintegratio,* art. 4.

4. *Ibid.,* art. 11.

5. In my opinion O. H. Pesch has shown with enough evidence that in the theology of Luther there prevails an existential theology that reflects "existentially" man's prayer, man's fear, and his trust in God, while the Catholic thinking to a great extent manifests a more "sapiential" approach that supposes the existential character of faith but extends the reflection beyond the existential realm (cf. n. 1, above).

6. Vatican II: Decree on Ecumenism, art. 14.

7. *Ibid.*

8. *Ibid.,* art. 15.

9. *Ibid.,* art. 17.

10. *Ibid.,* art. 23.

11. *Ibid.*

12. Erich Fromm, *The Heart of Man: Its Genius for Good and Evil* (Harper & Row, Publishers, Inc., 1964), p. 13.

13. James M. Gustafson, *Christ and the Moral Life* (Harper & Row, Publishers, Inc., 1968), p. ix.

14. Council of Trent, Sessio VI, cap. 8. Cf. Canon 9, Denzinger-Schonmetzer, *Ench. Symbolorum,* N. 1932. Cf. N. 1559.

15. Cf. Council of Trent, Sessio VI, Can. 32 and 33, Denzinger-Schonmetzer, N. 1582 and 1583.

16. Max Scheler, *Vom Ewigen im Menschen* (Leipzig: Der neue Geistverlag, 1923).

17. Cf. my book *The Christian Existentialist* (New York University Press, 1968), pp. 11 ff.

18. Rudolf Otto, *Das Heilige: Über das Irrationale in der Idee des Göttlichen und sein Verhältnis zum Rationalen* (1917; 30. Auflage, Munich: Beck, 1958).

19. I dedicated to this problem my book *Das Heilige und das Gute: Religion und Sittlichkeit in ihrem gegenseitigen Bezug* (Krailling vor Munich, 1950). In it I explored particularly the solutions given by Nicolai Hartmann, Immanuel Kant, Friedrich Daniel Schleiermacher, Emil Brunner, Rudolf Otto, Max Scheler, the Aristotelian and stoic ethics of self-fulfillment, the political ethics of "order" with their superficial "religious sanctions" in moral theology; and directing attention to those efforts which develop a vision, perspective, and vocabulary that show a closer synthesis without neglecting the necessary distinction between faith and morality.

20. It should not be forgotten that the legalistic type of moral theology was not the whole of Catholic moral theology. The French school of spirituality ("Cardinal Bérulle and his school") presented morality in the perspective of the "sacraments of faith." The German type of moral

theology (John Michael Sailor, John Baptist Hirscher, Deutinger, and many others) expressed very vigorously the unity between faith and morality as its fruit.

21. His whole *Church Dogmatics* III/4 is dedicated to this outlook.

22. Dorothee Sölle, *Phantasie und Gehorsam* (Stuttgart and Berlin: Kreuz-Verlag, 1968), is most critical of Karl Barth's view of *Glaubensgehorsam* as the chief character of Christian morality. It seems that she expresses the feeling of many Protestant theologians of the younger generation.

23. A good synthesis of this perspective is to be found in H. Richard Niebuhr's book *The Responsible Self* (Harper & Row, Publishers, Inc., 1963).

24. An introduction to this approach is in my book *The Law of Christ*, Vol. I (The Newman Press, 1961), pp. 35–53.

25. This religious perspective is splendidly developed by the various writings of John Bennett.

26. The book of Richard Luecke, *New Meanings for New Beings* (Fortress Press, 1964), expresses this awareness of the living God of history and the involvement of the element of faith.

27. I have great difficulty in finding the full dimension of salvation history in the ethics of Rudolf Bultmann. Cf. Thomas C. Oden, *Radical Obedience: The Ethics of Rudolf Bultmann* (The Westminster Press, 1964). In the ethics of Harvey Cox the open future does not fully integrate the past and does not fully affirm our hope of eternal life.

28. Cf. my essay "Dynamism and Continuity in a Personalistic Approach to Natural Law," Gene H. Outka and Paul Ramsey (eds.), *Norm and Context in Christian Ethics* (Charles Scribner's Sons, 1968), pp. 199–218.

29. Emil Brunner proposed as a more adequate name *Schöpfungsordnungen,* the created order, or the ordinations indicated by the Creator. Thus he too, but in a different way from Karl Barth, wants to remain within the limits indicated by the dogma of creation. But this name did not find universal consent; it seems also to be too static and does not express the complexity of moral knowledge and dynamism of persons who are sinners and just men at the same time, a fact of which Brunner was fully aware. In the world around us, there is also an investment of man's sins.

30. I mention here Confucius, since there is not only a prime importance given to man's "heart," to benevolence and kindness, but the whole is presented in gratitude toward the divine wisdom. "The share which Heaven has bestowed on the wise men are the virtues of kindness, justice, gentleness, and prudence. They all have their root in man's innermost being." (*Les Quatre Livres,* French and Latin trans. by S. Couvreur,

S.J., p. 616; Ho Kien Fou: Imprimerie de la Mission Catholique, 1895, p. 616.)

31. Vatican II: Dogmatic Constitution on the Church, *Lumen gentium*, art. 25.

32. Theodor Granderath, S.J., *Geschichte des Vatikanischen Konzils von seiner ersten Ankundigung bis zu seiner Vertagung*, Vol. III (Freiburg im Breisgau, St. Louis, Mo., etc., Herder & Herder, Inc., 1906), p. 476.

33. Council of Trent, Sessio IV, Denzinger-Schonmetzer, N. 1501.

✧ ✧ ✧ *Abraham Joshua Heschel, Professor of Jewish Ethics and Mysticism at the Jewish Theological Seminary of America, widely recognized as one of the outstanding interpreters of the Jewish religious tradition, served as the Harry Emerson Fosdick Visiting Professor at Union Theological Seminary for 1965–1966. His presence, spirit, and scholarship were warmly appreciated by the seminary community during his incumbency in the Fosdick professorship, one of the important events of Dr. Bennett's presidency. Rabbi Heschel received his Ph.D. in 1933 at the University of Berlin, and taught at Berlin and Frankfurt until the rise of Nazism led to his return to his native Warsaw. In 1939 he established the Institute for Jewish Learning in London. The next year he came to this country, where he taught at Hebrew Union College, in Cincinnati, before coming to New York the following year. Among his many books are* Man Is Not Alone *(1951),* God in Search of Man *(1955), and* The Insecurity of Freedom *(1966). He has been a leader in movements for peace, racial justice, and interfaith dialogue.*

Professor Heschel believes that mutual understanding among the religious communities is furthered when the deeper attitudes and concerns of each are frankly and thoughtfully expressed. For example, when a Christian speaks of the things of deepest religious concerns to him, he characteristically focuses on such themes as God, Christ, the Spirit, and the church. In an analogous way, in this essay Dr. Heschel sets forth simply but profoundly three central themes of Judaism: God, Torah, Israel.

3

GOD,
TORAH,
AND ISRAEL

❖ ❖ ❖ *Abraham J. Heschel*[1]

JUDAISM is a complex structure. It can neither be characterized exclusively as a theological doctrine, nor as a way of living according to the law, nor as a community. A religious Jew is a person committed to God, to his concern and teaching (Torah), who lives as part of a covenant community (Israel). Judaism revolves around three sacred entities: God, Torah, Israel. The Jew never stands alone before God; the Torah and Israel are always with him.

God as an isolated concept may be exceedingly hidden, vague, and general. In Jewish experience the relation between God and man is established as a concrete and genuine situation in finding an answer to the questions: What are the acts and moments in which God becomes manifest to man? What are the acts and moments in which man becomes attached to God? To the Jew, the Torah is the answer.

Jewish existence is not only the adherence to particular doctrines and observances but primarily the living *in* the spiritual order of the Jewish people, the living *in* the Jews of the past and *with* the Jews of the present. Not only is it a certain quality in the souls of the individuals but it is primarily involvement and participation in the covenant and community of Israel. It is more than an experience or a creed, more than the possession of psychic traits or the acceptance of theological doctrine; it is, above all, the living in a holy dimension, in a spiritual order. Our share in holiness we acquire by living in the Jewish community. What we do as individuals may be a trivial episode; what we attain as Israel causes us to grow into the infinite.

Since sanctity is associated with each of these three entities, the question arises whether they are all on the same level of holiness, whether they form part of a hierarchy, or whether a dialectic relationship among them exists that is too subtle to be stated in a simple brief statement.

Because of the power and preciousness of the three entities, there is a tendency to extol and to overstate one at the expense of the other two. Various movements in modern Judaism have tended to indulge in such extravagancy.

With some degree of justification it may be said that classical Reform Judaism has concentrated on ethical monotheism as the essence of Judaism. Secular nationalism has made the peoplehood of Israel its central concern, and neo-orthodoxy, in its eagerness to defend the traditional observances, has stressed the supremacy of the Torah and Law.

The purpose of this essay is an effort to clarify the relationship of God and Torah in the light of classical rabbinic literature, and to elucidate the classical rabbinic doctrine of the interdependence of the three entities.

I. GOD AND TORAH

The Torah, the comprehensive name for the revealed teachings of Judaism, has been an object of love and adoration. According to the school of Rabbi Akiba, the Torah has a concrete as well as a spiritual reality; it not only exists as a book in human possession; it also exists in heaven as well as on earth.[2] Indeed, the Hebrew term for revelation is literally "Torah from heaven."[3]

What is the relationship of Torah and God? What does the Torah mean to Israel?

The Torah is not only identified with the divine wisdom which preceded the existence of the world;[4] its worth surpasses the value of all things.

Two thousand years ago in Alexandria, we are told in a legend, a sage of the Greeks asked a sage of the Hebrews:

Why are you Jews so proud of your heritage? We Greeks have Homer, Plato, and Aristotle. What have you? Our sages have discovered the idea of the cosmos. What have yours done? How can you even venture to compare your intellectual heritage with ours?

"True," said the Jew, "you have discovered the cosmos. Yet what we have transcends even the mystery and vastness of the cosmos." "What can that be?" queried the Greek. Came the reply: "We have the Torah."[5]

This legend reflects a view not foreign to hyperbolic rabbinic thought. Not only does the Torah transcend the cosmos, but "any given part of the Torah is of greater importance than the cosmos."[6] The Torah determines both the essence and the existence of the universe. When God decided to create the Torah, say the rabbis, he consulted the Torah. It served as his blueprint for creation.[7] The nature of creation was determined through the Torah. Even the initial existence of the cosmos is dependent upon the Torah. "The existence of the Torah is a necessary condition for the existence of the cosmos."[8]

How vast is the cosmos! Yet somewhere in the dimension of space lies its limit. Is there an entity without any limit? Yes, said the enthusiastic rabbis, the Torah.[9]

Not only was the existence of the Torah the necessary requirement for the creation of the cosmos; it is also the necessary condition for its continued existence. The world was created on approval. Unless the Torah was accepted at Sinai, the cosmos would have to be returned to chaos. There could be a cosmos only with the Torah. The absence of the Torah would imply the absence of the universe. With Torah comes the divine blessing of an ordered creation. Without it, there is danger of a return to the abyss of cosmic confusion. The Torah is the ground of all beings. The creatures of heaven and earth cannot exist without it.[10]

When one gives a gift in love to another, part of the giver is given with the gift. The Torah is God's gift to his creation and to his creatures. When God gives the Torah, it is as if he gives of himself.[11]

A parable:

Once there was a king who had an only daughter whom another king married. When the latter wished to return to his country and take his wife with him, the father said, "My daughter, whom I have given you in marriage, is my only child. My love for her is great. I cannot part from her. Yet, I cannot ask you not to take her to your realm. It is now her proper home. Permit me this one request. To whatever distant place you take her now to live, always have a chamber ready for me that I may dwell with you and with her. For I can never consider really leaving my daughter."

So said God to Israel: "I have given you a Torah from which I cannot really part. I cannot tell you not to receive it in love. Yet, I request only this. Wherever you go with it, make for me a house wherein I may sojourn. As it is written: *Let them make me a sanctuary so that I may dwell among them*" (Ex. 25:8).[12]

Is not a child both a part of and apart from its parent? So is the Torah part of and apart from God. When Israel accepts the Torah, she accepts God.

A child's presence testifies to the life of its parent. The Torah testifies for God.

> Once a king had a daughter. He built her palaces with many great halls. His decree went forth: Whosoever is granted an audience with my daughter is to be considered as being in my presence. Whosoever dares to insult my daughter, it is as if he insulted me.[13]

The literary metaphors in which God's relation to the Torah is described may be compared to the rabbinic description of the relationship between the *Shekhinah* (God's indwelling or presence) and the community of Israel. Participation in the same events links them, one to the other. It is almost as if the fate of one determined the fate of the other. As reflections about the relationship between God and Israel develop, the interdependence of God and Israel becomes more emphatic. As the love between them intensifies, the father becomes dependent upon the daughter for love, devotion, and care. In effect, the daughter assumes the role of mother. Israel remains no longer the receptive child. God's actions are in a way determined by and dependent upon those of the child.[14]

The parent bears the child. Yet elements of the parent are borne by the child. Similarly, the Torah, which comes from God, carries the presence of God within its words. Since God is the source of all wisdom, the Torah is the treasure-house of all wisdom. *The spirit of God hovers over the waters*—these waters are the Torah. The Torah is all-inclusive. "Review its words again and again, all is contained in them."[15]

The child has qualities of the parent. Like God, the Torah transcends space and time. It is an element of heaven which was put upon the earth. It is eternity perceived through the given moment. Within it dwell secrets of perfection, visions of beatitude.

Perhaps the imagery describing the Torah is too exalting and consequently excessively audacious. Perhaps the image is too closely applied to the subject. Perhaps the Torah is identified too closely with divine wisdom, and there is a possibility of confusing the child with the parent. It is hardly acceptable, for example, to consider divine wisdom to be restricted to the Torah alone.

The tendency to assert a close identity between the Torah and God's wisdom may lead to the danger of making the Torah a substitute for God. One is tempted to understand the Torah not only as possessing a divine quality, as being saturated with divinity, but as being divinity itself, and consequently as being an object worthy of meditation and devotion in man's yearning to cleave to a higher reality than himself. In this view, divine wisdom is not only in the Torah; it is the Torah.

However, again and again we are admonished against taking a totalitarian view of the Torah. God is greater than the Torah. He who devotes himself only to Torah and does not cultivate awe of God is regarded as a failure.

Raba said:

> When man is led in for judgment in the next life, he is asked, "Did you deal honestly in business? Did you fix times for the study of the Torah? Did you engage in procreation? Did you hope for salvation? Did you engage in the dialectics of wisdom? Did you learn by means of deductive reasoning? Even so, if 'the awe of the Lord is his treasure,' it is well. If not, it is not well."[16]

From this, Rabbi Joseph of Trani, a Talmudist of the latter part of the sixteenth century, concludes: The study of Torah is worthless when not accompanied by awe and fear of heaven.[17]

There is an often-quoted remark that God has nothing else in this world but the four cubits of the Torah's law,[18] as if the law were the only treasure cherished by God. Other statements, however, insist: "The Holy One blessed be he, has nothing else in his world but awe and fear of heaven."[19] "The Holy One blessed be he, has in his treasury nought except a store of awe of heaven."[20]

In the liturgy asking blessings for the new Hebrew month, according to the Western European Jewish ritual, we pray for both "love of Torah and awe of heaven." One complements the other. Jewish religious consciousness must embrace both.

For all the extreme praise of the Torah, its real preciousness is not in its qualities, but in the fact that the Torah is God's Torah. The Torah is not an end in itself; it is transcended by God. The purpose of giving the Torah was to sanctify God's great name.[21]

The sanctity of the Torah is great. For example, one who leaves out or adds a letter to its text is compared to one who causes the entire world to be destroyed. Even so (says Rabbi Hiyya), it could still be asserted that it is better to remove a letter of the Torah than for God's name to be publicly desecrated.[22]

There are three cardinal sins: idolatry, adultery, and murder. More severe than they is the sin of desecrating God's name. "God shows indulgence toward idolatry, . . . adultery, . . . and murder, . . . but does not show indulgence to him who has profaned his name."[23]

There were many debates concerning the scope of the study of the Torah. When the religious obligations were listed, the study of the Torah was counted among those which have no limit to their performance. He who does more becomes more praiseworthy. After all the religious obligations had been enumerated, it was concluded that the study of the Torah is equivalent to them all.[24] The ideal is study for "its own sake," meaning God's sake, and not for the sake of the Torah. Occupation with the Torah for its sake means, "Because the Lord has commanded me, and not for the purpose of gaining recognition."[25]

Rabbi Bannah, a Palestinian Tanna of the third century, used to say: "Whoever occupies himself with the Torah for its own sake, his learning becomes an elixir of life for him. . . . But whosoever occupies himself with the Torah not for its sake, it becomes for him a deadly poison."[26]

This emphasis upon the correct motivation applies to all other commandments as well as to the study of the Torah.

An accepted statement of rabbinic tradition is that not study but the deed is the most important thing.[27] Together with this, Rabbi Jose, Palestinian Tanna of the second century, said, "All one's deeds should be for the sake of heaven."[28] The Mishnah, after dwelling upon all details of the sacrificial laws of animal and meal offerings, concludes with the general principle: "It is the same whether a man offers much or little, so long as he directs his heart to heaven."[29] The great sage Hillel was not praised for his learning alone. His greatest merit was that "all his deeds were for the sake of heaven."[30]

A favorite saying of Raba was, "The goal of wisdom is repentance and good deeds. . . . If one does good deeds for other motives than their own sake, it were better had he not been created."[31]

Rab, celebrated Babylonian Amora and founder of the academy of Sura (died 247), said: "Always let a man be occupied with Torah and religious precepts even if not for their own sake. For observance not for their own sake will eventually become observance for their own sake."[32] Commenting on this, Rabbi Isaiah Horowitz (1555–1630?) wrote: "While one is studying Torah with ulterior motives, in the course of one's study, one will learn that the tradition teaches that to act in such a way is a great sin. He then becomes encouraged to observe for the sake of the commandments themselves. However, preoccupation with the Torah because of ulterior motives is a sin in itself."[33]

Though expressions such as "awe or fear of God," "awe of heaven," "fear of sin," are common in rabbinic literature, there is no such expression as "awe or fear of Torah." One must always live in the awe of God (Deut. 6:13). To paraphrase an old rabbinic saying: One must not be in awe of the Torah but in awe of Him who gives the Torah.

In the Palestinian Talmud it is written:

> Nehemiah of Emmaus, the teacher of Rabbi Akiba, who learned all the minute peculiarities and details of the methodology of rabbinic exegesis from Rabbi Akiba, once asked, "What is the meaning of the verse, *One should be in awe of one's God*"? He said, "One must be in awe of God and his Torah."[34]

However, in the Babylonian Talmud, the story is reported differently:

> Nehemiah of Emmaus interpreted the verse, *One should be in awe of one's God,* to mean that one would not allow the awe of God to be extended to anything other than God. . . . Rabbi Akiba disagreed: the verse, *One must be in awe of God,* teaches that one should also be in awe of one's mentors.[35]

Should one be in awe of God's temple?

The verse reads, *You shall observe my Sabbaths and be in awe of my sanctuary* (Lev. 19:30). The expression "observe" was used in relation to the sanctuary. . . . As in the case of "observance" used in relation to the Sabbath, one does not revere the Sabbath but Him who commanded the observance of the Sabbath, so in the case of "awe" used in relation to the sanctuary, one is not to be in awe of the sanctuary, but Him who gave the commandment concerning the sanctuary.[36]

Said Rabbi Abraham ben David of Posquieres (twelfth century), "One should be in awe of God while in the sanctuary. One's awe should be directed to God, not to the sanctuary."[37]

To whom then will you compare me, that I should be like him? says the Holy One. (Isa. 40:25.) As God transcends the world, he transcends the Torah. Many rabbinic statements express this view. Suffice it here to note the general rule. The verse, *It is time for the Lord to act, They have made void thy Torah* (Ps. 119:126), was interpreted to mean: it is time to act for the Lord, set aside the Torah! Sometimes one should annul parts of the Torah to act for the Lord.[38]

Rabbi Joshua ben Korha insisted that one must first take upon himself the authority of God before accepting the authority of the Torah.[39]

The Torah is not to be understood in its own terms. Love of the Torah and awe of God are interrelated. Acts of loving-kindness and study of Torah must go together. The Torah does not stand alone. It stands with God and with man. Love of Torah links awe of God with the individual performance of deeds of loving-kindness toward one's fellowmen. The Torah is the knot wherein God and man are interlaced. However, he who accepts God's existence without accepting the authority of the Torah deviates from Judaism.

Rav Huna, Babylonian Amora (ca. 216–ca. 296), said, "He who occupies himself only with the study of Torah is as if he had no God."[40] According to Rabbi Jose, "He who says he has an interest only in the Torah has no interest even in the Torah."[41]

He who suggests that the Torah has a supremacy, not exceeded by any other being, and that belief in God (or attachment to Israel) is of secondary importance is guilty of extreme distortion. Though the divine is within the Torah, it also transcends the Torah. Even Moses, who received the Torah and achieved the highest level of prophetic attainment, knew that his prophetic illumination and grasp of the wisdom of God were not perfect.[42]

Though the Torah that Moses received is God's wisdom, it is inconceivable, scholars of later generations maintained, that the Torah he received is exactly the way it was in God's wisdom. Perhaps Moses did not receive the whole Torah, but only a small part of it,[43] only a small part of the all-inclusive store of God's wisdom, was revealed on earth. "Fifty gates of understanding were created in the world and all were given to Moses, except one."[44] The Torah in our hands is some of God's wisdom but not all of his wisdom. The Torah we have is the unripened fruit of heavenly wisdom."[45] Scripture does not capture the totality of the divine personality. God's mercy, for example, transcends all Biblical statements and expectations.

They asked Wisdom: What is the punishment of the sinner? Wisdom answered: *Evil pursues sinners* (Prov. 13:21). They asked Prophecy. And Prophecy answered: *The soul that sins shall die* (Ezek. 18:4). They then asked the Torah and she answered: Let him bring a guilt offering and it shall be forgiven unto him, as it says, *it may be acceptable in his behalf, in expiation for him* (Lev. 1:4). Finally, they asked the Holy One, blessed be he, who answered: Let him do repentance and it shall be forgiven unto him. For *good and upright is the Lord; therefore he instructs sinners in the way* (toward repentance) (Ps. 25:8).[46]

A Palestinian agadist, whose chronology is unknown, argued strenuously against the fate of bastards; namely, their being excluded, according to the law, from the community:

Again I saw all the oppressions that are practiced under the sun. And behold, the tears of the oppressed, and they had no one to comfort them! On the side of their oppressors there was power, and there was no one to comfort them (Eccl. 4:1). Daniel the Tailor interpreted the verse as applying to bastards. *And behold, the tears of the oppressed.* If the parents of these bastards committed transgression, why should their descendants suffer? If this man's father cohabited with a forbidden woman, what sin has his descendant committed and what concern is it of his? And there was no one to comfort them! But *on the side of their oppressors there was power.* This means Israel's Great Sanhedrin who comes to them with the power derived from the Torah and removes them from the fold, in virtue of the commandment, *A bastard shall not enter into the assembly of the Lord* (Deut. 23:3). *But they had no one to comfort them.* Says the Holy One blessed be he, It shall be my task to comfort them. Though in this world there is dross in them, in the World to Come says Zechariah (see Zech. 4:2), I have seem them all of pure gold.[47]

According to Nahmanides (born at Gerona, Spain, in 1194; died in Palestine about 1270), the Torah is not the all-inclusive guide to human behavior. "One can be a scoundrel within the letter of the Torah."[48]

It has been said: "He who is occupied with Torah is called a King and a Leader,"[49] and "He who studies Torah without ulterior motives, it is as though he built both the heavenly and the earthly Temple."[50] Nevertheless, it was believed that the rewards in the afterlife extended to the pious go beyond the attainment of wisdom and study of the Torah. A favorite saying of Rab was that in the future life "the pious will sit with their crowns on their heads feasting on the radiance of the divine presence."[51]

He who provides God with an image ascribes to him imperfection and negates his transcendence. To equate God with the Torah would be a grave distortion.

It is clear that the suggestion to equate the essence of God with the essence of the Torah has never even enticed the minds of the authors of the Talmud. They considered the Torah to be God's creation, his property, not his essence.

"Five possessions has the Holy One blessed be he, specifically declared his own in his world. These are: the Torah, the sanctuary, heaven and earth, Abraham and Israel."[52] The Torah is God's creation and his property, his wisdom and his will, but not he himself. Just as pantheism is foreign to the rabbinic mind, so would be the identification of God with the Torah. "With respect to the Holy One blessed be he, the world is his and the Torah is his."[53]

In contrast to the Muslim view of the Koran as the eternal uncreated Word, Maimonides insisted that all Jews agree "that the Torah is a created entity," brought into being in the same manner as all other created beings.

However, in the development of Jewish mysticism we come upon one statement that seems to contradict Maimonides' observation, a statement by Rabbi Menahem Recanati (ca. 1300), for which I know no parallel in Jewish literature. "God is incomplete without the Torah. The Torah is not something outside him, and he is not outside the Torah. Consequently, the mystic stated that God is the Torah."[54]

According to the Zohar, the Torah was emanated from divine wisdom. The Torah is connected to God. Therefore, "God is called the Torah"[55] since "the words of the Torah are in actuality the names of God."[56] Israel is the wick, the Torah the thread, and God's presence (*Shekhinah*) is the fire.[57] These are three entities each of which is connected to the other: God, the Torah, and Israel. "God and Israel, when together, are called one, but not when parted."[58] Similarly, "when a man separates himself from the Torah, he separates himself from God."[59]

The following statement is often quoted as having the Zohar for its source (late thirteenth century). Yet it is not found there. "The Torah, God, and Israel are one." The citation appears first among eighteenth-century authors.[60] The Torah and the world are God's possessions. The world is his, but he is not his world. The Torah is his, but he is not his Torah. The Torah is not in itself God, not his essence, but rather his wisdom and his will. Though the Torah pre-existed creation, it is not an eternal existent. Israel's relationship to Torah, however, is a commitment more basic than loyalty to any particular commandment. "Rabbi Jeremiah in the name of Rabbi Samuel bar Rabbi Isaac said: There are instances in which God excused Israel for the three cardinal sins of idolatry, adultery, and murder. Yet with regard to the sin of despising the Torah, we have no record of amnesty." How come? Paraphrasing the words of the prophet Jeremiah (Jer. 16:11), They have forsaken me and have not kept my Torah, he continued: "Would that they had forsaken me and kept my Torah."[61]

To regard this passage, however, as a declaration of the primary if not exclusive importance of studying Torah over concern for God is to pervert the meaning of the passage. Such perversion is made possible by overlooking the second part of the passage which reads as follows: "since by occupying themselves with the Torah, the light which she contains would have led them back to *me*."[62] It was not an ideal that the rabbis envisaged, but a last resort. Having forsaken all commandments, if the people had at least continued to study Torah, the light of the Torah would have brought them back to God.

It is, therefore, a distortion to interpret this passage to mean that Torah without fear or awe of God is acceptable, as if the importance of observance outweighs the centrality of faith.

The old rabbinic view that observance of Torah even without awe and fear of heaven is acceptable proposes that observance with improper ends in mind will lead to observance with proper ends in mind. "Rabbi Judah in the name of Rab said: A man should always occupy himself with Torah and good deeds, though it is not for their own sake, for out of doing good with an ulterior motive there comes about the service of God for its own sake, without an ulterior motive."[63]

Again and again we are taught that the Torah is not an end in itself. It is the gate through which one enters the court in which one finds awe of heaven. "Said Rabbi Yanni: Woe to him who has no court; woe to him who thinks the gate is the court. . . . And Rabbi Jonathan said: Woe to those scholars who occupy themselves with Torah and have not awe of the Lord."[64]

In a medieval Midrash we come upon a complaint against those saintly and righteous men whose dedication to the Torah surpasses their craving for the messianic kingdom.[65]

Rabbi Solomon Alami, an ethical writer who lived in Portugal in the fourteenth and fifteenth centuries, was an eyewitness of the persecutions of the Jews of Catalonia, Castile, and Aragon in 1391. Attempting to explain why so much suffering befell his people, he wrote:

> Let us search for the source of all these trials and sufferings, and we shall find that a state of dissolution prevails in the midst of us; that an evil spirit pervades our camp, which has split us into two parties. There are those of our brethren who expend all their energies in solving Talmudic problems and in writing numberless commentaries and novellae dealing in minute distinctions and interpretations, full of useless subtleties as thin as cobwebs. They diffuse darkness instead of light, and lower respect for the law. Others, again, clothe the Torah in strange garments, deck it with Grecian and other anti-Jewish ornaments, and endeavor to harmonize it with philosophy, which can only be detrimental to religion and lead ultimately to its decay.[66]

Rabbi Jehudah Loewe ben Bezelel of Prague (died 1609) pointed to the problem involved in the exuberant love of the Torah. The scholar who while studying is passionately absorbed in the love of the Torah is unable at that very moment to experience the love of God, since it is impossible to experience two loves simultaneously.[67]

The relationship between halachah and agadah in Judaism is reflected in the conception of the relationship between the Torah and God. Rabbi Mordechai Joseph of Isbitsa, a major figure in the history of the Hasidic movement, offers an important insight into this problem.

It has been foretold in the Bible that someday Ephraim will not be jealous of Judah and Judah will not harass Ephraim (Isa. 11:13). These two types (tribes) are always in conflict. Ephraim has been appointed by God to concentrate himself on the law and to be devoted to the commandments. This is why the prophet warns the people of Israel to observe the law strictly, *Lest he break out like fire in the house of Joseph* (Amos 5:6).

Judah has been appointed to concentrate on God and to be attached to him in all his ways. Therefore Judah is not satisfied to know the mere law but looks for God to reveal to him the depths of truth beyond the law itself. (For it is possible in law for a verdict to be correct according to the information which is available to the judges and yet to go against the truth. Cf. Shevout 29a, for example.) Judah refuses to be content with routine observance or perfunctory faith. Not content to do today what he did yesterday, he desires to find new light in His commandments every day. This insistence on fresh light sometimes drives Judah into doing actions for the sake of God which are against the strict law.

But in the future, we have been promised that Ephraim and Judah will no longer contend. God will show Ephraim that Judah's actions, even when they go outside the limits of the law, are always for His sake and not for any impure motive, and then there will be genuine understanding and peace between them.[68]

According to the method of "Judah," the Torah is not an end in itself. It has been said about the First Cause—"all existents need him and he does not need any one or all of them." Such a statement is not acceptable concerning the Torah. It needs us, it is not sufficient to itself.

II. God and Israel

According to rabbinic legend, the prophet Elijah, who did not die but ascended to heaven, not only was active as the helper in distress but also appeared to sages and saints assisting them in solving spiritual problems. Once, we are told, the following issue was submitted to him by a sage:

Two things I love wholeheartedly: the Torah and Israel. However, I am not sure which one I love more.

The response of Elijah was:

> The accepted opinion seems to suggest that the Torah is most important, as the verse reads, with regard to the Torah, *The Lord made me as the beginning of his way* (Prov. 8:22).[69] However, I think that not the Torah but Israel is most important. For the prophet has said: *Israel is holy to the Lord; the first fruits of his harvest* (Jer. 2:3).[70]

That which came first is to be cherished the most. Consequently, since the people Israel existed alone, first, without the Torah, it should be cherished more than the Torah. According to another source, reflecting apocalyptic thinking, Israel "existed (supernaturally) even before the world was created, as it says, *Remember thy congregation which thou hast gotten of old*" (Ps. 74:2).[71]

The extraordinary awareness of the endurance of Israel was expressed in an unsurpassed way by the prophet Jeremiah (Jer. 31:35–37).

> Thus says the Lord,
> who gives the sun for light by day
>   and the fixed order of the moon
>   and the stars for light by night,
> who stirs up the sea so that its waves roar—
>   the Lord of hosts is his name:
> "If this fixed order departs
>   from before me, says the Lord,
> then shall the descendants of Israel cease
>   from being a nation before me for ever."

These extraordinary words were echoed in the statement of Rabbi Joshua ben Levian, Amora of the first half of the third century, head of the school in Lydda in southern Palestine. "Israel can never die, neither in this world nor the world to come."[72] A world without Torah would be a world without Israel, and a world without Israel would be a world without the God of Israel.

Rabbi Simon bar Yohai of the second century said, "It is written, *For as the days of a tree shall be the days of my people* (Isa. 65:22). A 'tree' signifies the Torah, as it is stated, *It* (e.g., the Torah) *is a tree of life to them that lay hold upon it* (Prov. 3:18). Now which was created for the sake of which? Was the Torah created for the sake of Israel or vice versa? Surely, the Torah was created for the sake of Israel. Thus if the Torah endures for all eternity, how much more must Israel for whose sake it was created endure for all eternity?"[73]

Though the law demands strict observance of the latter, teleological consideration may dictate its suspension as, for example, for the purpose of saving human life, of saving the people. Perhaps the most striking expression of the relationship between the Torah and the people is the classical maxim by Rabbi Simeon ben Menasya, Palestinian Tanna of the second century, and contemporary of Rabbi Judah ha-Nasi, in his interpretation of Ex. 31:14, *You shall keep the Sabbath therefore, for it is holy unto you.* "The words 'unto you,' " he said, "imply that the Sabbath is given to you, and that you are not given to the Sabbath."[74]

The survival of Israel is an important consideration in dealing with the law.

Esther suggested to Mordechai: *Go gather all the Jews found in Sushan and fast for my sake. Do not eat or drink for three days* (Esth. 4:16). This was during the month of Nissan (April). Mordechai answered Esther: "I cannot abrogate the law set down in the Scroll on Fasting in which it is written, From the first day of the month of Nissan until the eighteenth of the month one may not fast. You would break this law by insisting that we fast three days, beginning with the fourteenth?" She responded, "Are you the chief elder of Israel? Then consider, if Israel is annihilated (according to the decree of Haman), what good will God's commandments for Israel be? If there is no Israel, why should there be a Torah?" . . . And so Samuel said, Mordechai pretended he was unaware of the law and declared the fast.[75]

III. Torah and Israel

It is customary to treat them as independent entities, as self-contained concepts with separate stature and independent validity. Nevertheless, these concepts are essentially related, one to the other. They are interdependent by virtue of their common source. Saadia Gaon was correct in asserting that Israel is a people only by virtue of its Torah,[76] that the only assurance for Israel's peoplehood is the Torah. On the other hand, Rabbi Halevi reminds us, "If there were no Jews, there would be no Torah."[77]

You are my witnesses, says the Lord, and I am God (Isa. 43:12). Rabbi Simeon ben Yochai (second century) took the sentence to mean: if you are my witnesses, I am God; if you cease to be my witnesses, I am not God.[78] This is a bold expression of the interdependence of God and Israel, a thought that occurs in various degrees of clarity in the history of Jewish theology. This particular statement maintains: If there are no witnesses, there is no God to be met. There is a mystery, an enigma, a darkness past finding out. For God to be present there have to be witnesses.[79]

The essence of Judaism is the awareness of the *reciprocity* of God and man, of man's *togetherness* with him who abides in eternal otherness. For the task of living is his and ours, and so is the responsibility. We have rights, not only obligations; our ultimate commitment is our ultimate privilege.

In interpreting Mal. 3:18, Rabbi Aha ben Ada said: "Then shall ye again discern between the righteous and the wicked," meaning: "between him who has faith and him who has not faith"; "between him that serveth God and him that serveth him not,"[80] meaning: "between him who serves God's *need* and him who does not serve God's *need*. One should not make of the Torah a spade with which to dig, a tool for personal use or a crown to magnify oneself."[81]

His need is a self-imposed concern. God is now in need of man, because he freely made him a partner in his enterprise, "a partner in the work of creation." "From the first day of creation the Holy One, blessed be he, longed to enter into *partnership* with the terrestrial world" to dwell with his creatures within the terrestrial world.[82] Expounding the verse in Gen. 17:1, the Midrash remarked: "in the view of Rabbi Johanan we need His honor; in the view of Rabbi Simeon ben Lakish He needs our honor."[83]

"When Israel performs the will of the Omnipresent, they add strength to the heavenly power; as it is said: *To God we render strength* (Ps. 60:14). When, however, Israel does not perform the will of the Omnipresent, they weaken—if it is possible to say so— the great power of Him who is above; as it is written, *Thou didst weaken the Rock that begot Thee* (Deut. 32:18)."[84]

Man's relationship to God is not one of passive reliance upon his omnipotence but one of active assistance. "The impious rely on their gods; . . . the righteous are the support of God."[85]

The Patriarchs are therefore called "the chariot of the Lord."[86]

He glories in me, He delights in me;
My crown of beauty He shall be.
His glory rests on me, and mine on Him;
He is near to me, when I call on Him.

(The Hymn of Glory)

To repeat, Jewish existence is not only the adherence to particular doctrines and observances, but primarily the living *in* the spiritual order of the Jewish people, the living *in* the Jews of the past and *with* the Jews of the present. It is not only a certain quality in the souls of the individuals, but it is primarily involvement and participation in the covenant and community of Israel. It is more than an experience or a creed, more than the possession of psychic traits or the acceptance of theological doctrine; it is, above all, the living in a holy dimension, in a spiritual order. Our share in holiness we acquire by living within the community. What we do as individuals may be a trivial episode; what we attain as Israel causes us to grow into the infinite.

NOTES

1. This essay, originally written in Hebrew, was translated into English by Byron Sherwin and subsequently revised by the author.
2. See Abraham J. Heschel, *Torah Min Ha-Shamayim b'Espaklaria shel Ha-Dorot* (*Theology of Ancient Judaism*, Vol. II) (London and New York: The Soncino Press, 1965), pp. 3 ff.
3. About another term for revelation, "Torah from Sinai," see Heschel, *op. cit.*, Vol. II, pp. 1 f.
4. See a discussion of this problem in Heschel, *op. cit.*, Vol. II, pp. 8 ff.
5. This story is mentioned in an essay by Deissman which regretfully I cannot locate now.
6. *Yerushalmi*, Peah 1:1 (15d).
7. *Genesis Rabba* 1:2.
8. *Tanhuma*, Tavo 3.
9. *Genesis Rabba* 10:1.
10. *Aboda Zara* 3b; *Sanhedrin* 99b.
11. *Exodus Rabba* 33:6; see also *Tanhuma, Terumah* 3.
12. *Exodus Rabba* 33:1; see *Leviticus Rabba* 30:13.
13. *Tanhuma*, Pekuday 4.

14. *Pesiktha de Rab Kahana* 1:4; see Abraham J. Heschel, *op. cit.,* Vol. I, pp. 66 ff.

15. *Aboth,* ch. Five, end.

16. *Shabbath* 31a.

17. *Response of the Marharit* (Joseph of Trani), Part I, #100.

18. *Berakoth* 8a.

19. *Shabbath* 31b.

20. *Berakoth* 33b.

21. *Yalkut Shimoni,* V'ethanan, #837.

22. *Yebamoth,* p. 79a.

23. *Leviticus Rabba* 22:6; *Midrash Tehillim* 27:2.

24. *Peah* 1:1.

25. Rashi to *Taanith* 7a.

26. *Taanith* 7a; *Sifre Deuteronomy,* Piska 306.

27. *Aboth* 1:17.

28. *Aboth* 2:12.

29. *Menachoth* 110a.

30. *Betzah* 16a.

31. *Berakoth* 17a.

32. *Pesachim* 50b; *Yerushalmi,* Hagiga 1:7 (76c).

33. *Shnei Luhoth HaBrit,* p. 371b; see also Yehiel Halperin's *Arche He Kinuyim,* "Aboda Zara," "All worship not performed for the sake of heaven is to be termed idolatry."

34. *Yerushalmi,* Berakoth 9:5.

35. *Kiddushin* 57a.

36. *Yebamoth* 6a-b; *Sifra,* Kedoshim 90d.

37. Rabbi ben David, *Commentary on Sifra, ibid.*

38. Rashi to *Berakoth* 54a.

39. *Berakoth* 2:2.

40. *Aboda Zara* 17b.

41. *Yebamoth* 109b.

42. *Yebamoth* 49b, Rashi *ad locum.*

43. Rabbi Moses Cordevero, *Shiur Koma,* ch. 121, Rabbi Moses Alshech, *Torath Moshe,* "Shmini," 9b.

44. *Rosh Ha Shanah* 21b.

45. *Genesis Rabba* 17:5.

46. *Pesiktha de Rab Kahana,* ch. 38 (ed. S. Buber), p. 158b; see Solomon Schecter, *Aspects of Rabbinic Theology* (The Macmillan Company, 1909), for a note on textual recensions and variants of this source, pp. 293 f., 294, n. 1.

47. *Leviticus Rabba* 32:8; see *Ecclesiastes Rabba* 4:1, and *Zohar,* Mishpatim, p. 113b.

48. *Commentary on the Torah,* "Kedoshim," beginning.

49. *Tanhuma,* "Tisah" 21.

50. *Sanhedrin* 99b.
51. *Berakoth* 17a.
52. *Aboth* 6:10.
53. *Kiddushin* 32a.
54. Rabbi Menachem Recanati, *Taamei Ha-Mitzvoth*, "Introduction." See Gershom G. Scholem, *On the Kabbalah and Its Symbolism* (New York, 1955), p. 44.
55. *Zohar*, Beshalach 60a.
56. *Zohar*, Yithro 90b.
57. *Tikunai Zohar* 421, 60b.
58. *Zohar*, Emor 93b.
59. *Zohar*, Va Yikra 21a.
60. Rabbi Moses Hayyim Luzzatto, *Adir Ba-Marom*, p. 61; Rabbi Hayyim of Velozhin, *Nefesh Ha Hayyim*, pp. 4, 11.
61. *Yerushalmi*, Hagigah 1:7 (76c); *Ekah Rabbathi*, Pesiktha 2; see also Rav in Nedarim 81a and Rabbi Jonah Gerondi quoted in the "Ran" *ad locum*.
62. *Pesachim* 50b; see *Taanith* 7a.
63. *Yoma* 72b, Rashi *ad locum*.
64. *Shabbat* 31a.
65. *Pesiktha Rabbathi*, ch. 34 (ed. Buber), 139a.
66. Rabbi Solomon Alami; *Iggereth Ha Musar*, ed. by A. M. Habermann, pp. 40 f.
67. *Tifereth Yisrael*, Introduction.
68. *Mei Ha Shiloach*, Va Yeshev.
69. There is an ancient belief in Judaism that wisdom, later identified with the Torah as well as the name of the Messiah and other entities, was created before the creation of the world. See H. A. Wolfson, *The Philosophy of the Church Fathers*, Vol. I (Cambridge University Press, 1956), pp. 156 ff.; Abraham J. Heschel, *op. cit.*, Vol. II, pp. 8 ff.
70. *Genesis Rabbathi*, p. 144; *Seder Elijah Rabbah*, ch. 15, p. 71; see Rabbi Samuel bar Rabbi Isaac at *Genesis Rabba* 1:4; also *Sifre Deuteronomy*, Re'eh #69, 74, 138, 141—"the last is most precious," compare *Mekilta of Rabbi Simeon Bar Yohai*, p. 31, and *Genesis Rabba* 78:8.
71. *Tanhuma* (ed. Buber), Noah 19.
72. *Menachoth* 53b. Maimonides, who lived in an age of severe persecutions of the Jewish people, went beyond these utterances in saying: "As it is impossible for God to cease to exist, so it is impossible for Israel to be destroyed and to disappear from the world." *Iggeret Teman*, ed. by A. Halkin (New York, 1952), p. 25. See Karl Barth, *Church Dogmatics*, Vol. III, Part 3, ed. by G. W. Bromiley and T. P. Torrance (Edinburgh: T. & T. Clark, 1958), p. 218: "The Jews can be despised and hated and oppressed and persecuted and even assimilated, but they

cannot really be touched; they cannot be exterminated; they cannot be destroyed. They are the only people that necessarily continue to exist, with the same certainty as that God is God."

73. *Ecclesiastes Rabba* 1:4,9; compare *Sifre Deuteronomy*, "Ekev," Piska 47.

74. *Mekilta*, Ki Tissa; compare Mark 2:27.

75. *Yalkut Shimoni*, Esther 1056.

76. *The Book of Beliefs and Opinions*, Treatise III, ch. 7, tr. by Samuel Rosenblatt (Yale University Press, 1948), p. 158.

77. *Kuzari*, II, 56; see *Seder Elijah Rabba*, p. 112. Compare John 4:22: "Salvation is from the Jews." See Raymond E. Brown (ed.), The Anchor Bible, *The Gospel According to John, ad locum.* In the Gospels, Israel carries the special sense that the people thus named is the people of God.

78. *Sifre Deuteronomy* 346.

79. *Seder Elijah Rabba*, ch. 21.

80. *Midrash Tehillim*, ch. 83:2.

81. *Midrash Tehillim* (ed. Buber), pp. 240 f.

82. *Numbers Rabba* 13:6; compare *Genesis Rabba* 3:9.

83. *Genesis Rabba* ch. 30; unlike *Theodor*, p. 277.

84. *Pesiktha de Rab Kahana* (ed. Buber), XXVI, p. 166b; compare the two versions.

85. *Genesis Rabba* 69:3.

86. *Genesis Rabba* 47:6; 82:6.

❖ ❖ ❖ *George W. Webber's odyssey from Harvard to Union and the inner-city ministry to the presidency of New York Theological Seminary has furnished the perspective from which he understands the life of the church and its ministry, especially to those caught in the throes of social turmoil. After college graduation and wartime service in the Navy he entered Union Seminary. In the year of his graduation, 1948, he was cofounder of the famous East Harlem Protestant Parish, and then served many years both as a member of the group ministry of the parish and as a faculty member at Union, where he became Dean of Students (1950–1957) and Associate Professor of Practical Theology. In 1963 he earned the Ph.D. degree from Columbia University. He has written* God's Colony in Man's World *(1960) and* The Congregation in Mission *(1964). In 1965 he helped to organize and became director of the Metropolitan Urban Service Training Facility (MUST); he was elected to his present post in 1969.*

Out of a life of active service in the inner city come these considerations concerning the task, the calling, and the resources of the church in facing the complex realities of change.

4

THEOLOGY,
THE CHURCHES,
AND THE MINISTRY

✧ ✧ ✧ *George W. Webber*

T HE INTELLECTUAL TASK of theology is never far removed from the practical life of a believing community. The developments in one are frequently affected by ferment in the other. In this reciprocal relationship, theology has consequences for the community of faith, and difficulties in the community of faith have consequences for the shaping of belief. A healthy spirit of direction within the churches often comes from, or results in, a sense of proclamatory assurance within theology; indecisiveness and uncertainty within the churches often accompany vagueness within the theological enterprise. Theological concern cannot be separated from the practical demands of ecclesiastical responsibility.

The contemporary Christian church is in trouble. Sometimes and in some places individual parishes are faithful to their Lord even when they are in severe conflict with their environment, but too often, as men like Gibson Winter, Peter Berger, and Martin Marty have pointed out, the churches have accommodated to their culture —becoming the introverted, complacent, irrelevant, "captives of suburbia" that only emit the "noise of solemn assemblies." Robert Spike, who was a parish minister before taking a denominational position that took him on travels all over the country, once remarked that while he knew as a local minister that churches were in trouble, he had no idea how bad things really were until he surveyed the wide scene from the standpoint of a traveling executive.

Discussion concerning the condition of the contemporary churches informs current theological debates, and often re-forms them. Whereas theology is concerned with divisions between liberals and conservatives, Protestants and Roman Catholics, theists and the "death of God" advocates, the debate concerning the church and its future often takes the form of a fight between those who would defend the residential congregation as the normative pattern for the Christian community and those who would plead for new or experimental types of witness and service.

The upshot of this debate over the condition of the churches is lengthy discussion of "renewal." This debate is often muddied badly by different presuppositions about the need for Christian community, the relevance of traditional faith to a secular age, and the meaning of revelation or other criteria of theological authority. Even the plea for "renewal" presents difficulty, for while no thinking person proposes to perpetuate the present inadequacies of ecclesiastical life, the word seems to connote a thrust toward the self-improvement of the churches without a necessary concern about the wider changes needed in the social order. So understood, it is probably an instance of basic introversion that stands in contradiction to the gospel admonition to lose one's life or to be a "church for others."

This chapter is concerned with the authentic witness of the church and the changes in theology and ecclesiology that seem necessary to bring about new health in the churches and their relationship to the common life of all mankind. The urgency of our times and faithfulness to Jesus Christ demand tremendous iconoclasm about contemporary ecclesiastical structures and practices. Those who recognize that "judgment begins with the household of faith" must not be written off as defectors, apostates, or heretics. Indeed, many such critics are, like the author of this chapter, profoundly committed to the Christian gospel and hold to certain basic convictions. For myself, these convictions include the following affirmations:

1. By the power of the Holy Spirit, Christ continues to call men to a missionary vocation, either as clergymen within existing churches or as missionaries in new situations. He locates them in Christian community for nurture and equipment and sends them into all aspects of service and witness. In short, God in his wisdom continues to evoke and sustain the church. The forms of community and mission may find drastically altered shapes in the years ahead, but they will reflect a continuity with the patterns of the New Testament.

2. Biblical language and Biblical perspectives upon the human situation provide the frame of reference from which, with integrity,

the contemporary Christian must continue to operate. The problem of relating Biblical concepts and imagery to a secular society is not essentially different in character from the missionary problem of past centuries when the gospel crossed barriers of geography, race, and culture. The gospel has always been a scandal and a stumbling block, and is so no more and no less in our day than in past epochs, but we must be sure that men stumble over the genuine gospel and not over our ineptitude with it.

3. The concrete events of contemporary history always provide the locus for the self-understanding of the church. This is to affirm that our problem is not merely to figure some new way to make the Christian message relevant in a rapidly changing urban world, as though to cure the present problem with a gimmick, but to ask what, in the light of Christ, are the meanings of contemporary events and what they require in terms of Christian witness and obedience. We must be theologically and ecclesiastically free enough to be truly obedient to our Lord; sufficiently obedient to be theologically and ecclesiastically creative.

I. The Situation We Confront

The immediate context for this discussion is the movement of American Protestantism since the end of World War II. The striking growth and acceptance of church life and institutions in much of American life has been followed, or succeeded, by a growing uncertainty as to the integrity of much of this activity. Tremendous ecclesiastical energy has been devoted in recent years to "church renewal," a response both to internal criticism and to the forceful emergence of "mission theology." Despite these developments, or perhaps because of them, the church at the moment seems largely stuck on dead center, caught between an urgent missionary understanding of the nature and purpose of the church and the fact of institutional inertia and rigidity that has come to be called "morphological fundamentalism." We will look first at the theological convictions central to a valid mission endeavor in the present world and then at the implications of these convictions for the work of the churches and their leaders.

As a small child, I remember hearing the minister at my church praying about our need to bring in the Kingdom of God. I genuinely assumed, as I suspect he did, that with a little more effort we might achieve this goal in the twentieth century. This is a Christendom mentality, the assumption that we shall bring the whole world under the sway of Christ. It is the assumption that underlies the conception of "a Christian society," that explains the normative character of baptism in Western European countries, and that makes Christians into a kind of conquering army described in Roman Catholic circles as "triumphalism."

In 1943, Abbé Godin, a Catholic priest with competent sociological training, published a book called, in its English translation, *France, Pagan?* He pointed out that the religious climate of France had undergone a fantastic change that was hardly noticed. What had been taken for granted, that France was a Roman Catholic country in a Christendom situation, was no longer true. While most Frenchmen still used the church for the cultic rites of baptism, marriage, and burial, in two of these cases they had to be carried into the church building! Less than 10 percent of the population had anything remotely like a meaningful relationship to the institution of the church. France was a pagan country. Godin's little book quickly led ecclesiastics in sectors of Protestant Christendom to check their situations. The results were identical or worse in such countries as England, Scotland, Sweden, and northern Germany. No wonder that at the first meeting of the World Council of Churches in Amsterdam in 1948 a major study was undertaken on the theme "the evangelization of man in modern mass society." A pagan, increasingly secular, society was challenging the assumptions of the churches at their very roots. The six years devoted to the study of evangelism in mass society made considerable progress in analyzing the shape of the emerging urban, technological society. But it also made clear the utter confusion in the churches over the meaning of evangelism.

This same pattern has been repeated over and over for the last twenty years. The churches have sought to understand and deal with a new historical situation, only to find that their traditional theological frame of reference is simply unable to comprehend the challenge. Every effort to alter practice, as in the area of evangelism, without a significant reordering of the theological basis of evangelism, simply has become a dead end.

The concrete historical situation in which the churches find themselves raises serious claims for mission and ministry. In the United States, the problems of human life in poverty, urban slums, and ghettos cry out to Christians for response. Serious response reveals severe conflicts, vagueness, or uncertainty that demand theological reformulation. And in turn, these result in new or redirected patterns of mission and ministry that may well be described as the reconsideration of conversion, the problem of Christianization, and the role of Christian competence. Let us look separately at each of the key factors in the task before us.

a. *The Reconsideration of Conversion.* In a variety of patterns and from various shades of theological backgrounds, Christians of all kinds have conveyed clearly to the world that they come with a vital message of salvation for all men. Implicit in this stance is an inevitable paternalism, knowing clearly that what we know and bring is essential for the well-being of the outsider. But at this moment in history, both in the developing nations of the world and in the slums and ghettos of the United States, anything whatsoever smacking of paternalism is in deep trouble. My black neighbor in a housing project in East Harlem couldn't care less about what God has done for Bill Webber. As a matter of fact, since I am white, middle class, and educated, I would have a hard time arguing that God did anything for me that I would not have been granted in a white society in any case. What the neighbor cares about is some *evidence* that God has done something for him. And he is not going to get this by anything I can *say.* The missionary abroad and the inner-city white pastor alike have been driven to ask whether the inescapable paternalism of traditional mission and evangelism is something they are stuck with or whether a fresh Biblical study may open up new understanding and fresh patterns of operation.

For example, open the Bible with this question in mind: Is the fundamental purpose of the Christian to convert men, to win men to Christ, or to save souls? This is traditional conservative language, but also it is close to the emphasis of the evangelism staffs of every denomination. A little scrutiny of the New Testament indicates that this emphasis on saving or winning souls is almost absent as a theme and that the typical evangelistic language and pattern of our practice is thoroughly uncongenial to the New Testament. Jesus harshly attacks the scribes and Pharisees for proselytism that sounds pretty much like normative American evangelism. Perhaps we have made the Biblical word "witness" into the active verb "win" and, as typical Americans, set out to take every possible scalp and to browbeat every respectable person into church membership. Further reflection on Scripture suggests that in the whole of the Bible, the call to faith is much more related to a task to be accomplished than to any matter of status. Perhaps we have made salvation seem to most men primarily a matter of a new status, a convert, baptized into the church, someone who says "yes" to Christ. This process may not make clear that acceptance of a new vocation is fundamentally a commitment to radical obedience to Christ. Isaiah 58:1–6 makes this point with dramatic emphasis. What is at stake is not faithfulness in religious duties, but responsibility for God's world.

Two further reflections emerge as one seeks to relate the evangelistic situation today to the insights of the Bible. One is the thrust of Matt., ch. 25, in which those who are "saved" are ignorant of their status. Is Jesus here suggesting that to be preoccupied with salvation, "with being saved," is a sign that we have not in fact become faithful to him? This passage certainly does raise havoc for the fundamentalistic approach to the outsider. The second consideration is simply the recognition that nowhere does the New Testament suggest that many men, hearing the word, seeing signs of the Kingdom or even confronted by Jesus in the flesh are going to accept the path of discipleship. Ecclesiastical preoccupation with making converts almost inevitably leads to evangelistic methods that are thoroughly incompatible with the gospel. In fact, they mislead men. *Any* emphasis upon man's action in winning or saving or making converts seems to be almost blasphemy, that is, taking into our own hands what is solely and uniquely the work of the Holy Spirit. The Christian's task is to sow the seed by word and deed, to be a sign of the Kingdom, and to leave the converting up to God. The sermon in Acts, ch. 2, where Peter confronts the throng on Pentecost is often taken as a vindication of evangelism in traditional patterns, but a careful study reveals quite the opposite thrust. The crowd gathered not at the invitation of a visiting evangelist, but upon seeing signs of the Kingdom. The power of the Holy Spirit became suddenly manifest. They gathered and were intrigued, confused, baffled, and demanded an explanation. This suggests that proclamation of the gospel almost inevitably must follow demonstration of the gospel. Peter sought to give meaning to what made no sense apart from the life and death and resurrection of Jesus of Nazareth. Note also that at the end of the sermon, he made no altar call, no pitch for conversion, but left the response to his witness entirely in the hands of the Holy Spirit.

Here then is an illustration of how one concrete situation, the impossibility of a paternalistic approach, can lead to a fresh understanding of the Biblical basis for mission. The task of the Christian can be explored in terms not of the lifeguard standing in the door of the church above the raging tides of the world, throwing life rings out to drowning men, but as one drowning man with others, pointing to the Christ who has saved them all. Paternalism is replaced by incarnation, the insistent New Testament demand that the Christian, like his Lord, empty himself and become a servant in the midst of the world's common life (Phil. 2:5–11).

b. *The Problem of Christianization.* Often in the early years of the East Harlem Protestant Parish we were challenged by churchmen who rather snidely suggested that they could see no difference between most of what we were doing and what any social work agency was about. They wanted to know what was Christian about our program and indicated that they felt we were nothing but humanitarians. Our response was often vigorously to defend our ministry, to seek to prove that we were authentically "Christian," and to claim that we were bringing the Christian "plus" to the East Harlem scene. But again, the facts gave us trouble. An examination of secular and Christian social work agencies generally showed that they did a better job and always paid better salaries. Further, in East Harlem, the places where one discovered signs of the Kingdom— that is, love, reconciliation, healing, compassion, justice—almost always tended to be in quite secular and unexpected places, while most Christians were locked up in ugly church buildings, quite away from the action. The tendency of Christian ministers to ignore the facts, to believe that their work was crucial, and to be opaque to the signs of the Kingdom found in secular service is perennial. It once affected me in the writing of the book *God's Colony Is Man's World.* In that book I talked about the world as though it could be healed only if it came to the church. I assumed that we were to colonize the world in the name of Jesus Christ and bring it into his Kingdom. After all, it seemed, the way God intended to get his work done in the world was through his church. "He has no other hands but ours." The imperialism and self-righteousness of such an approach was simply helpless before both the evidence in the community and the rigidity of the churches.

Back again to the Bible. Does God work only through the churches, do we bring Christ to a pagan community, or is the reverse the case? Christ is ahead of the church, calling us to join him in mission. This turns out to be an implication of the Last Judgment story in Matt., ch. 25; it is suggested in a host of passages in the Old Testament; and it suddenly makes sense in terms of the Gospel itself. The event of Jesus Christ is humanitarian through and through. Here God is affirming his love for men. Here we see in concrete, specific, historical embodiment precisely what it means to be human. Here we are called to discover and express our own humanity by accepting responsibility for God's world, seeking to live as participants in Christ's mission. Far from denying that what as Christians we do is "nothing but humanitarianism," we might pray that we might in fact be humanitarians for Christ's sake. Then the life of the Christian and of the Christian community would simply take its shape from the pattern of Christ's own incarnation, death, and resurrection, that is to say, by presence in the world, by servanthood, and by witness. In such light, the church becomes not the hands of Christ, but one instrument that God may use, "for he has made known to us in all wisdom and insight the mystery of his will, according to his purpose which he set forth in Christ" (Eph. 1:9).

c. *The Role of Christian Competence.* Out of concern for the world, the Christian approach has too often been paternalistic and imperialistic. It has also been self-righteous. In confronting East Harlem in 1948, we were appalled at the social disorder and sheer human misery in the community. Where in heaven's name had the social workers, teachers, and churches been to let such a mess develop? Thank God some eager Union Seminary graduates had arrived on the scene to get some changes made. We were armed with "the Christian ethical approach" to almost any problem you could name. While there might be some difficulty in applying our answers adequately, at least as Christians we knew what was right. This Sunday school logic, which holds that Christians are the good guys who know what is right and do it, proved to be singularly demonic.

Our ability to discern evil and to cry out against it was alarming enough to the committed change agents at work in the community, but our self-confidence was terrifying to them. It became obvious at once that even in one-to-one counseling situations, we did not in fact know what was best for the other person, what options were available, or what path they might follow. Our righteousness was shattered by the utter impossibility of knowing what was right or wrong in terms of affecting the significant social issue in the community. In 1965, for one illustration, the prophetic cry among militant groups was for "quality-integrated education." Anyone not lined up under that banner was a reactionary. By 1968, that line had been turned upside down by the emergence of black identity. Now the focus was on quality education in the ghetto and local control of policy. Those who still held for quality-integrated education were denounced as "white liberals." Finally it became clear that Christians are not called upon to play God, to assume that they know enough or can predict the consequences of actions in such manner that they can act with some unique competence and righteousness.

Once more, it has been fascinating to turn with these questions to Biblical study. There it begins to appear that Christian competence is not omniscient, but the freedom to love Christ and sin bravely. This recognition came as good news indeed. For the only alternatives, given the total ambiguity of significant involvement in the problems of the world, seemed to be either disengagement or self-deception. Certainly the churches have chosen one path or the other almost completely. Given the difficulty of knowing what is right in terms of areas of social change, the only way out for those who wish, in traditional terms, to be righteous is to cop out. Politics is dirty. Therefore, no Christian can be engaged. The other alternative is for a person to convince himself that his line of action is righteous and to fight on with holy self-righteousness. The church has engaged often enough in holy wars, blessing the self-interest of particular groups. The New Testament seems well aware of the ambiguity of involvement, but the freedom Christ bestows is precisely the freedom to transcend either disengagement or self-righteousness. "Sin bravely, love Christ and sin more bravely still," wrote Dietrich Bonhoeffer. Freedom is the ability to enter fully into responsibility in God's world, fighting against the principalities and powers that are as specific and real now as for Paul, and yet in the end depending upon the grace of God and trusting alone in his righteousness.

I would not argue that these are the only, or even the crucial, theological issues for the churches in our day, although for me, they have been the urgent points of reflection. A central concern here is also with the method that has been utilized in accepting the challenge of contemporary confrontations between the church with its traditional style and the events of a world in rapid social change as the call to enter into fresh dialogue with Scripture. In the encounter with the world, we are driven to a new appropriation of a Biblical faith. A new understanding of Biblical faith leads us with fresh eyes to appropriate the meaning of historical events and to reassess our commitments and involvement. This in turn has profound implications for the structure of mission and ministry.

II. Structured for Mission

The purpose of this section is to examine present thinking about the style of Christian community. The theological issues just considered have significant implications. So also does the fact that the whole world is now being caught up in an urban, technological, secular era of rapid social change. The symbol of our world is metropolis, not a city simply grown large, but a new reality in human history. In metropolis the elements that make up a man's life are separated in time and space from one another. He sleeps in one community, works in another, plays in a third. Ask most men two questions: (a) What are the most difficult decisions you have been asked to make in the past six months? and (b) Where did they occur? It is very likely that the arena where such decisions were required was far removed from his place of residence—where almost surely the man's church is located.

The point here is not that the church is failing but that it is being called upon to fulfill functions for which it is not equipped. A Sunday service can hardly be expected to equip a man for the different roles he must play and the varied demands of the worlds in which he lives. Just as, in secular terms, metropolis will choke itself to death unless political and social forms are devised that encompass the metropolitan region; so the church must also find a fresh way of understanding and serving humanity in this new society. The phrase *zone humaine* was coined in a World Council of Churches study as shorthand to describe an area in which cooperative church strategy needs to be developed (World Council of Churches, Department of Studies in Evangelism, *The Church for Others and The Church for the World,* pp. 30–33; Geneva, 1967). In most cases today, local congregations find their strength in residential neighborhoods, but it is equally important that structures of Christian community, service, and witness also take shape in the multiple communities and human groups of metropolis. In place of the sterile debate between those who would defend the residential parish to the death and those who insist that the parish is dead, a concept of *zone humaine,* requiring a variety of forms, both old and new, mutually supportive and equally essential, seems to make sense. Unfortunately, at this point in history, there are so few patterns other than the residential parish in operation that they are usually looked upon as experimental, novel, esoteric, tangential, rather than as essential components in Christ's mission in a *zone humaine.* The remarkable World Council of Churches study book, *The Church for Others,* provides an excellent summary of the thinking on this matter, followed by a preliminary, but very helpful, attempt to indicate some of the variety of forms that a responsible missionary vision might require.

a. *Ministries in the Public Sector.* Examples of this new form would be found in the emerging industrial missions of which the Detroit Industrial Mission has been the prototype in this country. Similarly the Metropolitan Associates of Philadelphia has proven to be a very remarkable attempt to find a "vehicle for relevant participation in the renewal of the city in the light of God's purposes for his creation." MAP found it necessary to create new styles of involvement for the Christians involved.

b. *Ministries for Social Change.* In recent years, as traditional social work approaches have seemed inadequate to get at fundamental social change, new patterns of action involvement have emerged. In a number of communities, Christian energy has taken shape in community organization, often following the insights of the Industrial Areas Foundation. Metro North in East Harlem is a good example of this approach. The style of the California Migrant Ministry would be another.

c. *Structures of Permanent Availability.* This form is oriented around long-term needs and provides, day and night, a place of guaranteed help and openness. The Life Line ministry in Sydney, Australia, the Exodus House for addicts in East Harlem, and a variety of Hospitality Houses would be examples. In most cases, services are made available without demanding involvement in return.

d. *Task Force Structure.* Increasingly, a normative pattern of Christian mission is a task force, called into being on an ecumenical basis, to meet a particular need or challenge. For the duration, it forms the basis of Christian community for the participants as together they develop strategy, seek guidance in prayer and study, and then act in the community. When the particular issue or function is no longer urgent, the group disbands.

For one illustration, a Bible study group in an inner-city parish is led to discuss the problem of education in the local schools. Out of this concern grows the determination to arouse parent and community support for quality schools. Enlisting others whose interest is shaped by this same focus, they now use their time together in Bible study in working on a strategy for effective involvement in educational change.

e. *Centers for Mission Coordination.* Traditional councils of churches are coming to see their function as centers for mission strategy, rather than as meeting places for churches and as agents to serve local parish needs. The council is asking about its function and how it might become a missionary structure on behalf of the *zone humaine.* Another model, often in cooperation with the council of churches, is the urban training center in the style of Metropolitan Urban Service Training (MUST) in New York. The purpose of MUST is to unlock the resources of the churches in terms of their public responsibility in the metropolis by pointing to the mission needs, providing insight into where resources of men and money are needed, and offering training required for effective participation in missionary action.

f. *The Residential Parish.* Despite the problems in the parish it surely needs to be seen as a specialized ministry, one among others. To be sure, it holds a primary place historically, and today remains the overwhelmingly dominant church structure. But the integrity of what the local congregation may hope to achieve in the years ahead will depend greatly on the development of the crucial, complementary forms of mission and ministry. Clearly, the function and style of such congregations needs serious attention, in order to undertake its proper share in Christ's total mission. While no longer is there any need to feel that the whole job belongs in the purview of the residential congregation, we can be equally emphatic in suggesting that the whole job cannot be done without the parish structure for certain situations to which it is still relevant.

The residential congregation is a problem. After fifteen years of intensive discussion of renewal, a host of denominational emphases on the mission of the congregation, and the best efforts of a generation of young clergy well briefed on mission theology, we still seem to be struck on dead center or going backward into an increasingly ghetto mentality. This is unfortunately true even where there is still vitality. Here let us assume that "renewal" as the center of attention for churchmen is a dead end. The implicit self-centeredness of trying to renew the church ought to have been a warning for those committed to a Lord who tells us we find our lives by losing them.

The experience and frustration of the renewal emphasis has taught several lessons. In the first place, the naïve assumption that the ordinary congregation could be expected to become a "congregation in mission" was doomed from the start. If the prophetic criticisms of Gibson Winter, Peter Berger, and Martin Marty are accurate, then most congregations are filled largely with men and women who have made no significant commitment to radical Christian obedience. We have no right to assume that they are converts who have relapsed, but must view them as men who never were committed in the first place. We dare not judge them as Christians gone AWOL, but accept the fact that our pews are filled with those who need no more be tried for apostasy than the secular community outside. To expect such a sociological grouping, gathered for familial, traditional, cultural, and personal reasons, to become a unified body of troops, engaged in Christ's mission, is simply silly.

The failure of the local congregation to undertake battles for just causes is rooted in its origins and composition. Except in the cases of congregations that have been gathered as victims of injustices (as in the slums and ghettos of big cities) the sociological analysis of the local congregation makes it manifest that this is not a vehicle which can bear the weight of conflict. The suburban church is composed of men whose self-interest is clearly threatened by the struggle for social justice and hence cannot be expected to undertake such struggles as a matter of easy course. Nor is the fact that ghetto congregations undertake social struggle necessarily a proof of the greater virtue of their members, for they are fellow victims whose self-interest is merely more closely aligned with the cause of the downtrodden than is the self-interest of suburban Christians.

Another lesson we have learned is that renewal attempts through the development of small groups in the congregation seem also largely to have failed. When the faith is studied apart from involvement in action, it seldom leads to significant new patterns of obedience. We must come to reflect in conjunction with involvement, rather than to cultivate spirituality in a vacuum of personal intimacy and self-scrutiny.

While there is no blueprint or scheme that can be applied to the problem of helping the congregation enter into mission, several clues come obviously to the fore. The starting point is simply to ask the question, What in this time and place is Christ's mission for this congregation?

Every congregation in America is located in the midst of obvious human problems and social dislocations from which it is escaping or hiding. The question for the congregation is simple: What is the task to which we are called in terms of Christ's concern for neighbor in our time and place? I have yet to find any congregation that did not have an urgent agenda at its doorstep, if it had eyes to see and ears to hear.

To cite an example: The success of a book such as *The Feminine Mystique* in suburban communities suggests that there is an urgent task of helping the American woman discover and exercise her full humanity. The chaos of teen-age life and the intensification of the generation gap indicate an urgent need for attention to nurture and family life in this fascinating world at the end of the twentieth century. Here are two agenda items, laid on the congregation by the world, demanding attention from the residential structure of Christian community.

The acceptance of God's agenda and entrance into Christ's mission has drastic structural implications. If we are concerned about nurture as a central task, then it is plain that we are playing games in much of present Christian education and failing to provide structures that have integrity when we speak of the church as a family. The sheer size and anonymity of many churches makes such rhetoric ridiculous. If we are to minister to families, we need family-type structures for our congregation.

When the concern is for mission in the community, then the task force pattern seems most appropriate. A congregation as such is rarely prepared or mature enough to take corporate action. But individuals must be set free from institutional involvement to respond to the needs along with others both from congregations and from the secular community. Perhaps the congregation might be likened to a vein of gold that needs to be mined. Within the total group there are those who can be set free, for the sake of Christ, in mission and ministry. Perhaps the vein will assay out at only five men per one hundred, but that would be a rich resource for mission in our time.

To change metaphors, perhaps the residential congregation is like a seedbed for responsible action agents in God's world. Nurtured in Christian traditions or brought from apathy or self-concern to a new freedom to be a Christ to their neighbor, a man or woman may no longer find participation in the residential congregation helpful or necessary and can freely enter into other styles of Christian community. Recently at an evening meeting a militant Negro woman was denouncing the churches and then describing her vital and impressive involvement in social change. Later she was asked about how she got to be so active. She told in glowing terms about the wonderful young priest that had almost literally dragged her out of her apathy and hopelessness in a slum apartment and set her on the path of a new life. Perhaps this is the function of the parish church—to call men from death to life, to give them a vision, to set them on a path, and not be threatened or distraught if or when they move beyond this locus of Christian community.

In this line of thought, the residential congregation, in large part, is like a boot camp, training the recruits in Christ's army. It is a place that provides a context in which to practice the style of Christian living, to take the risks of openness and honesty that the exercise of Christian freedom requires. In Eph. 4:1–16 there is a great description of the style of the community. Here one is to grow up to the maturity of Christ, to the stature of the fullness of one's humanity. The clues that make bodily growth possible are very specific. The first is to speak the truth in love. The second is to accept the gifts for the sake of *the whole body* with which each member has been endowed by the Holy Spirit. Finally, the body only grows when all parts are working properly. There is no room for passengers in such a community. The implications of this passage seem to require that we so structure our life in congregations that we have a context in which the style of Eph., ch. 4, can be realized, that is where men and women know each other in relationships that make it possible to risk speaking the truth in love, where they can discover, with the help of others, their gifts of the Spirit and practice their utilization, and in which the energy of each can be challenged for the sake of the good of all.

Lest I seem to be drifting back into an impossible ideal, let me be clear that I am arguing for the possibility in every present congregation of structures for those few, called by Christ, who want to follow him and are willing to enter into the sober discipline of discipleship. Some years ago, a Union graduate began his ministry as the student pastor at a large university. He determined to spend half his time doing what the Methodists expected and half doing the Lord's work. In addition to the big activity-centered program of the denomination, designed to provide a home away from home for Methodist students in the midst of the pagan campus, he sought out ten sophomores and ten juniors who committed themselves to spend ten hours a week in disciplined study and reflection focused on the question, "How do we live as Christians now on this university campus?" They did not function as a self-righteous elite, but as a remarkably effective leaven in the lump of the total program. Is this not in some sense a parable for the ministry of most of our present congregations? The challenge is to set free for mission those who accept the challenge, while continuing to plant the seed and till the soil of the congregational plot that is at hand.

III. IMPLICATIONS FOR THE CLERGY

The reformulation of mission theology calls for emerging patterns for the churches; these in turn put major demands upon the clergyman for a new set of skills and a new style of operation. The task of the seminary graduate in the life of the churches in the years ahead will not be easy. His preparation will need to be different from what it has been. He may even abjure ordination and employment as an ecclesiastic in any form. But it will be just as important, if not more so, to prepare and maintain a man in his ministry on the highest level of competence whether he is the ordained pastor of a congregation or works as a layman in a secular vocation.

a. *Growth in Maturity.* The essential starting point for every Christian, clergy and laymen alike, is growth in "the maturity of the fullness of Christ." This is a difficult area to assess and even more difficult to encourage, but the "formation" of the Christian is a matter of lifelong concern. The failure of seminaries to start a man on the right track can lead to continuing frustration over the years of his ministry.

Several years ago the topic of the annual twenty-four-hour faculty retreat at Union Seminary was the thinking of this student generation. Four able students were invited to discuss their goals and concerns as they prepared for their ministries. Also on hand to hear their presentation was Dr. Graham Blaine, head of the psychiatric services for Harvard College. In the evening, after the students had returned home, Dr. Blaine was asked to lead the faculty in a consideration of the views and development of these students. His major reaction was simply that these theological students seemed, even as college graduates, to be going through a period of adolescent identity crisis that needed to be successfully navigated if they were to become mature professionals. There was no denigration of the students intended. Dr. Blaine was just underlining the obvious experience of seminaries today. A high percentage of the student body arrives uncertain about faith and ambiguous about vocation. The real issue that needed attention was the role of the seminary in providing the context in which the student can attain mature manhood and grow "to the measure of the stature of the fullness of Christ."

Dr. Blaine had two suggestions. Using Erik Erikson, he argued for the need in the life of a young person for a "moratorium," a period when he in effect drops out of the academic tunnel that has determined his life for ten to fifteen years, cuts the umbilical cord with family and church, and seeks to discover his own values, understand himself, and come to some clarity about goals and vocation. This suggestion gave a very striking rationale to the metropolitan intern year for seminary students which Union developed in 1964. This program is designed to give students a year of life in the city as self-supporting, secularly employed human beings, living in an inner-city neighborhood and relating to the community as ordinary residents rather than as embryonic professionals. Five years of experience validated this program as a tremendous factor in the growth of that maturity so sorely needed for adequate professional success.

Dr. Blaine also suggested that students move beyond the "moratorium" period with the help of efficacious role models, men involved in the profession toward which they are heading whose own lives and vocational styles provide inspiration and challenge (but not blueprints) for the student. At this point, present seminary patterns are in real trouble. Neither the professor at the lectern nor the successful pastors in field placement situations are very useful to the student seeking patterns for ministry in the secular city. Words such as "enabler" and "equipper" seem far more relevant than "preacher" or "teacher" in finding role models. In the Metropolitan Intern Program, the major assignment of the clergy coordinator with each group of ten students was to help them function, to join themselves in an enterprise of learning whose results were dependent not on his charisma or scholarship, but on their own efforts. He was to be a theological resource person, a catalyst, a partner in a common effort to understand the city, the mission of the church, and themselves.

Under the presidency of John Bennett, Union has begun the process of developing educational patterns and a new style for the seminary community that recognized the need to take the student with a new seriousness. He is not to be seen only as a potential professional into whom knowledge must be poured and from whom competence in practice must be required, but as a person to be taken seriously where he is and helped to find his own maturity, faith, and vocation. Flexibility in curriculum, new teaching patterns, with the faculty and students discovering together the meaning of "dialogue," "partnership in learning," "Christian style of life." As a community, the seminary must be the locus of nurture and practice in discipleship. Its own pattern and style becomes a powerful increment for or against the maturity of the student.

Parenthetically, many of the emerging training centers for clergy find themselves giving much precious time to the maturity issue even with men long in the ministry. The "plunge" at the Urban Training Center in Chicago, for example, is designed to help men become open again to basic questions about themselves and their own maturity. UTC, the Clergy Intern Program in Cleveland, Metropolitan Urban Service Training in New York City, and other such programs all in effect provide for a man a moratorium period when he can dare examine with honesty and openness his own life as well as his own practice of ministry.

b. *Competence in Ministry*. For some years, signs of the malaise in the ranks of the clergy have been growing apace. The gradual diminution of able men applying for the B.D. degree is more than matched by the practicing clergy who are leaving the ranks of the ordained for secular employment. At MUST, week by week, clergy, often fine and committed men, drop in for advice about finding an alternative to parish ministry. Here I want to argue that at least some of this discontent and frustration is due, not to the sinfulness of their people or to morphological fundamentalism, but to the fact that they themselves are incompetent. This is a harsh word, but is meant to be a sign of hope. If part of the problem today is the fact that clergy are trying to use models and skills in ministry from another period, if they are untrained in the competencies that mission today requires, these are areas we can do something about.

Four areas of competence seem to emerge as essential elements for faithful ministry in a very wide range of specific vocational options open to the seminary graduate today, all the way from residential parish pastor to staff member of an industrial mission or a community organizer. Competence does not replace maturity, but neither does maturity or dedication serve Christ if a man is using inappropriate styles in ministry.

The first competence is the ability to analyze social issues. This can also be stated theologically as the ability to discover and analyze God's particular mission. Paul Abrecht, responsible for directing the World Council Studies on Rapid Social Change, reports that the saddest aspect of Christian mission around the world is the number of dedicated, selfless missionaries who, in the midst of social revolutions and rapid change, simply do not have the tools to understand what is happening around them and are condemned to irrelevance. In each of the major urban training centers in this country, the staffs spend an inordinate amount of time trying to help clergy gain competence in this area. The starting point for mission is God's action in history. The tools of social analysis are crucial for relevant participation in Christ's ministry.

The second competence has to do with institutional understanding. Clergy who demand that their congregations become devoted to mission without recognizing the essential requirements for institutional maintenance simply create a self-defeating situation. It is folly to expect a response from a congregation that its sociology makes quite impossible. Not long ago, a Union graduate accepted the pastorate of a city church and determined that it was going to become a congregation in mission. He did a good job of studying the needs of the community and defining the mission that needed to be undertaken. The church officers and key laymen read the renewal shelf, went on retreats, met in study groups. The only trouble was that the missionary vision of the pastor and the resources of the congregation in terms of age, present commitments, financial base, etc., simply did not fit. Faced with the fact that his base made the mission he demanded impossible, the pastor left for a job in the poverty program (I know at least a dozen Union graduates who will think this illustration refers to them). Here the issue remains one of competence. The pastor must understand the maintenance needs and actual potential of his congregation. He must count the cost before he seeks to build the mission. He must be a hard-nosed realist at this point. Too often he is simply foolish in demanding what is impossible and then falls prey to cynicism when the challenge is not met.

The third competence: "institutional manipulation." The basic clerical models still largely emphasized in seminaries are those of preacher, teacher, and pastor (in the limited sense of personal counselor or spiritual adviser). In terms of leading men and women into mission and ministry, these basic patterns are largely irrelevant as usually practiced. People no longer respond very readily to prophetic sermons, challenging them to action. The Biblical challenge comes alive far more often in a setting of give and take where genuine dialogue and confrontation cannot be avoided. The clergyman can rarely be the charismatic leader, at the head of the troops in battle. He must learn how to extract from the institution all that it is good for. He must mine the vein of ore effectively, with the skills that bring forth the riches of jobs well done.

In clergy workshops, we often begin by asking each man to write his job description, setting forth also his goals for himself and the congregation. I continue to be shocked at how few men respond to this assignment without a terrible struggle. Often they come back only with general theological statements about ministry or the vaguest objectives. It is apparent that they simply have not clearly in mind any specific goals for themselves and the parish, nor have they really any discipline in their ministry other than those imposed by the Sunday sermon, scheduled meetings, and parishioner demands. They are driven by the institution; they have not learned how to subvert it for God's purposes.

The final competence: "doing theology." Theological education is designed to produce men who are able to bring to bear on the events of our time the secular relevance of the gospel. They are called to look at social issues from the perspective of a Biblical faith. What is at stake is the ability to exercise the legitimate prophetic function of challenging the myths and ideologies of society seeking always to "tell it like it is." But it is no easy matter to be such a theological resource person. During the first year of MUST, we tried giving clergy each week a newspaper event and the Bible, asking them, after due reflection and study, to view the current events through eyes of faith. The exercise was usually a failure. We either spent time in a totally secular analysis, with no reference to Biblical faith, or we discussed the Bible, with no relation to the event. The men had acquired a tremendous amount of theological knowledge, but it was largely baggage that could not be unpacked and put to use. This is not meant to imply that the Bible directly answers modern social problems, but to affirm that the basic role of the seminary-trained minister is that of theological resource person as Christians seek to accept their mission in society.

These four areas of competence do not exhaust the list, but a correct list is not as important as the fact that when competency is the problem, this is something we can deal with. There are available now a variety of urban training and continuing education programs that can deal directly with developing competence in these and other areas. I suspect that normatively such training ought to be "on the job," so that reflection and practice, in concrete and responsible settings will provide all the material that is necessary for the training sessions. At MUST, we work with parish clergy who meet in small workshop groups each week for six months to a year, examining honestly and concretely their own practice of ministry.

c. *Forms of Ordained Ministry*: a footnote on the future. In the varied church forms of the *zone humaine* there certainly will be a wide range of demands on the seminary training personnel. The fact remains that the four basic competences just discussed suggest themselves as essential in most situations. They are the bedrock around which other skills can be developed. They enable the clergyman to be authentically a catalyst, an enabler, equipping the saints to live and serve in God's world with sensitivity and insight. He can help men reflect on their experiences, learn from their involvements, seek perspective on the demands, frustrations, and challenges in life. His location is likely to be in the midst of a small group that has gathered to reflect on a common missionary task and which uses him because of his Biblical expertise and skill in group process.

But the explicit future forms of ministry are anyone's guess. Here one need only take account of the legitimacy of wide experimentation. The time has come to allow and encourage the widest variety in structures and styles, even though they may seem to be mutually contradictory. There is no time left to debate about what is appropriate. It is far better to begin, and then, in the style of action-research, to become accountable and to learn from experiment, trial, and error. Unless we try to act, we will not learn.

I hope that the combination of personal maturity and competence for which we have argued in this section may produce a breed of men able to exercise their ministries with a new freedom from ecclesiastical inhibitions. Too often clergy wishing to experiment demand prior ecclesiastical approval. While there is far more freedom even within the most rigid ecclesiastical structures than many men are willing to risk, sometimes they must learn to bypass the higher authorities. Father Ford at Corpus Christi Roman Catholic Church near Union was far in advance of Vatican II in his ecumenical spirit. Asked how he had such freedom for action, he would reply, "I don't ask permission when I know I'll get the wrong answer." In a sense, only men with the personal freedom and maturity to risk being fired, who are not finally captive to the system will provide the revolutionary impetus the times require and the churches need.

Finally, one vital option today is some form of "tentmaking" ministry. As seminary-trained Protestants and Catholic clergy leave ordained positions and move into secular jobs, we make a profound mistake to treat them as defectors. They are precious men, educated and sophisticated theologians who are positioned precisely in the worlds of modern life which the church needs to penetrate. Many of them do in fact begin their new roles with a sober commitment to continue in Christ's ministry. But cast off by the ecclesiastical bureaucracy and unable to find a Christian community that seems in any way relevant to their new life, they quickly lose even the most tenuous bonds to the churches. Here is a challenge to all churches that must find a response and a form that permits such tentmaking to serve a crucial role in mission today.

IV. Conclusion

These are difficult times for the theological seminary, trying to prepare men for a ministry that often seems ephemeral and for a church that is uncertain and confused. Under John Bennett, Union has faced without flinching the harshness of the present challenge, been willing to examine its traditional forms and style without any holds barred, and undertaken a variety of new experiments whose implications are clearly radical and searching. One can only pray that the community will be open to the renewing power of the Holy Spirit, however strange and threatening that may be, in the confidence that God continues to call men to a missionary vocation, that faith must take shape in Christian community, and that such community requires men who are mature and competent. As in the past, so in the future, Union is committed to the task of equipping men for the ministry of Christ's church.

PART TWO

The Affairs and Thought
of the World

❖ ❖ ❖ *Roger Lincoln Shinn is John C. Bennett's successor as the William E. Dodge, Jr., Professor of Applied Christianity at Union Theological Seminary. He was educated at Heidelberg College, Union Theological Seminary, and Columbia University (Ph.D., 1951). During World War II he won the Silver Star as an infantry officer. He has also held teaching posts at Heidelberg College and Vanderbilt University. Among his many writings are* Tangled World *(1965) and* Man: The New Humanism *(1968). He is active in church and ecumenical affairs and has served as president of the Board for Homeland Ministries of the United Church of Christ and as a leader in the Conference on Church and Society, held at Geneva in 1966 under the auspices of the World Council of Churches. He has long been on the editorial board of* Christianity and Crisis, *and in addition to his teaching duties at Union acts as Dean of Instruction.*

Dr. Shinn's essay shows how the changes of the postwar decades have deeply affected Christian ethical thinking and suggests an agenda for the future of theological ethics.

5

THEOLOGICAL ETHICS:
RETROSPECT
AND PROSPECT

❖ ❖ ❖ *Roger L. Shinn*

THEOLOGICAL ETHICS is a bridge discipline. It studies the
meaning of Biblical faith for decision-making in the contemporary world—and it continuously reexplores Biblical faith under
the stimuli and pressures of moral decision in the present. Its freedom and its privilege are to investigate human life and society,
illuminated on the one hand by the Scriptural and theological tradition, and on the other hand by the newest knowledge of human
behavior reported by the news media and the scholarly work of behavioral scientists. The vocation of theological ethics is to maintain
the conversation between Biblical heritage and contemporary world.

The freedom and privilege of this vocation are also its temptations.
The church and its ethical thinkers may try to anchor life in a
seemingly secure past that obscures the meaning of responsibility
today. Or they may forsake the heritage of faith for some new idolatry. Either temptation leads to infidelity.

The same opportunities and temptations face theology per se,
especially in eras like our own when it has a preoccupation with
ethical issues and occasionally even defines its whole task in terms of
ethics.[1] But theology usually can, and often should, proceed deliberately. If contemporary theology wants to rethink traditional doctrines within the context of process philosophy, it may need a
generation or two for the job. But if ethicists need to rethink traditional responsibilities in the face of nuclear weapons or effective
contraceptives, they must move with some speed or their judgment
will come too late to matter.

Therefore theological ethics feels immediately the impact of social change. Sometimes it has the privilege and duty to initiate change; always it must observe and respond to change. Consequently recent decades have been a lively and confusing time for all Christians, not least for practitioners of the scholarly discipline of theological ethics, as they have sought the meaning of fidelity in contemporary history. Moreover, the history of ethics in this era, as this chapter will show, is an inseparable combination of intellectual and social history.

I. Emergence of a New Era

The self-consciousness of an epoch is not always a good guide to the historian who tries to find out what it did. Any generation is likely to misunderstand itself and, in particular, to exaggerate its own importance. We therefore might exercise some skepticism about the many claims that our own time is a revolutionary era. But massive objective data confirm the feeling most of us have in our bones that mankind is living through an age of momentous transformation. Whether we look at the population explosion, the scale and style of warfare, nuclear science and technology, achievements in transportation and communication, the battles of ideologies, computerization and automation, racial revolutions, or the changing map of the world, the evidences of vast transformations are joltingly evident.

The revolutionary movements are worldwide, and no one area can boast or despair over its determinative role in them. But certainly the United States, sometime in its recent past, entered a new age in its own visible and invisible life. It may well be, as Kenneth Boulding suggests, that ours is the time of a major world-historical transformation from civilization to "post-civilization,"[2] and that this nation has a unique role in the event.

We need not argue long over the time of the change. Any choice has something arbitrary about it. John Brooks makes a case for 1939 as "the watershed year between the older America and the newer one,"[3] the year of transition between economic depression and world war as the dominant social fact moving society. Nineteen thirty-nine was the year of the first regular transatlantic air service and the first public demonstration of television. John Meynard Keynes's economics was beginning to displace classical economic doctrines in the minds of public decision makers.[4] Most portentous of all, Niels Bohr came from Denmark to this country to discuss some issues of theoretical physics with Albert Einstein, with the result that the Columbia University laboratories began experiments confirming the possibility of nuclear fission. Einstein that same year wrote his famous letter to President Roosevelt, initiating the processes that were to produce nuclear weapons.

So 1939 will do as well as any year to symbolize the emergence of a new era, and it fits conveniently the pattern of this book. The record starts, then, with the time of transition when America, shaken by the Great Depression, was beginning to gird itself for war and international burdens on a scale previously unknown. I shall describe what happened with primary attention to the U.S.A., but with the recognition that thoughts and deeds elsewhere had much to do with the faith and life of America.

II. CHALLENGE TO TRADITION

The Christian church entered this new era of history with inadequate intellectual and ethical resources for its task. In part, this fact is no occasion for shame. The church shared the ignorance of educators, statesmen, sociologists, ecologists, and all men trying to find their way in an unfamiliar world. Unless the church makes pretentious claims for itself, it should not expect to be spared the confusions that assault mankind. But in part the unreadiness of the church was due to errors that might have been prevented by a better understanding of its own faith.

Three major ethical traditions had guided Christians, especially in America, as they sought to cope with the early twentieth century. The three were mutually inconsistent. Therefore some Christians chose one or another of them, and most lived with some confusion under the influence of all three.

The first of these was the theocratic tradition, derived from one strain in the Puritan heritage. It started from the unassailable premise that God is lord of all life, then went on to dubious attempts to impose the ethic of believers upon an unpersuaded society or to preserve an ethic of a past cultural situation in a changing present. A powerful Puritan creativity had once wrought profound influence upon northern Europe and America, but the latter-day descendants of the Puritans too often approached social problems with rigid legalism and prohibitions. An ethic that had once brought innovations came to stand primarily for restraint. Especially in the area of economics, the Puritan ethic (often entirely detached from Puritan faith) became a source of confusion in the face of complex industrial institutions, bewildering behavior of a market, and a fiscal system that acted more like a fate than a purposing providence.

The second was a pietistic tradition that sought to redeem souls and knew no answer for social problems except the transformation of individuals. It emphasized the saving religious experience and the sanctification of the individual. The evangelistic campaigns that had repeatedly swept through American life had entrenched the legacy of pietism—using that term in its broadest sense—in the American consciousness. The fervent charisma that once produced those movements had gradually become routinized, and the ethical consequence was a morality for personal conduct, often absorbing some of the Puritan legalisms but without the theocratic expectation of the Puritans. Hence the pietistic impulse, when joined with the American doctrine of separation of church and state, meant that religion came to be regarded increasingly as a private affair with little to say about major issues of public policy.

Challenging both these traditions was a third, younger movement: the Social Gospel. It might be described as one branch of the whole movement of liberal theology, by which Protestantism sought to maintain some credibility and power in the modern world. Something like a social gospel had emerged in the antislavery movements in the early nineteenth century, with their impulse to eradicate vast evils in the structures of society. But the distinctive Social Gospel developed toward the end of the nineteenth century and flowered in the twentieth. It sought to transform the world into the Kingdom of God, which its great prophet, Walter Rauschenbusch, described as "humanity organized according to the will of God."[5] Its high goal was the permeation of society with a justice and love that would change political, economic, racial, and international institutions as well as transform the hearts of men.

Most of the criticisms of the Social Gospel that later became voguish were entirely too glib. It is not true that the Social Gospel neglected the Bible; it took seriously the prophetic calls for justice and Jesus' concern for the poor, so often neglected by the church. Likewise, it is not true that the Social Gospel neglected the importance of sin; it saw and condemned sins that a complacent church had often tolerated. But it can be said that the Social Gospel—like all theologies—read the Bible selectively, and it was entirely too confident of the possibilities of overcoming sin. All in all, it adopted the assumptions of the Enlightenment and of liberal theology and culture on exactly the issues where those assumptions were to prove inadequate to comprehend the insidious and explosive power of evil, as the twentieth century was soon to meet it.

The American churchman in 1939, stunned by the Great Depression and uneasy at the news of Hitler's explosive rise in Europe, found none of these traditions adequate to the disturbing world. The dominant Christian ethic, a confused mix of the three traditions, faced either reformation or insignificance. The reformation, to be significant, would require both spiritual profundity and intellectual audacity. Unknown to the mass of churchmen, such a reformation was already under way.

III. The Emergence of Christian Realism

In 1932, Reinhold Niebuhr had published the ground-breaking book of the new era in Christian ethics: *Moral Man and Immoral Society*. Looking at a society that in both its rationalistic and religious impulses was steeped in "illusions and sentimentalities," he pointed to the role of power in the collective life of mankind. And he showed how the dominant ideas of justice in a society are the ideological rationalizations of the groups who hold power.

Niebuhr maintained that the "disproportion of power in society is the real root of social injustice,"[6] and he exposed the futility of the two most common hopes for progress toward justice. (*a*) Rationalists and educators were confident of the ability of reason to civilize man and harmonize conflict. But, said Niebuhr, while reason can indeed accomplish much, it is as likely to become the instrument of power as the impartial adjudicator of conflict. (*b*) Men of faith look to religious idealism to change the quality of life. Sometimes it does so. But, like reason, religion often becomes the weapon of the powerful. Or, when it overcomes men's grasps for power, it is likely to appeal to an ideal so remote and pure that it becomes irrelevant to the conflicts of better and worse that make up most of social life.

The polemical quality of Niebuhr's thought made it exhilarating to those whom it convinced, irritating to those whom it assaulted. Its polemics hit all three of the traditions that, as I have suggested earlier, nourished the American church. Under Niebuhr's astringent criticism the theocratic tradition appeared as too often the ideology of the comfortable, claiming divine sanction for its own class interests and avoiding the most urgent issues of social justice. The pietist tradition appeared as an evasion of conflict, obviously more congenial to the comfortable than to the victims of oppression. And the Social Gospel, of which Niebuhr was obviously the heir, although a very critical heir, appeared too hopeful and too pacifist to meet the realities of history.[7]

Niebuhr, both through his acute thinking and his personal leadership on many an ethical struggle, won increasing influence. Those who were not persuaded by his reasoning were sometimes persuaded by the course of events. The increasingly obvious threat of Hitler in Europe and the increasing American involvement, first indirect and then direct, in world war heightened the persuasiveness of many of his contentions.[8] The same events, combined with Niebuhr's increasing study of historical Christian ethics, led him to the discovery and appropriation of some of Augustine's ideas about history and Søren Kierkegaard's insights into human nature and experience.

To an earlier generation there might have seemed nothing less likely than the emergence of a theological ethic involving the critical appropriation of themes from such diverse thinkers as Augustine, Marx, and Kierkegaard—the whole enterprise conducted within a searching dialogue with contemporary culture and political-military events. But this is what appeared in *The Nature and Destiny of Man*,[9] Niebuhr's *magnum opus*.

By this time American theological ethics was thoroughly involved in conversation with the European theologies of Karl Barth, Emil Brunner, and the many others associated with the movement variously known as dialectical theology, theology of crisis, neo-orthodoxy, and neo-Reformation theology. It is worth noting that *Moral Man and Immoral Society* contained only two references to Barth, both incidental and critical. And while Barth had great influence in America, the temper of American ethics remained different from that of continental Europe.[10] Nevertheless, the reconstruction of Christian ethics in America was part of an international reconstruction of Protestant theology and ethics, carried out by many scholars in many lands and, more corporately, by study groups and assemblies of the World Council of Churches.

The style of ethics coming out of the reconstruction was frequently designated, in America, as Christian realism. Both words in that phrase are important. The ethic was Christian in its serious appropriation of Biblical motifs and classical doctrines: the uniqueness of Biblical revelation, the sinfulness of man and society, the judging and redeeming activity of God, the faith in justification by a divine grace that produces works worthy of repentance, the distinctive quality of Christian love. It was realistic in its criticism of naïve idealism or utopianism and its confrontation with the brute facts and power struggles of the contemporary world.

This Christian realism, at least at its best, was not an artificial combination of two unrelated motifs. It was realistic in its appropriation of Christian faith, and it was Christian—often recovering orthodox traditions neglected in the modern church—in its realism. It was alert both to the Word of God and to the latest news from European and Asiatic battlefronts, and it constantly sought the relation between the good news of the gospel and the daily news of the world.

When Waldo Beach and John C. Bennett summarized the chief developments in Christian ethics in the first half of the twentieth century, they (or their editor) chose the title "From the ethics of hope to the ethics of faith."[11] By this title they indicated the transformation of liberal Christian ethics by the criticisms of neo-Protestant theology. Although they appreciated the continuities in this history, they endorsed the newer criticisms of the old liberalism, especially those associated with Niebuhr. Even so, John Bennett occasionally remarked in those days that he hoped he would live long enough to see what would replace neo-orthodox theology. His hope obviously was not so much an aspiration to longevity as an awareness that further change was in the air and that a resurgence of some of the liberal motifs was likely. In this expectation he was prophetically accurate.

IV. Tensions Within Christian Realism

Christian realism developed as a highly dynamic style of ethical thought. It was not a fixed, codified position, but a sophisticated combination of diverse themes, often reacting with each other in considerable tension. Its richness of dialectical combinations made possible developments in many directions. The juxtaposition of eschatology and practical ethics, the sensitivity alike to the transcendence of God and the earthiness of the service of God, the commitment to political causes together with the awareness of the inadequacy of all such causes, the love of the world and the criticism of the same world, the certitude of faith and the uncertainties of frail human judgments—these were the stuff of an ethic powerful in impact and diverse in potentialities. Perhaps there was an inherent instability in so subtle a synthesis; perhaps the dynamism was not necessarily instable. But in any case the mode of thinking could move in a variety of directions. In time exactly that was to happen.

It is useful to note here some of the combinations of motifs that might persist in dialectical unity or that might fly apart. I describe these in the past tense, not to indicate that the movement is gone, but to place it in the historical context of its emergence and development.

—There was, to begin, the sharp break of Christian realism with the dominant culture-ethic of its time. This meant the appeal to a Biblical revelation that was distinct from the ideas generally approved by all high-minded people. Particularly in the European situation during the Nazi era there was an insistence on wrenching the Christian ethic loose from its cultural entanglements and asserting a word of divine judgment against men's pretensions and achievements. Yet there was concurrently an equal emphasis on the importance of involvement of the Christian in the struggles of mankind and a recognition that the church offered no sanctuary from the agonies of the world. Much of the genius of the movement inhered in this combination of movements—of cutting ties and reestablishing them, of diastasis and synthesis, as Paul Tillich put it. Yet at any time either tendency might dominate the other and establish a tone for the ethic.

—There was a simultaneous emphasis on the universality of sin in all men and causes, together with an insistence upon the importance of making distinctions between greater and lesser evils. The first motif kept in mind Christ's "Judge not that you be not judged." It forbade men to make self-righteous judgments in condemnation of others or to absolutize their own causes in conflict. The second motif impelled them to take sides against injustice in human conflicts —to support the nations threatened by Nazism, to work for the cause of laborers and colored peoples around the world, to join the efforts of political parties against other parties—without waiting for some perfect cause.

—Similarly there was a combination of gospel perfectionism with acute awareness of the imperfection of all human motives and plans. Self-giving *agape* was the standard by which all human actions were judged and found wanting; hence works-righteousness was to no avail and justification by grace became the only source of ethical security. But in the world where all choices were imperfect, it remained important to work for the rough justice that was achievable. Politics, defined as the art of the possible, required compromise. To try to import gospel perfectionism into political judgments, forgetting the workings of power, was foolish utopianism; yet to compromise without a troubled conscience was to yield to expediency. So men might fight wars or enter into the struggles of power politics, driven by love, yet always aware of the judgment of love and the need for penitence.

—There was a recognition that large collective groups—in particular, nations or social classes or ideological blocs—act in terms of their perceptions of their self-interest and are not capable of the kind of generosity or sacrifice that sometimes characterizes personal acts. When they claim to act for grander motives than the group interest, they heighten not their morality but their self-deception. Even, so, a Christian ethic must bring moral criticism to bear on these collectives, exposing their ideological pretensions and hypocrisies. It is not "realistic" to expect a nation to act contrary to its conception of its national interest, and a workable ethic must take this limitation into account. Yet Christian criticism has the task of exposing nationalistic idolatries and bringing moral criteria to bear on the many ways in which nations seek their national interest and relate it to the interests of others.

—There was a tentative quality in ethical judgments related to an urgent necessity for ethical action. The unqualified assurances of faith and the absolute purity of love did not translate into ethical absolutism on a policy level. Neither Biblical nor theological tradition told men directly what to do in the intricacies of human life. The right decision depended upon fallible human judgments about many a technical issue and about practical possibilities in a sinful world. Hence ethical theory warned against premature dogmatic judgments. This quality of restraint, by itself, might have led to suspension of judgment and inactivism, but Christian love and concern for justice drove the Christian realists to urgent activity. This ethical passion, in itself, might have led to a dogmatic fury if it had not been qualified by the awareness of the fallibility of men. The conflict between ardent commitments and tentative judgments would have been unbearable apart from justification by grace. Confident of justification, the Christian struggled for a cause, even though he knew he might be mistaken on many points. And he could struggle with furious energy, yet maintain some compassion toward the foe.

—Finally there was a constant interpenetration of eschatology and practical ethics, of awareness of the Kingdom of God and acknowledgment of the kingdoms of this world. Christian realism sought to maintain the relation between ultimate and proximate goals without confusing the one with the other. It was equally concerned for "impossible possibilities" and for practical programs. Its aspirations and efforts mingled the daring and the prudential.

Such an ethic, interweaving these various themes, could not possibly be static. Nor could there be uniformity of judgment within the camp. Its adherents might emphasize certain of its motifs extravagantly, then find correction from contrapuntal motifs within the same ethic. Christian realism might maintain a poise in motion; it could not settle down to a fixed position. Almost inevitably such an ethic would spin off various other ethics, as men drew upon one or another of its major themes. Even if there had been no challenge from outside, the ethic itself was bound to generate controversy. The impact of external events and currents of thought would heighten the controversy. Such, in fact, has been the case.

In August of 1968, in a reflective celebration and evaluation of this theological tradition, *Christianity and Crisis,* its journalistic voice for a quarter of a century, published a recorded conversation among some of its editors and contributors.[12] The lively argument among spokesmen for a considerable range of opinions made it evident that all the participants acknowledged a great debt to the reconstruction of Christian ethics called Christian realism. Yet all thought that contemporary history required reevaluation of that construction and some new ventures in ethical understanding.

The new ventures move in such a variety of ways that they cannot be described in a single chronological story. In the remainder of this account I shall therefore shift from narrative to description of a set of issues under simultaneous attack in the recent past and in the present.

V. The Uses and Abuses of Power

Traditional Protestant ethics in America was squeamish about power, although Protestants frequently used power without much inhibition. Churchmen preached to slaves about peace and humility while using the noose and the lash to enforce slavery. They talked to the poor of moderation and nonviolence, while using police power to enforce a system that maintained poverty. In part we must assume a conscious duplicity among slaveholders and robber barons who learned how to mingle profit and prayer. To an even greater degree we may detect a typically human ideology, in which the desire for reasonable resolutions of disputes by peaceful negotiation was a highly plausible ideal to men basically contented with the *status quo*.

Christian realism, as I have already described it, attacked this ideology, showing how power blocs often talked of peace and reason with little awareness of the actual uses of power. The new theological ethic asked men to be honest about power, to recognize its reality in the world. It paid tribute to the Christ who renounced the most obvious forms of power, but it exposed those who gave lip service to this ideal and had no real intention of practicing it.

Hence this ethic sought social justice, not by begging the powerful to be kind to the weak but by advocating shifts of power so that the weak could confront the strong. In international affairs it rejected the quasi-pacifist ethic that had won wide influence in the churches after the excessive attempts to join Christ to militarism in World War I. Hitler was for many Christians a refutation of pacifism as a political ethic, although not necessarily of pacifism as the vocation of Christians who, with no pretensions of political effectiveness, witness to gospel love even in desperate situations.

By mid-century two of the major facts of life required Christians to think further about power. The first of these was the destructive power of nuclear and thermonuclear weapons. If Nazism had refuted pacifism, the new weapons refuted all-out war as a sane international policy. A new ethic of "nuclear pacifism" arose among people who were unconvinced by traditional pacifism but judged pragmatically that no evil could justify nuclear overkill. Others half agreed, but could not accept the logical consequences of nuclear pacifism—unilateral nuclear disarmament—because they were convinced that, for the time being, the greatest single restraint against use of nuclear weapons was the existence of credible deterrents. Meanwhile "brushfire wars" and still graver nonnuclear wars went on, with the undeclared war in Vietnam actually engaging the nation's armies for a longer period than American involvement in either world war.

At present nobody is really convinced that the human race can survive several centuries of nuclear rivalry with escalating weapons races. Likewise, nobody believes that the world will be organized for peace without some structure of power. Christian ethics, like all political ethics, is struggling for a new comprehension of the uses and validity of power.

The second fact affecting Christian understanding of power was the changing contour of the racial crisis both in America and in many other parts of the world. The greatest charismatic leader of American Christianity in this century, Martin Luther King, Jr., died by the violence that he refused to employ. King was, in his own faith, a devout pacifist, committed to nonviolent methods, but he understood the uses of power. He fought the power blocs that victimized black people by a skillful combination of appeal to public conscience with a mobilization of power—economic, political, and judicial.

But King's methods sometimes met frustration, and his death was taken by some as a proof of the impotence of nonviolence. Black militants increasingly rejected the strategy of nonviolence. Ethical analysts pointed out that the systemic violence embodied in established power structures enforced by economic sanctions and police power may be fully as vicious as the sporadic violence of rebels. Christian ethics increasingly advocated the use of power to correct wrongs. Disturbed both by the evils of racism and the threat of heightened violence and counterviolence, Christian ethics is exploring once again the relationship of power to political responsibility. It is examining in myriad ways the morality of war, of worldwide and domestic revolution, of black power, of economic power as an instrument of protest and social change.

VI. Ambiguity and Commitment

The tendency to absolutize conflict, common enough in human history, has been a special temptation in American Christianity. The common culture has turned perplexing moral struggles into horse-opera melodrama, pitting clean-minded rangers against cattle rustlers, cowboys against Indians, national heroes against traitors, virile Americans against effete or insidious foreign foes. Americans could rarely fight a war without turning it into a crusade. In the decades following World War I the church frequently repented of its excessive ardor in sacralizing the national cause. A revulsion against overcommitment had much to do with the pacifist mood (sometimes a pacifist commitment) in the years that led up to World War II. Often peace propaganda, even in the face of the rising Nazi threat, made the point that an imperfect United States of America had no right to war against wrongs in others. As Nazi viciousness became increasingly obvious, churchmen with long memories wondered: must we now adopt the zealous militancy that hard experience has taught us to repent of?

Christian realism met the question by two simultaneous assertions. First, human conflict never sets perfect righteousness against total evil. But second, social life requires moral choices and commitments, even among ambiguous causes. Aware of both theses, a generation of Christians learned to make decisions among relative goods and evils. They fought a war against a demonic cause without claiming total virtue for themselves. They learned to understand politics as the art of the possible, to make commitments even as they recognized the flaws in their allies and in themselves, to opt for qualified goods and sometimes for lesser evils.

Such a stance, I have said above, is not easy to maintain. If men are going to dare great risks and commitments, must they not claim great validity for their causes? Conversely, if they are sensitive to the wrongs in all things human, will they not drift into indecision?

Frequently in the tepid postwar years, when heroes were few and leaders often faltered, society drifted into moral malaise. Social critics warned against the yearning for security and the drive for conformity. Awareness of the rents and patches in all garments of righteousness gave many the excuse for noncommitment. Observers lamented that even youth, who almost by definition should be crusading for *something*, lacked a cause.[13]

Then ethically sensitive Americans, or at least some of them, suddenly found a cause. Civil rights rescued them from the torpor of ambiguity. Once again they saw, or thought they saw, right embattled against wrong. When Martin Luther King confronted Bull Connor in Birmingham and (via television) in most of the homes of the nation, it seemed prissy to say that all men are sinners with mixed motives. When disciplined black youths absorbed the blows of raucous hoods without retaliation, it seemed irrelevant to comment that all causes are morally ambiguous.

While the classical period of the civil rights movement brought a joyful emancipation from ambiguity to eager idealists, it led to a revision of models among ethicists. The new models put greater emphasis on confrontation and subdued the emphasis on moral perplexity. Sometimes they elevated action above reflection, involvement above repentance, absolutism above negotiation.

Increasingly the new style dominated the Christian opposition to the war in Vietnam. But the questions arose as to whether it offered an adequate model for the intricacies of foreign policy. Was it really a good model for understanding the contest between Lyndon Johnson and Barry Goldwater? And if so, was it equally good for the test of strength between Robert Kennedy and Johnson, or Eugene McCarthy and Hubert Humphrey, or Humphrey and Richard Nixon? Was it even an adequate model for understanding the ethical issues of the race problem, when it moved out of the early civil rights struggle and into the tests of power between black militants and teachers' unions or city hall?

While the newly committed were jarred into a rediscovery of ambiguity in external social conflicts, they also sometimes discovered limitations in their own idealism. Some valiant white participants in the civil rights movement listened with pain to black complaints against the unconscious paternalism and messianism of the whites. They occasionally learned with horror that they had been therapeutically "acting out" their own resentments and projecting their inner conflicts on the world. Such recognition does not invalidate brave deeds—unless we foolishly refuse admiration to anything less than perfection. But such recognition does require a reassessment of the ethical question of ambiguity.

The basic issue remains. How does Christian ethics acknowledge the moral power of idealism, even of utopianism, while avoiding the dogmatism of those so sure of their own cause that they can have no understanding for an opponent? How does ethics encourage commitment without dogmatism? Paul Ramsey's tract for the times, *Who Speaks for the Church?*, was the cry of one Christian ethicist, haunted by the issues of ambiguity and perplexity in policy decisions against the ardent certitudes of other Christians, confident in their revolutionary polemics against established evils.[14] Without trying to referee the argument,[15] I can urge that it continue.

VII. The Debate Over Situational Ethics

The debate over situational ethics proceeded for several years before its public eruption. Inherent in Christian realism was a criticism of any idea that ethics was a deductive science in which a set of abstract principles could be applied directly to practical situations without taking seriously empirical data, the technical information and concepts provided by the social sciences, and the ambiguities of sin. I have noted above that a strain of Christian perfectionism lingered in the ethics of Reinhold Niebuhr, in tension with his attacks upon all perfectionism. This tension made possible variations both to the right and to the left of his own position.

John Bennett, seeing how easily "realism" might degenerate into expediency, has always been concerned to maintain some ethical guidelines to which men might refer even when circumstances required them to deviate from any assured standards. Sometimes he advocated "middle axioms" as practical guidelines or realizable goals somewhere between the perfection of Christian love and the sheer play of power.[16] Edward LeRoy Long, Jr., asked for a Protestant "casuistry" to help men relate ideals and principles to practice.[17]

Farther to the left were some of the students of H. Richard Niebuhr, impressed by Niebuhr's "relational" theology and ethics.[18] They argued that even Reinhold Niebuhr had not gone far enough in shaking loose from principles and deriving an ethic in concrete circumstances.

The scholarly debate was well summarized in 1965 by James Gustafson in an article entitled "Context Versus Principles: A Misplaced Debate in Christian Ethics."[19] Gustafson showed by a subtle analysis that any polarization of the issue was deceptively simple and that any real account of Christian ethics touched on at least four "base points": situational analysis, theological affirmations, moral principles, and the nature of the Christian's life in Christ.

This influential argument, while not intended to settle the debate, might have redirected it. But just as Gustafson was concluding that "the debate is no longer a fruitful one," the popular controversy over the issue was flaring into prominence. Prior to Gustafson and unmentioned by him, Bishop Robinson called for a "revolution in ethics" and a "new morality" in the best-selling *Honest to God*.[20] If Robinson later showed in *Christian Morals Today*[21] that he meant to direct his radical method to fairly conservative conclusions, Joseph Fletcher drew more unconventional conclusions and made "situation ethics" a household (or at least a campus-wide) term.[22] Fletcher's ethic is an up-dating and translating of the utilitarian hedonistic calculus,[23] set in a contemporary situation, and dependent upon theology only at the point of asserting a single indispensable faith-judgment—the positivism of love.

Popular discussion frequently equates Fletcher's situationalism with Paul Lehmann's contextualism, although both authors are concerned to emphasize the difference. Lehmann draws upon the tradition of Karl Barth and Dietrich Bonhoeffer, rather than of utilitarianism.[24] From Barth he draws the faith in a living God, whose activity is ceaselessly creative, calling for free obedience in new situations. From Bonhoeffer he draws the openness to the secular world in a new epoch of history. But Lehmann's contextualism includes at least three elements: the context of theology, the context of the Christian community or *koinonia,* and the context of the empirical situation. Hence he bases ethics on a perception of "what God is doing in the world to make and to keep human life human."[25] Fletcher needs the first two contexts only for the sake of his positivism of love; his emphasis is on the third.

These various forms of ethic have in common a deemphasis on ethical rules and principles, together with a belief that there is a peculiarly right thing to do in a given situation. For Barth there is a specific and certain will of God, although Barth is not clear on how man discerns it. For Lehmann the *koinonia* recognizes what God is doing. For Fletcher there is a calculation—it is subject to error, but error is subject to correction—of the best act in the situation. In all these forms of ethic it can be shown, as Paul Ramsey has shown,[26] that their advocates introduce more principles—even firm, unyielding principles—into their ethics than they are inclined to acknowledge. But it is important to recognize that their motive is not to enjoy a "permissive" ethic, but to develop an ethic that, freed from legalism, is creative and responsive. At this point the critics of situationalism—Ramsey and, in a more pragmatic way, Bennett—agree, but reply that love or obedience, unless these are to be empty words, produce some structure of ethics.[27]

There may be another motive in current situational ethics. Christian realism, particularly in Reinhold Niebuhr's formulations, put some Christians into what they considered an intolerable box. Niebuhr argued that perfectionism was impossible in a world of sin, that men had to compromise and (in a favorite quotation from Luther) "sin bravely," but that they should repent of their sin. For example, justice may demand that a soldier kill a foe; but he should kill in penitence. For Fletcher, if the act is the best of available choices in a situation, it requires no repentance.[28] For Niebuhr the repentance is in order; it is the world's sin that produces situations in which killing is necessary, and the killer has no moral right to separate himself from this sin in self-righteous pride. From Fletcher's viewpoint, Niebuhr burdens men with unnecessary feelings of guilt; from Niebuhr's viewpoint, Fletcher contributes to "the easy conscience of modern man."

VIII. HUMANISM AND SECULAR PASSION

No single characteristic is more notable in recent Christian ethics than the surge of humanistic motifs.[29] It is most dramatic in the career of Karl Barth, who once awoke Protestantism to the transcendence of God, echoing Søren Kierkegaard's message of the "infinite qualitative distinction between time and eternity."[30] The same Barth three and a half decades later, in an unembarrassed reversal of direction, declared that "God is human."[31]

This Protestant humanism has found a happy alliance with the Roman Catholic humanism of Vatican II, expressed in the *Pastoral Constitution on the Church in the Modern World* (*Gaudium et Spes*). As Catholic scholars have broken loose from the authoritarianism of past papal pronouncements and rigid interpretations of natural law, Protestant-Catholic discussions of ethics have moved ahead with unsuspicious cordiality and eagerness.

One consequence of this new humanism has been a secular passion, uncharacteristic of much of the history of Christian ethics. Its seminal and most influential expression came in Dietrich Bonhoeffer's prison letters. Bonhoeffer, whose theology and ethics were as Christocentric and incarnational as Barth's, called for a Christian "worldliness." This worldliness was no relaxation of, no retreat from, Biblical faith and ethics. Bonhoeffer said clearly: "I don't mean the shallow this-worldliness of the enlightened, of the busy, the comfortable or the lascivious. It's something much more profound than that, something in which the knowledge of death and resurrection is ever present."[32] This ethic might be understood as the consequence of taking with full seriousness the classical Biblical text, "For God so loved the world . . ." (John 3:16).

The new passion for the secular won enthusiastic response in America. Its double appeal—to Biblical faith and to contemporaneity—commended it to many theologians, especially of the postwar generation. In Harvey Cox's vivid expression it appealed to the church to welcome two facts that had often seemed frightening —the secularization and the urbanization of life.[33] Secularization, sometimes distinguished from an ideological secularism, won acclaim as an implication of, not a threat to, Christian faith.

If the neo-orthodoxy of a generation past had made a business of deflating men's false hopes, the new ethic sought to call men from frustration to authentic hope. Jürgen Moltmann's *Theology of Hope*, finding a secular meaning for Biblical eschatology by relating it to

Marxist revolutionary motifs, sought to reorient theology and ethics toward the future. The task of the Christian church, this young German theologian said, is to disclose to a "world of lost horizons" the "horizon of the future of the crucified Christ . . ."[34]

The fervent hopefulness of such versions of Christian ethics contrasts curiously with the familiar Christian criticism of utopianism, just as the occasional confidence of "the new left" contrasts with the frustration and despair that characterize much of world politics. Any program of Christian ethics for the days ahead will have to sort out once again the relation between eschatological and historical hope, between the valid and the illusory hopes that characterize men.

IX. The Relation of Christian Ethics to Philosophy and the Behavioral Sciences

Christian ethics always goes about its work, whether by design or inadvertence, in a variety of interrelationships with secular scholarly disciplines, chiefly philosophy and the social sciences. When it ignores these disciplines, it is most likely to be the victim of unrecognized and uninformed assumptions.

The ethics of liberal Christian theology frequently made an ally of philosophical idealism. As the early church had found Platonic idealism a congenial milieu of thought, so modern Christianity found in post-Kantian idealism a philosophy that took seriously freedom and ethics at a time when many philosophies seemed to exclude both. But just as an earlier church once turned from Platonism to Aristotelianism, so the modern church turned from idealism to more world-oriented philosophies.

The Christian realism that has offered the chief reference point for this chapter found a curious fascination in pragmatism. In many ways it preferred the pragmatism of William James to that of John Dewey. But in either case pragmatism took seriously the worlds of nature and society. Its ethical concern was not for past authorities or abstract laws, but for concrete events and decisions. Its future-thrusting style weighed the consequences of decisions in terms of their consequences for men. In all these ways Christian realism was pragmatic.

But this ethic never adopted Dewey's familiar theme that scientific method, if freed from authoritarian inhibitions, would achieve in the social arena the same triumphs it had won in physical nature and technology. In part the dissent from Dewey was clearly theological. Christian ethics adopted pragmatism within an eschatological faith that knew something about death and resurrection. There was a cruciform quality in this ethic that differentiated it, despite its concern for measurable social gains, from most secular pragmatism.

This theological criticism of pragmatism was reinforced by two philosophical strains that entered uneasily into conversation with pragmatism. One of these was Marxism, with its constant reminder of the role of conflict in human affairs and its warning that scientific reason might just as easily serve ideological bias as correct it. The other was existentialism, with its probing examination of the inner life of man and its recognition of a terror and exultancy that were hardly comprehended in the problem-solving model of ethics. Pragmatism alone, despite its fervent, crusading origins, had a tendency to become bland. The Marxist and existentialist strains in Christian ethics gave it both a toughness and a sensitivity that corresponded in fascinating ways with its Biblical origins. If the Christian-Marxist dialogues were largely interrupted, at least in America, during the era of Stalinism and its aftermath, they were renewed in the 1960's, occasionally with a strained reliance upon the "young Marx," who was discovered to be something of an existentialist, ignored by generations of orthodox Marxists.

The rise of logical positivism was rarely felt as a severe threat to Christian ethics. Logical positivism, especially in its brash juvenile forms, insisted that all theology and ethics was simply nonsense or emotive expression. But since it was obvious that all men, including the positivists, had to go on making personal and social decisions of momentous consequence, theological ethics simply kept at its work. No philosopher's polemic against ethics was likely to persuade the theologian that issues of war, race, poverty, and sex were inconsequential. The positivists' polemics could always be answered by an existentialist cry for decision or (more objectively) by the phenomenologists' descriptions of human experience.

Even so, the positivistic question, "How do you know?" haunted theological ethics and increased its tendency to avoid dependence upon metaphysical speculation or classical natural law or value theory. The theologian, meeting the positivist, might emphasize more than ever his reliance upon revelation or upon sheer existential decision or phenomenological description. But as the cruder forms of logical positivism gave way to more sophisticated linguistic analysis, the question shifted from "How do you know?" to "What do you mean?" To the extent that Christian ethicists were involved in moral crusades against social evils, *they knew* what they meant and did not take much time out for subtle theorizing about their language. But to the extent that they reflected on their words and actions, they had to analyze their meanings. Increasingly they found useful the ideas of linguistic philosophers.

Perhaps because of the activist tendencies in American theological ethics, there has been some impatience over the theoretical precision —sometimes approaching a modernized neo-scholasticism—of the linguistic analysts. For students of revolution or of the use of power, the refined studies of ethics and meta-ethics in contemporary philosophy are sometimes entirely too precious, at best an unneeded luxury, at worst a hideous diversion from more serious business. Yet the interaction between theological ethics and philosophical ethics is generating some lively thought on the meaning of ethical language and its relationship to man's other languages.

As important as philosophy for theological ethics are the social studies. Social and intellectual history has shown Christians how often their fixed moral ideas have been the expression of peculiar and temporary cultural situations. The sociological theories of Max Weber, appropriated by such Christian scholars as Ernst Troeltsch and R. H. Tawney, have enabled Christian ethics to examine its own configurations—to realize, for example, how the so-called "Protestant ethic" replaced the feudal economic ethic and must, in its turn, be criticized today. Any such inquiry forces the ethicist to ask similar questions of many past certitudes, whether they deal with war, politics, or sex.

The Social Gospel emphasized the importance of some understanding of economic processes, and economists were among the spokesmen for the Social Gospel. Increasingly, in the era of Christian realism, ethics became aware that sound policy-decisions are as dependent upon technical knowledge about the functioning of society as upon moral premises. The role of the lay expert—economist, sociologist, psychologist, or political technician—became important in the framing of ethical judgments about society. The Federal Council of Churches and later the National Council of Churches (like the denominations, on the one hand, and the World Council of Churches, on the other hand) saw the importance of including such specialists in its efforts to discover and illuminate the nature of ethical decisions in the contemporary world.

It is no longer necessary to argue that ethics requires the results of the social sciences if it is to enter into intelligent policy-making. That point has been made, at least in principle. The area of continuing controversy has to do with the methods of the social studies (as distinguished from the information they provide) as these relate to the methods of theological ethics. Peter Berger's work in the sociology of knowledge[35] and Gibson Winter's explorations of the models of the social sciences in relation to ethics[36] mark directions that ethics is required to explore.

X. AGENDA

The continuing agenda of Christian ethics includes all the issues I have described (sections V-IX above): the question of power, the tension between ambiguity and commitment, the thorny problems of situational ethics, the interest in humanism and secularization, the relation between theology and other intellectual disciplines. In each of these areas Christians live with a sense that they are venturing into unexplored realms. The erosion of past authorities and the emergence of new styles of self-understanding dominate ethical thinking in an era when announcements of revolution have become clichés.

Walter Lippmann describes something of the emergent task in his observation that men simply have not discovered workable governmental institutions for the contemporary world:

The challenge to democratic government does not come primarily from its avowed enemies, be they on the left or on the right. Nor does it come from the bogeymen that popular superstition conjures up to explain unpalatable facts. The challenge to democratic government arises from the fact it comes down to us from the Eighteenth and Nineteenth Centuries, from the age before the great technological revolutions of this century. It is this great technological revolution which has transformed not only our ways of living but, in its ramifications dealing with the structure and chemistry of the human personality, is remaking men themselves.[37]

Conceivably an abstract moral theology might go on with its analyses of right and wrong, oblivious to such a world history. But such an ethical exercise would be neither Biblical nor contemporary.

And it would certainly not be characteristic of the tradition of Christian ethics in America, where (as James Gustafson has rightly said), scholarship in Christian ethics has "clearly been motivated by concern for the actual state of public and private morality."[38] This "American" style runs the risk of slighting the careful scholarship characteristic alike of European theological ethics or of contemporary philosophical ethics, European or American. No doubt it needs the criticism of more academically oriented styles. But its genius is to keep in touch with human life.

The continuing agenda for Christian ethics requires a zest for contemporaneity and an eagerness for the future, conjoined with the historical and analytical studies that make possible an incisive criticism of all that is merely contemporary.

NOTES

1. The Ritschlian tradition, which found the meaning of theology in ethics, has come under severe attack in the twentieth century. But recently it has emerged in new forms. As Daniel Day Williams has noted, the declaration that "all theology is ethics," which would have delighted Ritschl, but then would have seemed "hopelessly quaint" between 1930 and 1960, is again in vogue. See Daniel Day Williams, "The New Theological Situation," *Theology Today*, Vol. XXIV, No. 4 (Jan., 1968), p. 447.

2. Kenneth Boulding, *The Meaning of the Twentieth Century* (Harper & Row, Publishers, Inc., 1964).

3. John Brooks, *The Great Leap* (Harper & Row, Publishers, Inc., 1966), p. 11.

4. Keynes's major work, *The General Theory of Employment, Interest and Money* (London: Macmillan & Co., Ltd., 1936), was published three years before. Statements of his ideas had, of course, begun to seep into public consciousness some years sooner.

5. Walter Rauschenbusch, *A Theology for the Social Gospel* (The Macmillan Company, 1917), p. 142.

6. Reinhold Niebuhr, *Moral Man and Immoral Society* (Charles Scribner's Sons, 1932), p. 163.

7. The Social Gospel was not uniformly pacifist. Within it were some strict pacifists and many semi-pacifists who looked to international organizations (the League of Nations) and the Kellogg-Briand Peace Pact to make wars unnecessary. A more Marxist wing rejected "imperialist" wars but emphasized the necessity of class conflict. Niebuhr ob-

viously shared many of the concerns of the Marxists, but his thinking was far more subtle than the doctrinaire Marxism of the 1930's. On the pacifist issue, he was once president of the pacifist Fellowship of Reconciliation. Even in his resignation from that group and his renunciation of the pacifist ethic, he continued to regard international war as "suicidal." See "Why I Leave the F.O.R.," *The Christian Century*, Vol. LI, No. 1 (Jan. 3, 1934), pp. 17–19.

8. In one other respect Niebuhr's argument had to wait longer for popular vindication. The Black Power movement of the 1960's could almost use *Moral Man and Immoral Society* as a textbook for many of its aims—although not for the drive of some of its advocates for racial separatism. Niebuhr wrote that "when collective power, whether in the form of imperialism or class domination, exploits weakness, it can never be dislodged unless power is raised against it." Referring specifically to the American Negroes, Niebuhr predicted that their "most minimum demands" would "seem exorbitant to the dominant whites" and that they could never expect to "win full justice" by methods of accommodation in a conflict caused by "the disproportion of power in society" (pp. xii, xvii).

9. Reinhold Niebuhr, *The Nature and Destiny of Man* (Vol. I, *Human Nature*, 1941; Vol. II, *Human Destiny*, 1943; Charles Scribner's Sons).

10. Religious journalism often exaggerated and misconstrued the differences, as did some theological polemics against "continental theology." Almost any statement of the differences results in an overcategorization, in which some Americans find themselves friendly to continental thought and some Europeans find themselves friendly to American ideas. But there was a difference, which became evident at the Evanston Assembly of the World Council of Churches in 1954. The difference was recognized and symbolized, without the popular caricatures, in the two addresses on Christian hope by Edmund Schlink of Heidelberg and Robert L. Calhoun of Yale. See *The Christian Century*, Vol. LXXI, No. 34 (Aug. 25, 1954), pp. 1002–1011.

11. See the symposium, *Protestant Thought in the Twentieth Century*, ed. by Arnold S. Nash (The Macmillan Company, 1951).

12. "Christian Realism: Retrospect and Prospect," A Symposium by John C. Bennett, Harvey Cox, Roger L. Shinn, Richard Shaull, Alan Geyer, Tom F. Driver, and Robert W. Lynn, *Christianity and Crisis*, Vol. XXVIII, No. 14 (Aug. 5, 1968), pp. 175–190.

13. In a famous book David Riesman and his colleagues described the "other-directed" character type that they saw emerging increasingly on the American scene. See David Riesman with Nathan Glazer and Reuel Denney, *The Lonely Crowd* (Yale University Press, 1950). As late as 1965, Kenneth Keniston published *The Uncommitted: Alienated*

Youth in American Society (Harcourt, Brace & World, Inc., 1965). A few years later Keniston described a quite different phenomenon in *Young Radicals: Notes on Committed Youth* (Harcourt, Brace & World, Inc., 1968).

14. Paul Ramsey, *Who Speaks for the Church?* A Critique of the 1966 Geneva Conference on Church and Society (The Abingdon Press, 1967).

15. I have already done a bit of that in "Paul Ramsey's Challenge to Ecumenical Ethics," *Christianity and Crisis*, Vol. XXVII, No. 18 (Oct. 30, 1967), pp. 243–247.

16. Among several of Bennett's writings, perhaps the most sustained exposition of this position is in *Christian Ethics and Social Policy* (Charles Scribner's Sons, 1946). More than any other American ethicist, Bennett influenced and drew upon the work of the World Council of Churches and its predecessor Life and Work movement.

17. Edward LeRoy Long, Jr., *Conscience and Compromise* (The Westminster Press, 1954).

18. The theological premises are expressed in *The Meaning of Revelation* (The Macmillan Company, 1946). The ethic is elaborated in *Christ and Culture* (Harper & Brothers, 1951), where it is suggested that love is too abstract to characterize the ethic of Jesus, which is better described in terms of loyalty, devotion, or "consent to Being." The theme is further developed in the posthumously published book, *The Responsible Self* (Harper & Row, Publishers, Inc., 1963), where Richard Niebuhr proposes that an ethic of response is preferable to either the classical deontological or teleological styles of ethics.

19. First published in *Harvard Theological Review*, April, 1965. Reprinted in *New Theology No. 3*, edited by Martin E. Marty and Dean G. Peerman (The Macmillan Company, 1966).

20. John A. T. Robinson, *Honest to God* (The Westminster Press, 1963).

21. John A. T. Robinson, *Christian Morals Today* (The Westminster Press, 1964).

22. Joseph Fletcher, *Situation Ethics: The New Morality* (The Westminster Press, 1966). Robinson's *Honest to God* drew upon Fletcher's preliminary sketch of his own position, "The New Look in Christian Ethics," *Harvard Divinity Bulletin*, Vol. XXIV, No. 1 (Oct. 1959), pp. 7–18. Fletcher's book-length discussion then followed Robinson's book.

23. Hedonism, in the utilitarian sense, does not refer solely to cheap pleasures. It is concerned for the greatest happiness of the greatest number. For Fletcher, "all ethics are happiness ethics" (*Situation Ethics*, p. 96). Because he uses the term "hedonism" in an individualistic sense, he prefers to describe his own ethics as an *agapeic* calculus.

24. Paul Lehmann, *Ethics in a Christian Context* (Harper & Row, Publishers, Inc., 1963).

25. *Ibid.,* p. 117.

26. Paul Ramsey, *Deeds and Rules in Christian Ethics* (Charles Scribner's Sons, 1967).

27. For a discussion in depth of the issues, see the symposium, *Norm and Context in Christian Ethics,* ed. by Gene H. Outka and Paul Ramsey (Charles Scribner's Sons, 1968).

28. In the most dramatic and controversial sentence he ever wrote, Fletcher said: "On a vast scale of 'agapeic calculus' President Truman made his decision about the A-bombs on Hiroshima and Nagasaki" (*Situation Ethics,* p. 98). Fletcher's method, more sophisticated than the single conclusion just quoted, is quite open to discussion as to whether the calculations were accurate. But if they were correct and were made out of a desire for justice (which in his system is the same as love distributed), there would be no reason for Truman both to make the decision and repent for it.

29. I have traced this story in somewhat more detail in my book *Man: The New Humanism* (The Westminster Press, 1968).

30. Karl Barth, *The Epistle to the Romans,* tr. from the sixth edition by Edwyn C. Hoskyns (London: Oxford University Press, 1933), "Preface to the Second Edition," p. 10. Original date, 1921.

31. Karl Barth, *The Humanity of God,* tr. by John Newton Thomas (John Knox Press, 1960), p. 51. Original date, 1956.

32. Dietrich Bonhoeffer, *Letters and Papers from Prison,* tr. by Reginald Fuller (The Macmillan Company, 1967), pp. 225–226.

33. Harvey Cox, *The Secular City* (The Macmillan Company, 1965).

34. Jürgen Moltmann, *Theology of Hope,* tr. by James W. Leitch (Harper & Row, Publishers, Inc., 1967), p. 338. Cf. Moltmann, *Religion, Revolution, and the Future* (Charles Scribner's Sons, 1969).

35. Peter Berger and Thomas Luckmann, *The Social Construction of Reality* (Doubleday & Company, Inc., 1967).

36. Gibson Winter, *Elements for a Social Ethic. Scientific and Ethical Perspectives on Social Process* (The Macmillan Company, 1966).

37. Walter Lippmann, Column, "Today and Tomorrow," *New York World Journal Tribune,* March 16, 1967.

38. James Gustafson, "Christian Ethics," in Paul Ramsey (ed.), *Religion* (Humanistic Scholarship in America: The Princeton Studies; Prentice-Hall, Inc., 1965), p. 287.

✧ ✧ ✧ *Douglas E. Sturm was educated at Hiram College and the Divinity School of the University of Chicago, which granted him the doctorate in philosophy in 1959. His formal education was interrupted by a term of service as Executive Secretary of Christian Action under the chairmanship of John Bennett. He has been cited for outstanding teaching at Bucknell University, where he is Associate Professor of Religion and Political Science and chairman of the Department of Religion. He has focused his scholarly concerns on interdisciplinary work in religion, politics, and law. He was Fellow in Law and Philosophy at Harvard Law School and has done research in political thought at the British Museum. Articles from his pen have been published in a number of books and journals, including* Journal of Religion, Journal of Politics, *and* Stanford Law Review.

The following essay explores the theoretical relationships between political-legal thought and theological-ethical thought.

6

ASPECTS
OF THE INTERPENETRATION
OF RELIGION AND POLITICS[1]

❖ ❖ ❖ *Douglas E. Sturm*

THE QUESTION of this essay is that of the relationship between religion and politics. At first blush, these two activities of humankind seem far distant from each other in their preoccupations and interests.

On the one side, religion is highly personal and concerns matters of ultimacy. In Whitehead's phrasing, religion is what man does with his solitariness. That is, religion in its elegance is the most intimate of human expressions. It touches on and manifests the innermost thoughts, feelings, and aspirations of the human soul. It is a delicate and sensitive matter. It betokens the profoundest depths of human yearning and directs the mind to the farthest reaches of human destiny.

On the other side, politics is obviously public and concerns matters of the moment. It is often excused as the art of the possible. Its time is the immediate. Its locus is the marketplace. Its facial expression is that of harsh determination and fierce contention. At best, politics results in compromise; at worst, it moves into battle. And at all times it leaves some men scarred, weary, and suffering while it exalts others, even if only for a time, into positions of power, glory, and honor.

It is no wonder that religion is consigned to the heavenly sphere, permitting politics to occupy the terrestrial. The City of God and the city of man seem at least distinct, and perhaps irreconcilable. Indeed, the temptation to effect a total separation of the two spheres is strong.

But a total separation is resisted, and properly so. Religion and politics are, after all, both activities engaged in by the same men. While they may be distinguishable, they cannot be unrelatable unless man is, by nature or condition, a split being. To ascertain or to define the relationship, however, is by no means an easy matter, and clearly it is not a task that admits of a high degree of certainty or of a single result.

Over the past several decades there have been a number of significant attempts by American Protestant Christians to demonstrate the relevance of their faith to political matters in the form of statements and in the form of direct action. None thought that the political expression was exhaustive of the faith, but at the same time none considered the relationship to be merely tangential. They have not, to be sure, spoken with one voice, nor have they acted in concert. They have differed not only in their approval or disapproval of particular policies and in their stand on concrete issues. They have differed as well in their methods, in their approaches, in the level on which they determined to draw the line of connection, in the manner in which they thought political action by men of religion was appropriate. The differences are as instructive as the common effort to demonstrate the relationship between the spheres of religion and politics.

There is a need at this time, however, for the construction of a general theory of the connection between these two spheres of human activity, a theory that provides a broad, inclusive framework within which these more narrowly circumscribed emphases on the relevance of faith to politics can be cast and that is attentive both to theological understandings and to issues and trends in modern political analysis. The primary purpose of this essay is to suggest the beginnings of such a general theory. More precisely, its purpose is to suggest, in a preliminary but systematic form, a series of points at which religion and politics interpenetrate.

As a preparatory step, I shall delineate six relatively distinguishable emphases in American Protestant Christian thought and action, each representing a different nuance in relating religion and politics. It is important to observe, given the purpose of this essay, that each of these emphases has an analogical counterpart in political analysis. The nature of the counterpart will be characterized in the delineation of the six positions.

In the chart (page opposite), the positions in column A emphasize ideals and goals, while those in column B emphasize methods and strategies of action. The distinction between the columns is between what to do and how to do it; it is between the content, the level, the source of the norms of action and the means by which effective action is possible or appropriate action is directed. These positions are not absolutely distinct. There is overlapping among them, but this overlapping does not obliterate the difference of emphasis among these ways of relating religion and politics.

AMERICAN PROTESTANT EMPHASES ON THE RELATION BETWEEN RELIGION AND POLITICS	
A Emphasis on Principles of Action	B Emphasis on Methods of Action
1. Ultimate principles 2. Intermediate principles 3. Intuitional response	1. Balance/rebalance of power 2. Official/elite action 3. Interest/pressure group action

The *ultimate principles* emphasis derives from the farthest reach of religious vision. Resting uneasily in the injustices and sufferings of immediate circumstance, it aspires to actualize man's final good in uncompromising and pure form. It views political realities from a soteriological standpoint. To the extent that political institutions and relationships fail to embody the ultimate good for man, this emphasis takes on a revolutionary, transformative character. It is the obligation of the *homo religiosus* to "Christianize the social order" (Rauschenbusch), to establish the Kingdom of God on earth, to implement the principles of the "social creed." The analogue in political thought that is not overtly religious is a utopianism that is deemed practicable. Within the past few decades political utopianism has been a *rara avis*, except among some Marxists. More recently, however, it has been manifested afresh among those revolutionary and radical movements actively seeking to bring about a new, even if ill-defined, order in the world.

Those who emphasize *intermediate principles* generally view ultimate principles as, by themselves, nonoperational partly because they are too general, vague, and imprecise to indicate what exact form political relationships should assume and partly because they fail to provide for the often rather narrow limitations on possible action imposed by the actual historical process. The alternative is to formulate "middle axioms" (Oldham; J. C. Bennett) or "directions for decision and action" (P. Ramsey).[2] Such principles are intermediate in the sense that, on the one side, they are informed by the ultimate dimension of religious vision but, on the other side, they are designed to provide some fairly definite, even if open and pliable, instruction for policy formation. Because of their operational design, intermediate principles are subject to reconsideration, revision, and rejection as times change and as the nature of the issues requiring political decision alter. The counterpart of the intermediate principles emphasis in nonreligious political analysis is the "policy orientation" from whose perspective the first task of political science is the clarification of goals or values defined operationally. The statement of goals and values establishes the basis for the construction of theory and hypothesis, for the pursuit of empirical studies, and for the advancement of desirable courses of action.[3]

According to the *intuitional response* emphasis, the nature of appropriate action in political affairs as in all affairs cannot be determined at a distance from the context of action. Appropriate action consists in an immediate and positive response to the activity or will of God within the decision-making situation. Principles, ultimate or intermediate, are deceptive and obstructive. If principles, defined beforehand, are determinative of decision, the result might well be unjust, wrong, incorrect—for each situation is novel and possessed of its own unique requirements. Moreover, the will of God is free and not determinable by principles formulated by men. To be sure, those espousing this emphasis do not advocate a kind of blessed ignorance about the social and political facts relevant to the situation of decision. Nonetheless they assert that a proper decision is dictated not by facts alone, but by a faithful response to the will of God within the factual situation. The nearest analogy to this emphasis in nonreligious political analysis is "incrementalism" (Charles Lindblom), a form of decision-making theory that eschews both hierarchy in organization and rigidity in rules and principles in favor of disjointed, flexible, open-ended, pluralistic processes of policy formation and decision-making.[4] Perhaps there is an even closer counterpart in legal theory in the school advocating *freie Rechtsfindung* (E. Ehrlich), the "free finding of the law"—that is, each court case should be decided by the judge freely and openly according to its particular and unique merits.[5]

One of the most influential reactions against the ultimate principles emphasis involves a radical reconception of politics and of human relations generally as unending struggle and conflict. From this perspective one may articulate all the finest ideals conceivable and design institutions reflective of the principles of the Kingdom of God—but to concentrate on ideals and institutions is to neglect the realities of history within which successful action depends upon one's relative degree of power. Generally the best that can be accomplished is an occasional, tentative, and precarious balance of power. This emphasis on the *balance and rebalance of power,* either in its more overtly religious form or in its more explicitly political form, does not necessarily entail the rejection of principles.[6] But it does entail the acknowledgment that principles, ultimate or intermediate, must be bent, twisted, and compromised in order to achieve whatever modicum of goodness is possible within the concourse of history. Moreover, it entails skepticism about appeals to the will of God and wariness about incrementalism. The former may be merely a rhetorical cloaking of an actual power struggle, and the latter fails to take into account radical discrepancies in the distribution of power and influence in society.

The *official or elite action* emphasis shifts the focus of social and political analysis from power factors to structural factors. Relationships are not sheer conflicts of power. They have a relatively systemic quality about them. In sociological categories, social and political systems consist of interrelated roles. In more religious language, men are located and associated by virtue of various vocations or offices. What one can do and what one ought to do in political affairs is dependent upon one's role or vocation within the system. Generally, the wisest and most effective decisions are made in the appropriate office. So it is urged that actual decisions about public policy are best left to the "office of political prudence" (P. Ramsey) or that the most appropriate method to bring religious influence to bear on policy decisions is to provide organizations and centers for professionals—statesmen, lawyers, etc.—to reflect about the relations of their faith to their official responsibilities and duties. In a variant of this approach, the social structure in any given area of political policy formation is understood as roughly divisible into three groups: an elite that in fact makes the final decision; a mass that is affected by, but that has a negligible effect on, the decision; and an intervening elite that may, if it exerts the effort, influence the general quality and direction of decisions. The last group is the deliberate focus of attention of some Christian ethicists concerned with political affairs. This emphasis is paralleled in nonreligious political analysis in various forms and uses of role theory and elite theory.[7]

The *interest or pressure group action* emphasis assumes a pluralistic conception of society, according to which societies (or at least modern societies) are composed of multiple, overlapping groups—formal and informal, complex and simple, large and small, long-lasting and ephemeral. Each group struggles to maintain its existence and to further its aggregate of interests both by securing and deepening the intensity of its members' loyalty and by exerting pressure on other groups, including the relatively formalized institutions of government. Yet government itself, it is understood, consists of multiple, overlapping, more and less formalized groups that are often at cross-purposes with each other. Public policies and social decisions are thus not the result of clearheaded, deductively logical thought, involving a careful meshing of principles operationally defined and of knowledge scientifically derived; nor are they the result of some official or group of officials fulfilling the duties of their vocation. They are rather the result of a confused interplay of a large number of groups and organizations, official and unofficial, each of whose degree of influence it may be well-nigh impossible to trace. This conception of society in the form of "group theory" (Bentley, David Truman, E. Latham) has been highly influential in political science. And it appears to underlie the efforts of various church bodies and religious organizations to participate actively in the pluralistic group process through lobbying, demonstrations, publications, public statements on particular issues, and contributions to political campaigns.

There are alternative ways to reconstruct the history of American Protestant approaches to politics of the last several decades. Additional emphases might be distinguished (such as negative emphases —deliberate withdrawal or apathy). Different combinations of those listed above are possible (such as the subclassification of group theory as a form of power politics). An entirely different mode of analyzing the history of Protestant political thought might be adopted (including a more developmental mode). The purpose here, however, is to circumscribe emphases that might constitute in themselves important but fragmentary contributions to a more inclusive theory. That is, from the perspective developed in this essay, each of the major approaches to politics characterized—from the Social Gospel (ultimate principles) through Christian political realism (balance of power) to various forms of contextualism (intuitional response; official/elite action), *et alia*—provides a concentration that should in some fashion be included in a more general theoretical framework. And among the needs of the present moment is precisely a general theory of the relationship between religion and politics. What follows is a systematic agenda for such a theory incorporating but also modifying these six emphases.

A general theory of the connection between religion and politics must, given its character, stand astride two spheres, two forms of discourse, two concerns. It must indicate points at which the two interpenetrate and areas where each might contribute to the enlightenment and edification of the other. The two spheres are not, however, on a par. As developed here, while religion is neither handmaiden nor queen of politics, it is the more fundamental of the two in the matter of perspective or orientation. On the other hand, politics is of vital importance in the matter of action or expression, and the disciplines of politics have much to provide in the analysis and interpretation of the political act.

There are six related parts to the agenda, each part epitomized in a proposition. The first two parts deal with religious orientation, the first discussing in general terms the connection between religion and politics, the second providing a statement about the content of the basic orientation of Jewish-Christian faith. The other four parts deal with aspects of the political act, indicating the need for theories that are, respectively, of a structural, developmental, programmatic, and eschatological character.

ASPECTS OF THE INTERPENETRATION OF RELIGION AND POLITICS

Religious Orientation

I. General	II. Particular
Religion and Political Culture	Jewish-Christian Faith and Political Models

Political Act

Input: Political Situation

III. Structural	IV. Developmental
Religion and Political Theory	Religion and Political Change

Output: Political Response

V. Programmatic	VI. Eschatological
Religion and Political Design and Decision-Making	Religion and Political Values

The sketch as a whole is tentative and suggestive. It is meant to indicate and to illustrate that the range of issues in the connection between religion and politics extends far beyond, even as it includes, immediate and pressing matters of state. The essay presupposes that, even in the midst of social and political problems that desperately require solution or amelioration, there is a need for a consideration of fundamental theory. The happiest of circumstances, of course, is where thought and action, the theoretical and the practical are conjoined in a mutually enriching and critical alliance.

Proposition I. Given an understanding of religion as most generally but most essentially "ultimate concern" (Tillich), it follows that all the associations, decisions, and actions of men, including those of a political character, are fundamentally expressions of a religion of some kind.

The question of definition is unavoidable in a theory of the connection between religion and politics. In Proposition I, Tillich's definition of religion is adopted, namely, "Religion, in the largest and most basic sense of the word, is ultimate concern."[8] Within the framework of this definition, each person has multiple concerns— vital, cognitive, aesthetic, social—but at any given time these multiple concerns are organized around some central, determinative, singularly important, basic concern. The basic concern may not be clearly articulated; it may be tenuous and unsteady. But for the moment to the person involved, it is ultimate. It is this ultimacy of a concern that constitutes its religiousness. Thus each person's life is through and through informed by religion, faith, ultimate concern, or, in the terms of Louis Monden, S.J., a "fundamental option" or "basic choice."[9]

There is a virtually identical position presented by H. Richard Niebuhr in a definition of faith as "the attitude and action of confidence in, and fidelity to, certain realities as the sources of value and the objects of loyalty."[10] So conceived, faith is a fundamental and universal personal attitude. All men have a faith of some sort and thus all men live in relation to something that functions as god to them, for the object of faith—that is, the source or center of value, the object of loyalty in which one has confidence and to which one is devoted—is one's god. In Tillich's terms, ultimate concern always stands in relation to some object; it is "concern about what is experienced as ultimate," and what is experienced as ultimate is, by definition, a god.[11]

This conception of religion or faith is obviously formal. The possible types of faith are legion. The possible objects that might function as gods are innumerable. Nationalism, internationalism, humanism, aestheticism, racism, careerism, drunkenness, sex—seemingly distant from traditional modes of religious expression—might nonetheless function as forms of faith. And, as H. Richard Niebuhr especially reminds us, polytheism, far from being a primitive, archaic, and precivilized mode of religion is, with its unstable and vacillating character, among the most prevalent of modern expressions of faith.

This conception of religion precludes the possibility of a "postreligious era." That *certain* religions are moribund and that *certain* gods are dead may be so. Whether or not it is so is an empirical question. But the demise of one means the rising of another. Indeed the rising and dying of the gods of mankind is a continuous and complex process. On this level of analysis, the coming and going of the gods is independent of the vitally important question of the relative goodness, truth, adequacy, elegance, or validity of any particular form of faith. But even without raising that question, this definition of the nature of religion constitutes a potentially useful interpretative category for analyzing all sorts of realities, including political realities.

In this connection, it should be noted that faith or religion as ultimate concern is a characteristic—the fundamentally defining characteristic—not only of personal existence, but of social and political existence as well. Augustine's definition of a people as "an assemblage of reasonable beings bound together by a common agreement as to the objects of their love" affirms this equation.[12] The character of a people depends upon the character of what they love. The term "love" employed in this context by Augustine is synonymous with the usage of the term "religion" in Proposition I. It indicates a basic orientation to a center of value, an object of loyalty; it is ultimate concern. In this sense, a political society is most basically defined by the common orientation of its members, by its religion.

Admittedly, for empirical purposes, this general equation of religion as the defining characteristic of a people should be subjected to refinement, for the degree of agreement and the intensity of commitment among a group of persons on this level does vary. Nonetheless, intriguingly, one of the major developments in modern political analysis has arrived at essentially the same position. At the beginning of this century, the primary focus of attention in political analysis was on the structural factors of politics, that is, on the formal patterns and institutions of government. Later, the focus shifted to political parties, pressure and interest groups, actual pockets of power and influence within society, that is, the infrastructural factors of politics. This shift gave rise to group theory and the theory of politics as power. But most recently, an increasing amount of attention has been devoted to the notion of political culture.[13]

Political culture consists in the fundamental orientations of people toward social and political objects. It includes cognitive, affective, and evaluational components. It is more deeply founded and more generally pervasive than "opinions" and "attitudes." It includes expectations about and dispositions toward other persons— public and private, familiar and strange, fellow nationals and aliens. It includes basic values, emotional attachments, and existential beliefs.

In political analysis, the immediate concern is the relation of operationally distinguishable aspects of the orientations of particular persons to politically relevant objects. But these distinguishable aspects are embedded in and expressive of the general cultural milieu of the people. They are functions of an inclusive "framework of orientation and devotion" (Fromm), of a total "belief system," which in turn is informed by an ultimate concern. Thus, at this point, there is an important connection between religion and politics, and in this sense, political systems and structures, political policies, movements and conflicts are, in their most elemental aspect, expressive of religion.[14]

This is not to assert that *all* political policies and conflicts are in *all* respects *directly* dictated by the religious factor such that, for instance, contenders for differing policies on a particular issue are of diametrically opposed religious orientations or that those supporting the same policy are religiously in full agreement. But this perspective does provide for an important level of analysis that is neglected if attention is limited to structural and infrastructural factors.

Moreover, it calls for some revision of the political theories according to which one of the key marks of political modernization is "secularity."[15] The precise meaning of secularity in these theories is often obscure. It seems to include the type of values and goals desired (this-worldly as opposed to otherworldly) and the manner in which those values and goals are pursued (pragmatic as opposed to dogmatic). But it is always contrasted as standing in inverse proportion with sacrality. Political modernization is thus taken to mean an increase in secularity and a corresponding decrease in sacrality.[16] The congruity of this concept of political development and Auguste Comte's periodization of history is perhaps not wholly accidental. But Proposition I requires at least a terminological revision of this theory.

Proposition II. Within the Jewish-Christian religious tradition, the true God is understood to be most centrally characterized as love. Faith within this tradition is thus active in love, which here means the drive toward the continuous formation of creative community of all with all.

A second stage in the construction of a general theory of the connection between religion and politics involves the definition of a particular religious orientation and an indication of its relevance in the understanding of politics. The orientation adopted in Proposition II is that formulated by Daniel Day Williams.

God's unity is His goodness. God's goodness is His love. God's love is that creative and redemptive power which works unceasingly in all times and places to bring to fulfillment a universal community of free and loving beings.[17]

Proposition II casts Judaism and Christianity together as manifesting essentially the same fundamental orientation, the same ultimate concern, namely, toward the God who is love. This statement is not intended to gloss over important differences between these two religious traditions or among the multiple subgroups within each of the traditions. There are indeed grossly different histories, variant styles of expression, alternative emphases, divergent understandings — and these differences have at times broken out in bitter dissension, even to the distortion and subversion of what is here considered the genuine and innermost essence of the traditions. Nonetheless, the thesis is tendered that the God of Abraham, Isaac, and Jacob, the God of Moses and the prophets, is the same God that is revealed in Jesus Christ, and that is the God whose nature is love.

From this perspective, the immediate sociopolitical effect of both the Exodus event and the Christ event was the formation of a new community—a community for whose members love was the basic orientation, aspiration, obligation, vision, and yearning. Such a community is a relationship in which, by intention, "the members of a society are so related that the freedom, uniqueness, and power of each serves the freedom, uniqueness, and growth of all the other members."[18] Either immediately or after a time of reflection the realization emerged that the full depth of love drives toward the actualization of "universal community . . . in which each member is more free, more mature, more powerful through what he gives to and receives from every other member. . . ."[19]

The term "creative" in Proposition II qualifies "community" in order to stress the nonstatic character of this conception. Man is a purposive, creative, free being, and love, when it becomes the expressive content of his ultimate concern does not preempt, although it does permeate, the detail of his concerns, intentions, and actions. At least in part because of the purposive nature of man, each individual person, each particular association, indeed each moment of existence is unique, and love as the drive to community must attend to this uniqueness. Thus the community of love, even if it could be and were universally actualized, is a process continuously open to new possibilities of concrete particularization and arrangement.

Moreover, the freedom of human existence constantly keeps open the possibility of alternative ultimate concerns, and thus of estrangement, alienation, or on the sociopolitical level, the formation of human relations that are only fragmentarily and pervertedly expressive of creative community. In more traditional theological terms, man is created in the image of God, that is as a creative and loving being. But man sins, which means the distortion of the image of God, the violation of the law of love, the corruption of community. God's redemptive work is oriented toward the restoration of the image and thus the reformation of creative community.

If it is the case that an ultimate concern is the basis or source of patterns of action and forms of thought, one may ask about the precise relevance of the conception of Jewish-Christian faith formulated above to the understanding of politics, to the basic "orienting concept" (David Easton) of political research or the model employed in political theory.[20] Orienting concepts and models, it should be noted, are not merely useful tools, perhaps inescapable if unwittingly present in the scientific investigation and interpretation of politics; they have as well an impact upon the actual operation of political systems. The conception of politics as fundamentally a struggle for power, for instance, has had evident influence in the policies and decisions of politicians.

The selection of criteria to assess the relative adequacy of a particular model is a difficult but crucial methodological question. From the perspective of Propositions I and II, one of the criteria should be the capacity of the model or orienting concept to take account of the religious realities of the human situation, especially as they bear on political processes. More narrowly, given the framework of Jewish-Christian faith, one of the criteria should be the capacity of the model to take into account the dynamics of creative community, which elsewhere I have designated the "communicative association."[21]

The latter term indicates a possibly fruitful connection with a seminal development in recent political theory, namely, the use of communications and control systems as a conceptual model in the construction of a general theory of politics with both empirical and normative components. The connection is more than terminological. The degree of possible congruity between the communications model, at least as developed by Karl W. Deutsch,[22] and the concept of creative community is striking.

Briefly, within the framework of the communications model, politics is understood to be a communal and a purposive enterprise. More precisely, a political system is an autonomous or self-steering process involving the coordination of human efforts and expectations for the attainment of social goals. The crucial factor in this conception of the political system is the system's dependence upon information for the sake of its survival and for the realization of its purposes.

The successful operation of a political system depends largely upon information about its environment, about the results of its action on the environment, about its own inner workings, and about its past history and traditions. To be informed, a system must possess a capacity to absorb, a readiness to listen, to see, to appreciate, to empathize, an ability to learn—for only by means of these capacities and abilities can a system receive, sort out, be influenced by and benefit from information.

These capacities are located in, among other places, a system's "feedback mechanisms." Any political system that is successful in any degree in its survival and in the realization of its purposes must possess a network of feedback mechanisms. The more receptive, sensitive, and adaptable the network of feedback mechanisms, and the more a system is open to the possibility of change, even in its purposes and in the structure of its operation on the basis of information received and interpreted—the more probable the system's success. But what must remain constant as an overriding purpose is the preservation of an autonomous process of communal purpose-seeking.

Pursuing the implications of this model, Deutsch observes: "As regards the eventual chances of survival of any autonomous system, we found them to depend to a decisive extent on its range of relationships to events and information from outside its own limits. In the long run, these chances may thus depend in good part not only on its ability to continue to remake and restructure itself, but to achieve integrative relationships with others."[23] The danger of nationalism, for instance, is that it will lead to an inability to assimilate experience, a narrowing or closure of channels of communication, a dwindling of the capacity to understand other peoples or cultures. In this sense, nationalism is, paradoxically, a force threatening the viability of the nation. Conversely, a political system flourishes in direct proportion to the relative depth and extent of its intercommunication with individuals, groups, and societies throughout the world, including those within its own boundaries.

In Deutsch's understanding, the communications model has implications for both the empirical investigation and the normative evaluation of political systems. It has already been extensively used for the former purpose, although, as Deutsch rightly observes, its normative implications have been left largely undeveloped.[24] However, in both its empirical and its normative aspects, the communications model requires a serious modification of the theory of politics as power (cf. the balance/rebalance of power emphasis)[25] and a recasting of the group theory of politics (cf. the pressure/interest group action emphasis).

In general, I am suggesting that in the construction of a general theory of the connection between religion and politics, it is desirable to consider the relative compatibility of the fundamental notions or orienting concepts in both areas. In particular, I am suggesting that there is an interesting and fruitful congruity between the conception of creative community as expressive of the Jewish-Christian form of ultimate concern and the communications model in political thought.

Proposition III. In the drive toward the continuous formation and re-formation of creative community, love seeks out knowledge of the situation of action in its particularity and in its connectedness.

Proposition IV. In the drive toward the continuous formation and re-formation of creative community, love seeks out knowledge of the possibilities of action and the agencies of social and political change.

Politics involves processes of policy formation and action that are, in a simplified version that distorts their full complexity, two-sided. This two-sidedness is reflected in the last four propositions of the essay. To use the terminology of the communications model, the input side consists of messages about the character of the situation of action, and the output side consists of a response to the situation as understood. Propositions III and IV taken together represent the former side, stipulating that, from the perspective of Jewish-Christian faith as presented in Proposition II, the input of information, of knowledge, is a requisite of proper or fitting action.

These two propositions are formulated separately in order to indicate two dimensions of information—structural and developmental. They indicate the need for both a theory of social and political structure and a theory of social and political change. The division is artificial and in some respects untenable, but is maintained to stress the relative difference in focus. As Amitai and Eva Etzioni have remarked, "Even in a fully integrated theory, whereas statements on high levels of abstraction will probably be applicable to both structure and process, concrete statements may deal with one rather than the other."[26] Both propositions center on the situation of action and both raise the question of the character of a situation.

One of the emphases of much contemporary Protestant analysis has been that each situation of action, as each individual person and each association, has its own particular character. This is a fundamental theme of the intuitional response approach to politics. It is a central principle of "situation ethics" (Joseph Fletcher). It underlies the formulation of the "law of specification," viz., "All persons ought, in any given situation, to develop the value or values specifically relevant to that situation."[27]

This emphasis is obviously compatible with the orienting concept of creative community (Proposition II), but an important question is whether particularity means absolute uniqueness. If so, then knowledge, in the ordinary sense of the term, is impossible or at least useless. The assumption of Propositions III and IV is that significant knowledge is possible; that particularity includes similarities and differences, congruities and contrasts; and that, from the orientation of Proposition II, knowledge of the situation of action is desirable if not obligatory for the most fitting action.

But what kind of knowledge? There is a well-known statement by Martin Luther that seems to minimize the importance of abstract, formalized, sophisticated knowledge.

> A Christian who lives in . . . faith has no need of a teacher of good works, but whatever he finds to do he does, and all is well done. . . . This we may see in a common human example. When a man and a woman love and are pleased with each other, and thoroughly believe in their love, who teaches them how they are to behave, what they are to do, leave undone, say, not say, think? Confidence alone teaches them all this, and more. . . . So a Christian who lives in this confidence toward God, knows all things, can do all things, undertakes all things, that are to be done, and does everything cheerfully and freely.[28]

A possible connotation of this statement is that all that is necessary for good, right, or fitting action is faith, confidence or trust in the true God, a good will. No special knowledge is required.

Yet perhaps the statement does not exclude knowledge. Note especially Luther's homiletical illustration. The apparent spontaneity of the interaction of man and wife or lover and beloved rests, in fact, partially on a culturally transmitted knowledge, to employ sociological terms, of the expectations, norms, obligations, and responsibilities of a set of role relations. In addition, it rests partially on an intimate (even if not wholly accurate) acquaintance with and knowledge of the surroundings or context of role behavior. Thus appropriate action, even in this most personal of relations, depends on a combination of confidence and knowledge, even if the knowledge is not highly sophisticated or the result of formal education or scientific investigation.

This is the equation that underlies the proposal that persons acting in their official capacity make the wisest and best decisions in their assigned spheres of action (cf. official action emphasis). Officials possess a fund of specialized knowledge about their roles and about the matters with which their roles are concerned that generally no one else can fully comprehend or appreciate. This applies not only to lover and beloved, but also to corporation executives, presidents and rulers of nations, chairmen of political parties, cabinet ministers, military leaders, members of specialized professions.

Incidentally, what might easily and unfortunately be neglected in this approach to political knowledge is the office or role of the citizen. Admittedly, the precise expectations and obligations of the citizen may be culturally ill-defined and may vary in content from society to society. But within the framework of the concept of creative community (Proposition II), the role of a citizen includes active participation in the formulation of political policies.

There are serious limitations, however, in culturally transmitted role knowledge, particularly where the situation of action is in the realm of politics. This is acknowledged in the reliance of government officials upon "technical experts," in the appointment of commissions to undertake special studies of particular problems and issues, in the occasional (perhaps too occasional) use of "Brandeis briefs" and masters in American law courts.

The implication is that an adequate understanding of a situation of political action depends on scientific knowledge, and if so, that the religious orientation of Proposition II drives toward a consideration of developments within and the results of the social and political sciences. This is not a startling conclusion, however greatly violated it tends to be in practice, but it does raise a problem that is worthy of some comment, a problem already approached in the comment on Proposition II.

In this respect, David Easton's remark regarding political science is of interest: "The headlong pace at which empirical data can now be accumulated threatens to inundate the scientific enterprise with an overwhelming and virtually irresistible flood. Some powerful counterforce is required to spare the discipline from being buried under an avalanche of knowledge that can only gain momentum through the decades if it thunders on unchecked."[29] Easton's remedy to control and give meaning to the flood of data is theory construction, the formation of a conceptual pattern that will provide a means of arranging and classifying data, and of making sense and assessing the relevance of bits of research. However, the proposed remedy, as Easton is aware, contains its own difficulties. Indeed, it raises issues which indicate that the connection between religion and politics is by no means uncomplicated even at the point of deriving knowledge about a situation of political action. It would be quite insufficient to say, for instance, without radical qualification, that the social and political sciences simply provide facts, whereas religion is the ultimate source out of which goals are set, problems defined, and solutions sought.

Perhaps what should be said is that the relation between religion and politics is or should be dialectical and mutually critical. That is, on the surface the social and political sciences are directed properly toward empirical discovery, but the results of scientific investigation are not pure data or sheer empirical fact. Rather, the pursuit, classification, ordering, presentation, and interpretation of empirical data —even the understanding of what constitutes empirical data—are inextricably bound up with theoretical conveyances, with conceptual constructs. And, surely, one's ultimate concern will influence and inform, in however distant a way, the frame of reference, the basic concepts, the fundamental categories of scientific work.

Thus while, on the one hand, empirical discovery may result in the reconstruction of theory, at least negatively (that is, by disproof), on the other hand, empirical discovery is itself contingent in large degree on expectations and investigations set by theoretical categories that in turn are influenced by religious orientation. Indeed, the very effort at any sort of empirical discovery at all is itself motivated in its ultimate dimension by religious orientation. All of this means, of course, that one must be cautious and critical in the appropriation of scientific knowledge about the situation of action, for the religious orientation of the giver and the receiver of knowledge may not be compatible.

Thus religion, as defined in Proposition I, impinges not only on the basic understanding of politics as asserted in the commentary on Proposition II. It is also involved in the derivation of knowledge about the character of a situation of action. It is involved there in at least three ways. First, religion is a dimension in the situation itself. This is acknowledged in the increasing attention devoted to political culture in political science. Second, religion is an influence in the construction of theory, which is in turn a fundamental component in the interpretation of the character of a situation. Third, from any given particular religious perspective, what is presented as scientific knowledge about any situation must be taken with the proverbial grain of critical salt.

In the light of the third point, note David Easton's statement: "No one way of conceptualizing any major area of human behavior will do full justice to all its variety and complexity. Each type of theoretical orientation brings to the surface a different set of problems, provides unique insights and emphases, and thereby makes it possible for alternative and even competing theories to be equally and simultaneously useful, although often for quite different purposes."[30] Yet from the standpoint of the religious perspective in Proposition II, one of the emphases that should not be ignored, one of the concepts that should be central in any characterization of the situation of action is that of process, history, change, movement—for integral to the notion of creative community is the understanding of man, personally and socially, as purposive, intentional, processual.

Consequently, Jacques Maritain's neglected notion of historical constellation, historical climate, historical sky is worth exploring. According to Maritain, social and political philosophy ought to take cognizance of the "radical irreversibility of historical movement" whereby "humanity, borne on by this irresistible movement, passes underneath various historical constellations, typically different constellations that create for the principles of culture specifically different conditions of realization."[31] That is, there is an intelligible difference among periods of history, and this difference is relevant to the mode of appropriate conduct, to the actualization of the impetus of love to form creative community. Structural analysis of the situation of action must therefore be complemented by historical-developmental analysis; a theory of political systems must incorporate a theory of political change, including Maritain's emphasis on the linear periodization of history, but extending to other issues as well.

Each of the six Protestant approaches to politics characterized in an earlier section of this essay[32] assumes, more or less openly, some understanding of the processes and possibilities of political change. The emphases on balance of power, official action, and group action bring the issue deliberately to the fore, yet even in combination their scope is too narrow. They are limited in the time span considered, focusing primarily on the immediate or the short range in the supposition that such a focus is more "realistic" or "relevant." Thus they tend to neglect the broad sweep of historical processes as expressed in the Maritain quotation. They are limited as well in the factors conceived as productive of change, ignoring particularly one of the forces that is receiving close attention in the discipline of comparative politics and that, as observed above (Proposition I), constitutes an important link in the connection between religion and politics, namely, political culture.

That comparative politics is particularly concerned with the dimension of change is indicated in the pivotal status in both theory and research of the concepts of political development, political mobilization, and political modernization. As defined, the concepts of development and modernization contain echoes of some of the grand historical periodizations of the nineteenth century—e.g., Comte, Marx, Tönnies, Maine. Yet nowadays there is an effort to define the concepts of the stages of development (for instance, primitive, traditional, modern) more operationally and to employ them in scientific investigation more meticulously. This has resulted in an increased awareness of the multiplicity and the combinatorial complexity of the variables in the process of development and has made difficult any attempt to reduce political change to any simple sequential scheme of stages of development. That in itself is a significant datum in the move to arrive at some understanding of the character of a situation of action.

But of particular significance given the purpose of this essay is the thesis that cultural factors are crucial in social and political development, the thesis that the orientations, expectations, sensibilities, loyalties, understandings of a people are decisive in the direction and the character of the more specifically political aspects of their relationships. That is, whether or not an existent political system is viable or an envisioned political system is possible; whether or not a set of particular political policies will be acceptable and effective; what degree of flexibility, adaptability, tolerability of innovation in political program is available within a given society depends in large part upon the character of its political culture, even though economic and other extracultural variables cannot be ignored.

This raises the question of the sources and transmitters of political culture, of the agencies of political socialization. Almond and Verba have argued, on the basis of extensive evidence, that *education* is the most important variable in determining political culture.[33] Means and modes of *communication* have been singled out for special investigation.[34] David Apter has proposed that the diffusion of the *ideology of modern science* is an especially critical agency in the formation of a particular political orientation.[35] And the influence of specifically *political and legal processes*—political party patterns, governmental practices, legal procedures—in the production of political culture has been cited, indicating an element of circularity or causal reciprocity in the relation between culture and politics.[36]

In any case, it seems obvious that anyone who aspires to actualize a vision of a desirable political community, anyone promoting political modernization and social development must ascertain which are the key agencies in political acculturation, the extent to which they are manipulatable, and how or whether it is possible through these means to accelerate and direct political change.

All of this combined with the thesis of Proposition I means that religion, as the profoundest level of political culture, is among the decisive factors in determining the possibilities of political change. Indeed, as defined, religion is a positive force in modernization despite the usual definition of modernization as involving the decline of religion.[37] But religion is not merely an agency of change; it is a fundamental aspect of both development and stability, disruption and preservation, revolution and integration, radicalism and conservatism. The precise political function of a particular religious orientation will depend upon its specific character and the specific character of its historical context. One of the tasks of a general theory of the connection between religion and politics might well be to unpack this general statement into a set of operational hypotheses correlating types of religious orientation and types of historical situation.

Despite its difficulties, Tillich's concept of *kairos*, derived from a religious source, provides an instructive insight both for a theory of political change and for the overall attempt to characterize a situation of action. A *kairos* is a time that is rich in significance, open to creative possibility, ripe in content. It is an epochal moment, a moment in which radical transformation is at hand. Time, according to Tillich, has direction, periodization, qualitative differences precisely because of *kairos*. "All great changes in history are accompanied by a strong consciousness of a kairos at hand."[38] The idea of *kairos* is compatible with Maritain's notion of changing historical constellations, but in both cases, one of the problems is how to discern the presence of *kairos* or the emergence of a new epoch. It may be that the art, the poetry, the literature of a time expresses more clearly than social, political, economic patterns the critical character of the period and the ripeness of history for adventurous action. At the very least, however, the idea of *kairos* may be a reminder of the occasional radically creative character of history and may shake the mind loose from thinking in too narrowly prescribed terms and categories about the situation of action. A *kairos* is indeed not only a moment for possibly novel action; it is, as well, an openness to new forms of thought, to new modes of conceiving and understanding both the character of reality in general and the structure and dynamics of the human situation in particular.[39]

Proposition V. In the light of knowledge about the situation of action in its structural and developmental aspects, love actualizes that possibility which seems most nearly to embody creative community.

Proposition VI. While immersed in the immediate processes of history both reflectively and actively, love reminds one to raise ever and again the critical question of ultimate purpose, final goal.

It was affirmed above that Propositions III and IV, in conjunction, stipulate that from the standpoint of Jewish-Christian faith, the input of information about the structure and development of a situation of action is a requisite of proper action. Propositions V and VI, on the other hand, are concerned with output, with the response to the information received. They stipulate that the fundamental aim, direction, purpose, intention of action is creative community. The distinction between the two propositions is not absolute; rather the difference is one of stress. Proposition V is programmatic. Its concern is with the delineation of alternative courses, the formulation of policies, the making of decisions. But both vertically and horizontally, in its ultimate dimension and in its farthest reach, it shades off into the central eschatological concentration of Proposition VI, namely, the concentration on the chief end of man.

The dominant concern of each of the six Protestant approaches to politics characterized above is programmatic. The thesis of this essay is that there is need for a general theory of the connection between religion and politics and that there are spheres of analysis related to but distinguishable from the programmatic that deserve serious attention. Yet the singular importance of programmatic matters cannot be denied. Moreover each of the approaches indicated provides some contribution of value in this connection. This is written in the spirit of the suggestion by Edward LeRoy Long, Jr., who, after describing the divergent motifs that have recurred throughout the history of Christian ethics, urges the rejection of "polemical exclusion" and the adoption of the method of "comprehensive complementarity."[40]

On one level, on that which I shall call "design," this suggestion might be satisfied by a programmatic construction consisting of long-, medium-, and short-range projections. This is at least one mode of conceiving the relationship among ultimate principles, intermediate principles and immediate response. Despite the connotation of the notion of "range," however, it would be improper to conceive this relationship as "spatial," that is, as involving varying distances. It is temporal, and because of its temporality, it is wrong to consider only short-range projections as realistic and to pass off long-range projections as irrelevancies. It is wrong precisely because it is, to turn the criticism back upon the critic, unrealistic—if to be realistic means to be attentive to operative social forces and effective social possibilities. As Whitehead has argued, great ideas and general notions have creative power; they generate stirrings within the souls of men. To put this in the terms of modern political analysis, they enter into the makings of political culture. As such, "impractical ideals are a programme for reform . . . not to be criticized by immediate possibilities."[41]

The germination of future styles of man's social and political life occurs within the instant present. While there is no gainsaying the durability and strength of power factors, of economic and organizational realities in social and political action, it would be equally foolhardy to ignore the power of ideas, at least in the long range. Indeed, one important element in the strength of economic and political institutions lies in their acceptability in the minds of men.

The ideas about which Whitehead was writing were of greatest generality and the history of their ingression into the cultures and institutions of men was long and remains incomplete. A more medium-range projection is formulated in Jacques Maritain's concept of a "concrete historical ideal" or "prospective image," which is the programmatic counterpart of his notion of historical constellation or historical climate. Maritain distinguishes between a utopia and a concrete historical ideal. A utopia is an abstract mental construct "isolated from existence at any particular time and from any particular historical climate, and expressing an absolute *maximum* of social and political perfection."[42] A concrete historical ideal, on the other hand, is an essence related to a particular historical period, calling forth a mode of social and political perfection relative to the given lines of that period. It is an end of action that incorporates the directional forces of the period but requires the active participation of men for its realization. Maritain himself constructs a concrete historical ideal for the modern epoch in the West and contrasts it with what he considers the appropriate historical ideal for the medieval period.

"Middle axioms," in John C. Bennett's usage of the term, is expressive of the same medium-range projection, although his illustrations are more particularized and more immediately operational than Maritain's model for modern Western society.[43]

The point is that the concern for immediate relevance must not blind one to forces operating within present circumstances of a long- and medium-range significance. Whitehead's "adventures of ideas" and Maritain's "prospective images" refer not just to distant times and faraway places, but to the moment of instant action. This is an apology for social and political blueprints, for designs that may seem on some levels impracticable but that may nonetheless contribute to the molding and shaping of political processes. At the same time, to take seriously the communications model of political systems delineated above, such blueprints and designs should be subjected to constant redrafting in the light of information feedback about the course of events.

From this perspective, emphasis on intuitional response and efforts at immediate and appreciable impact on political affairs should not be rejected, but they should be modified to include place for the designing and redesigning of long- and medium-range images of man's communal existence. A hard-nosed realism may fail to discern the full scope of possibilities and of cultural and social forces actually present—and "where there is no vision, the people perish."

The neglect of long- and medium-range aspects of politics is a charge that applies not only to Protestants concerned with political affairs. A few years ago, P. H. Partridge leveled it as well against the field of political science.

> It seems to me that recent political science has suffered from concentrating so heavily on the study of short-term political events (e.g., the study of the single election), on the act of "decision-making," on "bargaining models" and so on. This may have had advantages from the point of view of concreteness, empirical exactness and rigour. But it has brought about a very drastic abstraction from a great deal of political reality.[44]

There is yet another aspect of the programmatic side of the relation between religion and politics, related particularly to the question of the methods of decision-making and action. Politics, especially on its most conscious level, entails the coordination of efforts in the attainment of social goals. Its decisions are thus in important respects social at each point within the political system. They are social both in their origin and in their impact. Decision-making of a social character is of the essence of political processes. Institutions and organizations are often deliberately created methods to arrive at the solution of problems, the resolution of conflicts, the formulation of programs, the administration of policies—all involving the making of decisions. And even if not created with full deliberation, they function toward the same end.

But modes of decision-making vary widely. The venerable division of types of government into democracy, aristocracy, monarchy and their perverse counterparts (ochlocracy, oligarchy, tyranny) is one means of classifying modes of political decision-making. But that scheme is limited. One must include as well negotiation, election, delegation of authority, adversary system, trial by ordeal and its counterpart in war, parliamentary diplomacy, consensus, polyarchy, and the like.

More important than classification is the question of appropriateness. This question becomes particularly keen in the area of social decision where there is disagreement, lack of unanimity, an absence of consensus. And it becomes pressing as well where knowledge about the situation of action is fragmentary and skimpy, or where expertise is confined but where the decision is bound to have widespread impact.[45]

There is a curiosity about the question of the appropriateness of divergent modes of decision-making—namely, its answer itself entails a decision. This puzzle is no mere idle curiosity. In the political arena it is crucial. It might be suggested that the ability to make the initial decision about methods of decision-making is precisely the ability to form a political society. Perhaps that ability is contingent upon a common orientation, a common set of values, a common purposiveness, a common religiousness underlying all other differences among the persons involved.

From the standpoint of Jewish-Christian faith, the most crucial valuational question is the extent to which methods of decision-making are conducive to or expressive of creative community. In the past, Protestant theorists have tended to concentrate on two matters —the relative legitimacy of war and the relative preferability of democracy as methods of decision-making. What I would propose is that while violence and autocracy constitute particularly visible issues in the appropriateness of decision-making, they are only parts of a larger political problem, and that the question of participation and creative involvement should be raised about all sorts and conditions and areas of man's communal existence.

Among the questions relevant to this context is that of both *whether* and *how* specifically religious organizations, official and unofficial, should participate in processes of political decision. The question of *whether* religious organizations should participate underlies discussions of the "right of the church to intervene" (William Temple),[46] the "competence" or "proper task" of religious bodies (P. Ramsey),[47] and the "role of the church" (John C. Bennett)[48] in political affairs. But at least equally important in this same context is the question of *how* a religious organization (or for that matter any organization) decides to intervene, by what procedures it decides both what position it should assume and how it should go about pressing that position.

From the perspective of Proposition II, the limiting principle, although not the sole consideration, on both these questions is the principle of creative community. That is, political issues bear more or less directly on the actualization of creative community.[49] The more direct the bearing, the more appropriate it is for organizations representing Jewish-Christian faith to resist those forces, cultural and structural, that are violative of, and to support those forces that are conducive to, creative community. The less direct the bearing, the less appropriate it would be for such organizations to engage in the issue. On the other hand, the religious organization should certainly not violate the implications of its own faith in the process by which it makes its own decisions—including its decisions about the character of the situation of political action, about whether it is fitting for the organization to intervene, about what its position should be and how it should intervene.

One of the implications of this discussion is that the two components of the programmatic dimension of the political act, the component of design (long, medium, and short range) and the component of decision-making, are interactive. That is, designs should include patterns for the making of decisions. But, on the other hand, the very articulation and projection of designs constitute in themselves problems of decision-making, especially where the designs are of a social and political character.

From the perspective of Jewish-Christian faith, a simplicity of final aim, a singularity of ultimate purpose, pervades all the complexities, compromises, and difficulties of design and decision-making. The ultimate purpose is the drive behind the attempt to attain knowledge about the situation of action, and it constitutes the central directive force in the programmatic response to knowledge. Its content is indicated in the eschatological vision of Judaism and Christianity, the vision of a day when all peoples "shall beat their swords into plowshares, and their spears into pruning hooks; nation shall not lift up sword against nation, neither shall they learn war any more." On that day "the wolf shall dwell with the lamb, and the leopard shall lie down with the kid, and the calf and the lion and the fatling together, and a little child shall lead them. . . . They shall not hurt or destroy in all my holy mountain; for the earth shall be full of the knowledge of the Lord, as the waters cover the sea.[50]

But eschatological visions and concepts are two-edged swords— they both promise fulfillment and threaten judgment. Note the parable recorded in the Gospel of Matthew (Ch. 25:31–46). When the Son of Man comes, he will take his seat, and all the nations (note: not individuals, but nations!) shall be gathered, and he will judge them. In accordance with the way in which they have dealt with the hungry, the thirsty, the stranger, the naked, the sick, and the imprisoned—they shall either inherit God's Kingdom or be cast into everlasting fire.

In other words, the eschatological vision, the vision of the ultimate goal and final good of human existence is a reminder of the ambiguity of history. Men and nations act within history according to the faith, the knowledge, the love they possess. But their faith may be weak or idolatrous; their knowledge may be limited or distorted; their love may be feeble or frail. Consequently the eschatological vision is a vision of the ultimate good—the full and unqualified actualization of creative community; but it is at the same time a harsh judgment upon the poor, fragmentary, partial embodiments of creative community at any moment within the historical process.

The historical process presents the man of faith always with a structure of both limitations and possibilities. An acknowledgment of the limitations of any particular historical occasion is valuable to instill a sense of humility, a means of preventing or at least mitigating self-righteousness and hypocrisy. On the other hand, an acknowledgment of the possibilities inherent within each historical occasion is valuable as a goad to creative action.

To quote Ernst Troeltsch:

The task of damming and controlling [the stream of historical life] is . . . essentially incapable of completion and essentially unending; and yet it is always soluble and practicable in each new case. A radical and absolute solution does not exist: there are only working, partial, synthetically uniting solutions. . . . In history itself there are only relative victories; and these relative victories themselves vary greatly in power and depth, according to time and circumstances.[51]

Yet without the eschatological vision, there is no final goal, and no ultimate standard by which the struggles of history are made meaningful and by which the accomplishments of history are judged.[52] And this is true even if Rudolf Bultmann is correct, that man is always and forever between the times.[53]

This doctrine of the ultimate good or final purpose of man is relevant to at least one in Robert A. Dahl's list of "the most hotly disputed issues in modern political analysis," namely, "what are the proper sources, grounds, or foundations for political values?"[54] This issue has become peculiarly contentious because of what Arnold Brecht has called the "real crisis in Western *scientific theory*"—that is, "the rise of the theoretical opinion that no scientific choice between ultimate values can be made."[55] This opinion is expressed in the "Gulf Doctrine," that logically there is an "unbridgeable gulf" between is and ought, between facts and values, between scientific statements, which are about matters of fact, including the fact that evaluations of a kind have occurred and may or will occur, and statements about the validity of the ultimate norms or standards on which evaluations are grounded or ought to be grounded.[56] Whether or in what sense the validation of ultimate values is a matter of scientific investigation may depend on what one understands to constitute the boundaries of science.[57] But in any case, the question of the grounding, validation, justification of political values cannot be silenced. It is crucial in both political theory and practice.

The eschatological orientation of Jewish-Christian faith precludes some of the answers that have been given to the question of justification. For one thing, from this perspective, the eschatological vision of faith is not the result of subjective imagining or psychological fantasy. It derives, by claim, from an apprehension of the creative and redemptive working of God. And this working of God is understood to be an objective datum, the most basic fact apart from which the world could not be. How this can be demonstrated to be the case is a knotty question of theological and philosophical method. But, whatever the answer, any form of sheer preferentialism or unqualified subjectivism on the level of justifying ultimate values in the political process would seem to be excluded, although given the nature of creative community, preferentialism is not excluded on all levels.

Moreover, the eschatological vision is of the fulfillment of mankind, the restoration of the *imago Dei,* the actualization of the essential destiny of humanity. This is to say that the eschaton is the ultimate purposiveness of man—but of man *qua* man, not man merely in his capacity as butcher or baker, father or son, citizen or soldier, Jew or Gentile. Jewish-Christian faith is, within its own terms, humanistic, if humanism means to draw a line at the violation of the essential ends of man's humanity—his creativeness and his communality. From this perspective, all political processes, patterns, and policies must, in the final analysis, be judged in a relational manner, in relation to the essential and universal humanity of man within the context of the universe as a whole. To the extent that any set of political values or any justification of political values fails to conform to this norm, it is excluded.

To conclude, the spheres of the heavenly and the terrestrial are neither unrelated nor identical. They may seem unrelated or at least distant when the grandeur of religious vision is contrasted with the miserable realities of political life. But they are seen to be inseparable when the implications and levels of meaning in both spheres are examined closely. In pursuing the relationship this essay has been more illustrative than exhaustive and has concentrated on the theoretical rather than on the practical. But this is not to deny the importance of the practical. It is, rather, to focus attention upon the need for more extensive, systematic, theoretical reflection upon the interpenetration of religion and politics in the conviction that the clarification of ideas is a requisite to responsible action.

NOTES

1. This essay was prepared while I held a post-doctoral fellowship for cross-disciplinary studies from the Society for Religion in Higher Education. I am indebted to Prof. Wm. B. Gwyn for assistance during its preparation.

2. See Paul Ramsey, *Who Speaks for the Church?* (Abingdon Press, 1967), *passim*, esp. pp. 16 ff.

3. See Harold D. Lasswell, "The Policy Orientation," in Harold D. Lasswell and Daniel Lerner (eds.), *The Policy Sciences* (Stanford University Press, 1951); Harold D. Lasswell, "The Democratic Character," in Harold D. Lasswell, *Political Writings* (The Free Press of Glencoe, Inc., 1951). See also the procedure employed in Robert A. Dahl and Charles E. Lindblom, *Politics, Economics, and Welfare* (Harper & Brothers, 1953). Both the *ultimate principles* and the *intermediate principles* emphases are, in the classification scheme provided in the recent study of Christian ethics by Edward LeRoy Long, Jr., *A Survey of Christian Ethics* (Oxford University Press, Inc., 1967), expressive of the "prescriptive motif." The *intuitional response* emphasis is an instance of the "relational motif." Long's helpful and illuminating study became accessible to me only after the initial sketch of this essay was completed.

4. David Braybrooke and Charles E. Lindblom, *A Strategy of Decision: Policy Evaluation as a Social Process* (London: Collier-Macmillan, Ltd., 1963); Charles E. Lindblom, *The Intelligence of Democracy: Decision-Making Through Mutual Adjustment* (The Free Press of Glencoe, Inc., 1965).

5. Eugen Ehrlich, *Fundamental Principles of the Sociology of Law,* tr. by Walter L. Moll (Harvard University Press, 1936), *passim,* especially references to Ehrlich's 1903 lecture "Freie Rechtsfindung und freie Rechtswissenschaft." See also Georg Cohn, *Existenzialismus und Rechtswissenschaft* (Basel: Kommissionsverlag Helbing and Lichtenhahn, 1955).

6. Reinhold Niebuhr and Hans Morgenthau are perhaps the best-known theorists whose positions tend to represent the balance/rebalance of power emphasis.

7. Role theory and elite theory are, of course, quite different both in origins and in focus. Nonetheless, I have, with a bit of a strain, placed them into a single category because of the tendency of some religious groups—for example, the Ecumenical Institutes and the Council on Religion and International Affairs—to treat certain classes or occupational groupings of persons as of particular significance in political matters.

8. Paul Tillich, *Theology of Culture* (Oxford University Press, Inc., 1959), pp. 7–8.

9. Louis Monden, S.J., *Sin, Liberty, and Law,* tr. by Joseph Donceel, S.J. (Sheed & Ward, 1965), pp. 30 ff.

10. H. Richard Niebuhr, *Radical Monotheism and Western Culture* (London: Faber & Faber, Ltd., 1961), p. 16.

11. Paul Tillich, *Dynamics of Faith* (London: George Allen & Unwin Ltd., 1957), pp. 9 f.

12. Augustine, *De Civitate Dei*, xix, 24.

13. See, e.g., Gabriel A. Almond and Sidney Verba, *The Civic Culture* (Little, Brown and Company, 1965), and Lucien W. Pye and Sidney Verba (eds.), *Political Culture and Political Development* (Princeton University Press, 1965).

14. Elsewhere I have argued that a similar connecting point is demonstrable in the relation between religion and law—"Three Contexts of Law," *Journal of Religion*, Vol. XLVII, No. 2 (April, 1967), pp. 127–145.

15. See, e.g., Gabriel Almond and G. Bingham Powell, Jr., *Comparative Politics: A Developmental Approach* (Little, Brown and Company, 1966), Ch. 11.

16. See, e.g., David E. Apter, *The Politics of Modernization* (The University of Chicago Press, 1967), Ch. 1.

17. Daniel Day Williams, *God's Grace and Man's Hope* (Harper & Brothers, 1949), p. 64.

18. *Ibid.*, p. 151.

19. *Ibid.*, p. 79.

20. David Easton, *The Political System* (Alfred A. Knopf, Inc., 1960), Ch. 4.

21. "The Communicative Association: The One and the Many in Human Society," *Journal of Religion*, Vol. XLVIII, No. 2 (April, 1968), pp. 189–204.

22. Karl W. Deutsch, *Nationalism and Social Communication* (The MIT Press, 1953); Karl W. Deutsch, *The Nerves of Government* (The Free Press of Glencoe, Inc., 1966).

23. Karl W. Deutsch, *Self-referent Symbols and Self-referent Communication Patterns: A Note on Some Pessimistic Theories of Politics* (Department of Humanities, Massachusetts Institute of Technology, 1954), *Publications in the Humanities*, No. 8, p. 644.

24. See "Introduction—The Study of Political Communication and Control, 1962–1966," in Deutsch, *The Nerves of Government*, pp. vii–xxiii.

25. See Deutsch's discussion of the politics of power versus the politics of growth in his book *The Nerves of Government*, Ch. 14.

26. Amitai and Eva Etzioni (eds.), *Social Change* (Basic Books, Inc., 1964), p. 75.

27. This is a formulation of Edgar S. Brightman quoted and used in Walter G. Muelder, *Moral Law in Christian Social Ethics* (John Knox Press, 1966), pp. 52, 90–94.

28. Martin Luther, *Treatise on Good Works*, v and vi.

29. David Easton, *A Framework for Political Analysis* (Prentice-Hall, Inc., 1965), p. 134.

30. *Ibid.*, p. 23.

31. Joseph W. Evans and Leo R. Ward (eds.), *The Social and Political Philosophy of Jacques Maritain* (London: Geoffrey Bles, Ltd., 1956), p. 265.

32. See above p. 145.

33. See Almond and Verba, *op. cit.*, pp. 315–324.

34. See Lucien W. Pye (ed.), *Communications and Political Development* (Princeton University Press, 1963).

35. See Apter, *op. cit.*, Ch. 9.

36. Thus, as faith begets faith, so presumably democracy begets democracy, oligarchy begets oligarchy, etc. Compare in this connection Roger E. Money-Kyrle's "spiral theory" in his book *Psychoanalysis and Politics: A Contribution to the Psychology of Politics and Morals* (W. W. Norton & Company, Inc., 1951) and Harry Eckstein's 1961 monograph, *A Theory of Stable Democracy*, republished in *Division and Cohesion in Democracy: A Study of Norway* (Princeton University Press, 1966).

37. See, e.g., Werner Levi, "Religion and Political Development: A Theoretical Analysis," *Bucknell Review*, Vol. XV, No. 2 (May, 1967), pp. 70–95.

38. Paul Tillich, *The Protestant Era* (London: James Nesbit & Co., Ltd., 1951), p. 173.

39. With the stress of Propositions III and IV on the desirability of knowledge about the situation of action, some acknowledgment should be given to the massive attempt of Friedrich A. Hayek in his book *The Constitution of Liberty* (London: Routledge & Kegan Paul, 1960) to construct a theory of liberal constitutionalism on the basis of the premise that men are invariably ignorant about their situation. See a similar emphasis in the writings of Lindblom, *The Intelligence of Democracy*, and in Thomas Landon Thorson, *The Logic of Democracy* (Holt, Rinehart and Winston, Inc., 1962).

40. Edward LeRoy Long, Jr., *op. cit.*, Chs. 19 and 20.

41. Alfred North Whitehead, *Adventures of Ideas* (London: Cambridge University Press, 1933), pp. 52 f.

42. Evans and Ward (eds.), *op. cit.*, p. 290.

43. John C. Bennett, *Christian Social Action* (London: Lutterworth Press, 1954).

44. P. H. Partridge, "Politics, Philosophy, Ideology," in Anthony Quinton (ed.), *Political Philosophy* (London: Oxford University Press, 1967), n. 2, pp. 47 f. This essay was published originally in 1966. Compare, however, the recent long-range projection of an empirical character by Herman F. Kahn and Anthony J. Wiener, *The Year 2000* (The Macmillan Company, 1967), a product of the Hudson Institute. Clearly there is a place for long-range projections of a normative character, and this is a task in which theologians, philosophers, and social scientists should be involved together.

45. There are, of course, many factors that bear on the question of the most appropriate mode of decision-making such as the type of decision being made (see, e.g., Lon L. Fuller, *The Morality of Law* [Yale University Press, 1964], Ch. 4); the character of the political situation (see, e.g., J. P. Nettl, *Political Mobilization* [London: Faber & Faber, Ltd., 1967]); and, not least, the values that are held to be desirable or inviolable (see, e.g., Dahl and Lindblom, *op. cit.*).

46. William Temple, *Christianity and the Social Order* (Harmondsworth: Penguin Books, Ltd., 1942).

47. Ramsey, *op. cit.*

48. Bennett, *op. cit.*

49. Cf. *per analogia* the "law of the closeness of relation" in H Emil Brunner, *Revelation and Reason*, tr. by Olive Wyon (London: SCM Press, Ltd., 1947), p. 383.

50. Isa. 2:4; 11:6–9.

51. Ernst Troeltsch, *Christian Thought: Its History and Application* (London: University of London Press, Ltd., 1923), pp. 128–129.

52. See Williams, *op. cit.*, pp. 134–135.

53. Rudolf Bultmann, *Existence and Faith*, tr. and ed. by Schubert M. Ogden (London: Hodder & Stoughton, Ltd., 1961), pp. 248 ff.

54. Robert A. Dahl, *Modern Political Analysis* (Prentice-Hall, Inc., 1963), p. 100.

55. Arnold Brecht, *Political Theory: The Foundations of Twentieth-Century Political Thought* (Princeton University Press, 1959), p. 9.

56. *Ibid.*, pp. 127, 483 f.

57. See Thomas Landon Thorson's critique of Brecht in Thorson, *op. cit.*, pp. 94 ff.

❖ ❖ ❖ *Kenneth Winfred Thompson has made impressive contribu-*
tions to the study of international affairs, with particular
attention to their ethical dimensions. After graduation from
Augustana College and service as an Army officer in World
War II, he earned his M.A. and Ph.D. degrees at the Univer-
sity of Chicago. He taught there and at Northwestern Uni-
versity in the fields of political science and international rela-
tions. In 1955 he became associated with the Rockefeller
Foundation, becoming director for social sciences in 1960
and vice-president the following year. He has authored and
coauthored a number of books and written many articles and
chapters, including one on "Ethical Aspects of the Nuclear
Dilemma," in a volume edited by John Bennett, Nuclear
Weapons and the Conflict of Conscience *(1962). Among*
his own books are Christian Ethics and the Dilemmas of
Foreign Policy *(1959) and* The Moral Issue in Statecraft
(1966). Dr. Thompson serves on many boards and commit-
tees, including the Board of Directors of Union Seminary, and
has been a consultant to the State Department's Advisory
Committee on International Organization Affairs.

His essay reviews the enormous contribution of thinkers
such as John Bennett to the development of a realistic Chris-
tian ethic of responsibility in foreign affairs. Noting both its
strengths in the past and its limitations in the present, he
suggests modifications for this perspective which show promise
of fruitfulness for the future.

7

THEOLOGY

AND

INTERNATIONAL RELATIONS

✧ ✧ ✧ *Kenneth W. Thompson*

OVER THE YEARS religious leaders have concerned themselves with issues related to war and peace. Some have periodically expressed concern and anguish over urgent problems. Journals and sermons abound in testimony for or against particular policies: World War II, Suez, Vietnam. Other leaders have rushed to the barricades in defense of deeply held convictions about such matters as conscientious objection, disarmament, and the United Nations. These interventions have worked an influence on the trend and character of American thought, especially among the ethically sensitive and socially conscious of each generation. The young and dedicated in every age group have drawn inspiration from these approaches. Yet the combined effect of this thinking has had no more than occasional influence on policy makers, whose work has gone forward largely divorced from the thinking of religious leaders. While religious and moral witness has touched the American conscience, it has not shaped the practice of foreign policy. Down to the present day a wide gulf separates the great bulk of religious witness from diplomatic practice.

But a handful of theological leaders has demonstrated a sustained generalized interest in international relations backed by solid study of the field. Perhaps the most conspicuous examples are found in the work and writings of the two senior editors of *Christianity and Crisis*, Reinhold Niebuhr and John Bennett. Each has lived and labored during periods of ferment and change in religious thinking. Each has had "the courage to change" perspectives and viewpoints as conditions and circumstances varied. Their work can best be understood against the background of four major periods of theology and international relations. By understanding these periods we are enabled to appreciate and to understand the contributions of these men, a contribution of sustained and generalized importance.

I. THE THEOLOGY OF IDEALISM

American thinking in the period between the two world wars was heavily isolationist. This attitude had deep roots in the unique geographical position of the United States. We were a far-flung continental land mass capable of economic growth and political development with a minimum of "entangling alliances." We were relatively free of the commitments that were familiar in Britain and Europe. On the surface it seemed that there was little need for involvement in the struggles of Europe or the necessity to preserve some measure of equilibrium in the power situation there or in Asia.

The major thrust of the theological writing in this period was outspokenly idealistic. It was marked by a self-conscious indictment of American isolationism and indifference. Journals such as *The Christian Century* and organizations such as the National Council of Churches struck out against the prevailing trend of belief and practice that resulted in American withdrawal from the problems of the rest of the world. But even the theologians did not see as clearly as they should have that the United States had far more international involvements than most people realized.

Within this situation the American people rejected membership in the League of Nations. The high prophet and major architect of the League had been repudiated by his own people and had given his life in a futile defense of internationalism. His message fell on deaf ears and there was lacking a concert of national political movements capable of providing legislative and popular support for his "Grand Design." He had been himself, particularly in his later years, a theologian of sorts doing battle against "the forces of evil." His allies in death became more numerous than his supporters in life, particularly among religious leaders, international lawyers, and idealists in all walks of life.

Furthermore, there was a natural convergence of thought between the bold and simple tenets of Wilsonianism and the idealistic temper of theology. Both dealt in essentials. Both saw the world as it ought to be, not as it was. Both found distasteful political give-and-take; both eschewed compromise and concessions; both resisted ambiguous means. Therefore, theologians in search of a credible international program which was not offensive to nobler ends found it in the doctrine of Woodrow Wilson. With Wilson, they affirmed that the evils and high costs of international relations would be mitigated by turning to transnational institutions.

The trouble with this approach was not its error but its insufficiency. Mankind through the ages has tirelessly searched for new machinery for improving the conduct of interstate relations. Procedures and institutions, however, are no more effective than the environment permits. They are limited by the social and political setting that determines what commitments and loyalties men will have to the goals and practices of institutions. Those who called for a new world order found it comforting to point to symptoms that would be removed, to forms that would be changed, and to legal tenets that would be altered by adoption of these plans. The underlying political and social realities, however, are the determining forces for nations as they operate within their institutional frameworks. If nations cannot afford to depart from ancient practices, no new constitutional arrangements will alter this fact. If leaders are in the habit of giving priority to their own national security, no amount of rhetoric concerning international security will change this fact.

Another circumstance that prevented responsible leaders vested with authority from accepting the theology of idealism stemmed from the fact that this nation had already made commitments and undertaken responsibilities that were departures from isolationism. It was true that the foes of Woodrow Wilson had overturned his particular version of American participation in the world. It was not the case, however, that the United States had retreated and pulled back on every front from assuming international obligations. Indeed, our representatives were continually linking us economically and politically with peoples in distant areas. We participated in international naval conferences, we had commerce and trade around the world, and our action or inaction played a vital role in deterring or encouraging ambitious leaders bent on expanding their influence in Europe and in Asia. The history of the Stimson Doctrine and American vacillation on the question of our guaranteeing the security of weaker nations in Asian countries provides an example or a case in point.

The effect of the United States on the rest of the world, and conversely our response to events far from our shores can also be seen in the sources of the worst depression this country has experienced.

It was the crisis of the Credit Anstalt in Austria that precipitated the beginnings of the severest economic decline in our history. This decline in turn had influence on all the economies of Western Europe and of Latin America.

Thus the issue was not so much whether the United States had a moral obligation to involve itself in world affairs but what form that involvement should take and on what social and economic arrangements it should be based. A United States indifferent to the fate of countries in other parts of the world would be little more helpful within the League of Nations than outside the framework of that international organization. Theoretically at least it would have been possible for the United States to participate in world affairs wisely and consistently outside the League of Nations no less than inside it. In any case, the distinction that had been drawn and disseminated by legal and spiritual idealists between a good American policy based on involvement in the new international organization and a bad one based on separating us from the League ignored two important realities. It ignored the milieu and setting of international politics in a state-centered world. At the same time it overlooked the network of commitments this nation had made quite unnoticed in far-flung corners of the world. In doing so, both its diagnosis of the international problem and its prescription for transcending it proved more confusing than helpful.

On one side, as practiced in the past, the theology of idealism asked too much of the United States. It called on policy makers to transform the international environment in one sweep by ridding the world of the time-honored instruments and actions that nations had always employed to safeguard their national security—military strength, alliances, and security arrangements. Idealists forgot that even a bold and heedless state acting upon these premises would have limited influence on others. It might offer itself as a sacrificial example to the harsh realities of the international jungle but nations had done this before without exerting effects on others. The Low Countries before World War II had sought not to offend their more powerful neighbors by the display of even minor power or strength. But their weakness had little influence on the mighty juggernaut the Nazis unleashed upon all of Europe. The United States, following World War II, set an example of the wholesale dismantling of a massive military establishment, but no historian can show that this led to comparable steps by Soviet military planners. Nor did it evoke worldwide disarmament within the framework of the new United

Nations. And with the mounting threat of Soviet might at the center of Europe and the subsequent conflict in Korea, the trend for the United States as well was reversed and overturned several times over.

On the other side, as a continuing philosophy, the theology of idealism asks too little of nations by minimizing the importance of meeting international responsibilities and commitments around the world. It has next to nothing to say about security guarantees particularly when they take on a less than universal character. It speaks in derogatory terms of the maintenance of a balance of power. It casts doubt upon policies that involve coming to the aid of a threatened and embattled nation-state. In short, its very idealism and internationalism are profoundly isolationist where the use of the existing limited instruments of international order are involved. It is willing to be wholeheartedly internationalist and responsible for security everywhere in the world if and when an idealized international system comes into being. Its sense of responsibility verges on the irresponsible where peace and order depend on the existing machinery of international order.

These failures and limitations led to the call for a new theology— a theology more attuned to an age of crisis and conflict. In the wake of questioning the dominant theology, new thinkers appeared on the horizon, some of the ablest centering around the journal *Christianity and Crisis*. Their influence redirected American approaches by theologians to war and peace. They included the principal architect in this country of the theology of responsibility, the senior editor of the journal, Reinhold Niebuhr.

II. THE THEOLOGY OF RESPONSIBILITY

There is tension, if not contradiction, in the fact that theologians must stand in judgment on those who wield power without themselves being forced to carry this burden. The degree of tension is minimized on the domestic front because many of the functions within national governments involve orderly constitutional processes and rational and routinized bureaucratic procedures. Actions are carried out within a broad constitutional framework where law and justice are generally defined. On the international front, however, there is no consensus among states as to the framework within which foreign relations are conducted. Some states pursue policies aimed at maintaining the *status quo*. Others are dedicated to overthrowing it.

Law and justice are filtered through national aims and interests that largely determine the content they give to law and justice. Whatever the lip service that states may give them, the rules of the international system are frequently in dispute since somewhere in the world there are states bent on changing them. There is division between the haves and the have-nots, colonial and nationalist powers, communist and democratic states, new and old nations. Even if the circumstances were such that no important nation or group were bent on overturning a particular international order, the interpretation they give it would put them at odds with one another at certain important points.

What is the role of the responsible state or statesman, or for that matter the theologian, in this kind of international system? This question was posed in the 1930's not in the abstract but in brutal and crushing military terms. Talk of law and justice proved impotent in deterring the sweep of the mighty armies of Adolf Hitler across the face of Europe. The League debated and passed resolutions, but in the end it was powerless and was unable to halt the march of German and Italian power. Chamberlain's Britain tried appeasement, but the appetites of the aggressors were only further whetted. Neither world public opinion, which proved to be a collection of divergent voices from the international community, nor the appeals of essentially reasonable leaders were able to deter Nazi or Fascist imperialism.

What did the theology of responsibility have to say in these circumstances? How was it to address itself to the violent and irrational impulses that generated a series of imperialist thrusts that soon left the whole of Europe within the grasp of a single aggressive power?

The spokesmen for a theology of responsibility were first and foremost Christian or Jewish realists. They knew in their bones that civilized nations cannot responsibly stand aside while one power, or a consortium of powers, gains hegemony over an entire continent. Men such as Niebuhr had learned this in the crucible of local politics. They knew that justice on the local scene was a product of some form of equilibrium of power. The Liberal party in New York had grown up to balance the monopoly of power that otherwise would rest in the state Democratic party. But these spokesmen of a new theology of responsibility were also students of history and sociology. The lessons of the past had taught them that whether the threat was Napoleonic France, monarchist Spain, or present-day

Germany, the challenge of a power to control the whole of the European continent must not go unanswered. Their theology was derived in part from Augustine, who had written classically about the power dimension of moral decision, and in part from the sociology of Max Weber who had written convincingly on the ethics of responsibility.

Responsibility in an age of crisis meant more than a retreat to institutional or legal affirmations. It required will and commitment, blood and treasure. There came a time when invoking the prestige of the League was not enough nor was talking of compromise and accommodation enough, although responsibility required that all these remedies be tried and exhausted. At some stage, tragic as it seemed, there could no longer be any alternative to meeting power with power, force with force, commitments with commitments. Once the aims and objectives of the Nazis and Fascists were seen as unlimited in character, there was need for more than words or threats if their worldwide mission was to be turned back.

For those who espoused a theology of responsibility the judgment of their colleagues was harsh. Idealists invoked the Sermon on the Mount and the historic creed of religious and secular pacifism. Others called into play the doctrines of the world community. Not the Grand Alliance but the agencies of world law should be the deterrent. Yet no one could show that turning the other cheek would protect the helpless and powerless from Hitler whether in Central Europe, in the Low Countries, or in the Scandinavian lands. An individualistic ethic that offered reasonable guidance for relating man to man was largely irrelevant where great and massive collectivities fired by national passions were involved. Nor was it reasonable to call on an international assembly whose strength had been sapped by defections and by failure to pose a responsible deterrent to aggressive powers. If the League of Nations had proven unable to protect little Ethiopia from the overextended power of Mussolini, who could expect it to resist the mighty German juggernaut?

In the end, it was clear that what counted was not so much what the League declared or resolved but what its individual members were willing and able to do. France and England had vacillated and finally gone their separate ways in successive crises facing the League. If either or both had been prepared to resist imperialism early in the crisis, the image of the allies as defenseless and unable to stem the tide might not have encouraged further adventures by aggressors in Europe. The United States at the eleventh hour had the choice of reacting in kind or of joining their allies (all of them be-latedly) in halting a military movement that had gained enormous momentum and power.

The theology of responsibility postulated that power in the world presupposes responsibility. The failure of will and responsibility had invited aggression. Now the task of those who had the means of restoring the peace of Europe was to join together in the defense of those whose freedom was being snuffed out. Failing that, the freedom of those who had the power (whether latent or in being) to assure national survival would in turn disappear. First France and then England, having slept as the threat appeared and mounted, would be overrun unless there was a revival of national responsibility against aggression.

This story of the defense and preservation of freedom is a finished chapter in the history of mankind. The theology of responsibility had been tested by events. While few would be bold enough to claim the relevance of this approach for all time, it proved the best guide for statesmen and ethicists of the day. It was clear that the relative security which came with the defeat of Hitler could scarcely have been gained in any other way. And those who sought to relate ethics to international politics then helped men to understand that the price of peace was the responsible use of countervailing power.

III. The Theology of Pluralism

The world after World War II was a different world from that with which the prewar theologians of responsibility had been obliged to deal. Not two world systems—those of aggressors and those of peacemakers—but a great variety of political regimes came into being.

At first this world was viewed through the perspective of those who spoke of communist and noncommunist states. Indeed the only states that mattered at the outset of this discussion were the two superpowers, the Soviet Union and the United States. Each of them had those requirements for universal world leadership which had in the past led to rivalry and conflict. They both were centers of enor-mous power and influence, possessed far-flung geographic empires, had governments that provided models for the rest of the world, and were the capitals of strongly held political ideologies. It was tempting to substitute the Soviet Union for Nazi Germany, and the United States for the Allied powers, and to apply tenets of the theology of

responsibility in evaluating them. This way of viewing the struggle
was plausible to anyone studying postwar foreign relations. The
Soviet Union emerged from World War II possessing great military
and political power and newly acquired prestige. Its ideology under
Stalin was that of first-generation revolutionaries who looked forward to a comparatively early communization of much of the world.
Whereas in World War II, Russian survival had required emphasis
upon the preservation of communism in one country, following
victory, the Soviet Union found it reasonable to expect the stabiliza-
tion of its system within and the expansion of its influence beyond
its historic confines.

The Red Army was stationed in the center of Europe on the
boundaries of a divided Germany and inside the territory of an
expanded Soviet empire. It seemed clear that unless this expansion
could be arrested, the Soviet Union would replace Hitler's Germany
as the principal hegemonial power in Europe. Therefore circumstances called for the building up of "situations of strength" to
replace the power vacuums into which Russian influence could flow.
The basic principle underlying the Marshall Plan and the Truman
Doctrine was the need for a reconstructed Europe in which free and
independent nations could work out their destiny without having to
be politically and economically dependent upon the Soviet Union.

All this had the ring of sound moral and political thinking. It grew
out of earlier experience with threats to peace in Europe. It reflected
what sensitive students of politics and religion had learned from the
study of the interwar period. Moreover, the application of a firm
and responsible policy of deterrence to the spread of Communism,
as organized and led from Moscow, proved to be a largely successful
policy in restoring the economy and the security of Europe.

Before much time had elapsed, however, the necessity of
widening the horizons of this approach became clear. The evidence
soon mounted that the Soviet Union was both more and less of a
threat than Nazi Germany had been. It was more of a threat because
it possessed a persuasive political ideology. It had a program that
offered some kind of salvation for oppressed people. Particularly
men and nations existing on the borderline between starvation and
survival found it an appealing doctrine. Soviet Communism was less
of a threat in the military field. Whereas Nazi Germany pursued a
military strategy from beginning to end, the Soviet Union, perhaps
because it saw the eventual triumph of Communism, was more apt
to be patient in the use of nonmilitary techniques. Thus the risk of

outright global conflict was a serious but not an immediate threat. Responses on the part of other nations required strategies more complex and varied. These included economic and social programs as well as military preparation.

Furthermore, Communism within and outside the Soviet Union was no monolith. It was different in the Stalinist era from under Khrushchev and it changed again when Brezhnev and Kosygin came to power. Communism and socialism around the world were even more many-sided. The Yugoslav experiment in state planning looked different and had other roots than the Communism of Mao Tse-tung in China. Romania, Poland, and Hungary evolved their own Communist systems so that containment or deterrence no longer meant applying counterforces to a single rigid system everywhere in the world.

In addition to communism a richly varied pattern of nation-state development grew up elsewhere in the world. The new states of Africa and Asia, whatever their constitutional arrangements, bore little resemblance to the older states of Europe and America. New concepts such as "guided democracy" and "one-party democracy" came into everyday political parlance. A blending of various liberal and collectivist methods and techniques was developed in these new states. A country like Tanzania drew economically, politically, and educationally on approaches and people from Western Europe, Britain, the United States, and the Communist world. It was not surprising to find in developing universities two or three acting heads of departments recruited from Poland working alongside other heads of departments who came from the United States or Canada.

In other words it was difficult to use traditional political or ideological terms in talking about the characteristics of these new regimes or their objectives and intentions. What was common and self-evident as one viewed their development was the immense variety they reflected. To build an international order it was no longer enough to resist the expansion of one or two nations or to keep the spirit of one or more ideologies within bounds. The real issue became one of assisting the orderly and peaceful development of new societies along some kind of internationally acceptable course, of minimizing poverty and illiteracy, and of encouraging opportunity for education, of giving assistance to those who sought constructive national development and of keeping in check a growing sense of alienation and despair that could only breed extremism and military adventurism.

A plural world required plural approaches to peace and order. It was no longer enough to talk of resistance to this or that imperialist force. There was need for human and material resources, new and innovative technologies, wiser allocation of limited resources, extension of cooperation within a region including regional trade, and the growth of a sense of responsibility by those most directly concerned.

This kind of world required that something be added to the doctrine of responsibility, resulting in a theology of pluralism. A more complex set of concepts was needed; a greater appreciation for variety was called for. Theologians such as John Bennett gave increasing stress to these considerations. They were critical of statesmen who failed to recognize the diversity and pluralism of world society. They denounced those who spoke as though all Communist states were the same. They were impatient when leaders acted in recognition of a pluralistic world but did not account for their actions by setting forth new doctrines that reflected the facts. In this the theologians performed their historic, prophetic function of challenging men to reach out for new principles that were ignored or unarticulated in practical politics or diplomatic encounters. (Perhaps if the theologians had experienced more of the anguish of having to interpret their actions not to one but to many publics and being held accountable for them, they would have been more forgiving.) In any event, a new world had come into being, and the theology of pluralism sought to grant it legitimacy for citizens and leaders alike.

IV. The Theology of Change

The several trends that are reflected in earlier stages of evolving theological approaches have come to a head in the recent expression of a theology of change. Beginning in 1946, the world experienced profound change. Upwards of a billion people found that political realities and the legitimacy myths under which they had lived had been changed. New nations, swept along by winds of change, came into being; old empires came crashing down. (It is worth noting that a liberal empire such as the British Empire accepted change and gave independence to its colonies voluntarily. The Soviet Empire, a product of World War II, has felt the winds of change within its satellites but has not chosen to loosen the bonds and grant them autonomy.)

Other profound and far-reaching changes were at work. The

maxim that war was an instrument of national policy, or that war, in Clausewitz' terms, was a continuation of diplomacy by other means, came into question. The incredible destructiveness of thermonuclear weapons guaranteed that victor and defeated nation alike would both be the victims. The equation of rational warfare was upset if not overthrown.

At the same time other forces were at work transforming modern thought. Young men and young thinkers who had witnessed the legislation of moral purposes in the civil rights crusade called for a similar attack on the problem of war and conflict. Ironically, they sought their goals by escalating domestic conflict but justified this as a means of overthrowing a corrupt society. Much as the pressures before World War II had mounted for eliminating war, so in more rational and persuasive terms young minds called for the elimination of war in the late 1960's. As they saw it, war was the servant of unjust causes: witness Vietnam. War was a product of the military industrial establishment: note the gains that privileged groups enjoyed. War was a diversion from civil pursuits: witness the neglect of the problems of the cities. Whereas young men in the 1930's had called for the outlawry of war, they asked in the 1960's that men put an embargo or boycott on it. The use of demonstrations and mass appeals came to be the basis for influencing the course of history. These movements for change were not the product of a few young men in one country. They were the expression of a worldwide phenomenon having deep roots in the rebellion of youth against the wrongdoings of society.

The theology of change called for a spirit of impatience with both past and present. It needed its scapegoats and found them in leading decision makers. It required slogans reminiscent of those after World War II which saw war as the product of a handful of munitions makers.

But the movement went farther and struck deeper roots. It was geared to a growing awareness that thermonuclear war would be an act of madness. It generated support from young people who wanted to get on with the business of improving society. It came at a time when the worldwide trend of abandoning all ideologies for a more pragmatic approach to our problems was being challenged. The benefits of pragmatism and realism lie in their understanding that problems can be tackled on their merits; their liabilities, little inspiration or uplift in an approach that calls for routine hard work on each successive problem.

A vacuum had grown up in the realm of ideals. For a time young people found a way of filling it with commitments to civil rights causes. As time went on, however, there was need for something more. They searched for a more generalized theory. Someone had to be held accountable for the gap between the ideals men proposed and their failure to realize them. This was possible in our society because never before had there been such freedom of expression, never such affluence and abundance for those who labor, including those who read and write, never such concern among conservatives and liberals alike for helping the downtrodden and the oppressed. In order to go beyond the pragmatic efforts that were thus made possible by the world of change, young people and the new theology felt compelled to judge reform by more absolute goals.

The theology of change tended to be a one-directional approach. It looked forward from things as they were or are to the ideal of what things ought to be. It had little taste for measuring backward to things as they used to be. In short it had little sense of history. Nor was it willing to measure laterally the conditions of other societies elsewhere on this earth. By and large, theologians of change knew less about history and the rest of the world than might have been hoped. Therefore, while their thought was attuned to the time and to the forces of change, it failed to provide the standard against which to judge itself.

In this context the philosophy that can boast the strongest sense of history and the wisest perspective of change is still the theology of responsibility. Perhaps the challenge for tomorrow is to find ways of marrying the wisdom of this approach with the vitality of the theology of change. There is wisdom and relevance for the day in each emerging theology. It would be misleading to say that one theology is universal and the others geared solely to the era in which they have prevailed. Yet each partakes of qualities that belong to a particular complex of problems. Each is a response to a set of issues. Each is intended to give meaning to a complicated and baffling set of facts with which men have been obliged to come to terms.

V. The Call for a New Synthesis

Theologians of the future, therefore, will face the challenge of sorting out and defining the points at which earlier theologies have relevance. They cannot long escape the need to relate and reintegrate historic approaches. It should be within the reach of our ablest and boldest minds to lay down certain guidelines or working hypotheses concerning the timelessness of these great historic adventures in thought. This task is the unfinished business of the theology of international relations. It constitutes the agenda of the future.

A few concepts and proposals for the future may be worthy of enumeration in the form more of questions than of conclusions. First, the shape of the future will be a design for change. We face vast and far-reaching transformations in the numbers and makeup of the world's population, the circumstances under which men live, the pressures for survival and a better life, the relationships between rich and poor, young and old, the privileged and the oppressed. How will theology deal with these changes? What will it have to say about life in the twenty-first century? How can it avoid, on the one hand, sanctifying forces and peoples who represent the pell-mell rush toward change and, on the other hand, dignifying time-encrusted factors from the past? Where should it direct the main thrust of its judgments? How can it avoid both neutrality and self-righteousness respecting the good and evil embedded in both the new and the old? Where is the balancing force that will enable beneficiaries of change from becoming its high priests? Who will speak against praise of novelty for novelty's sake? And with the explosions of knowledge that have both great civilizing and destructive potential, who will turn revolutionary movements from destructive drives to civilizing effects while preserving the dynamism of change? And through it all, who can speak both to and for the poor, the young, and the alienated and in doing so maintain the dialogue for peace?

Second, where are the moral and intellectual resources that prepare men for living in a pluralistic world? How can one find the route to peace and understanding when the differences between societies loom larger than their commonalty? How can the point of community be found between societies that live on their differences, whose polities depend for their strength and political survival on accentuating what distinguishes them from the others? We need to remind ourselves that the fuel of nationalism is the self-consciousness that societies are different, that tutelage is contrary to human nature, and that social cohesiveness requires an external threat. Totalitarian leaders justify elaborate superstructures of power on the claim that outsiders are plotting their destruction. And finally, how can we reconcile respect for differences ("let many flowers bloom") without obscuring the fact that within and between the communist and democratic world order there are better and worse regimes. In short, does pluralism indicate that man's quest for the good society and the best political regime is a mere illusion that men have pursued for two thousand years?

Third, is it possible that responsibility is a concept of a different, more universal quality than either pluralism or change? Must not responsibility, with its emphasis on the wise and prudent exercise of authority and the clear recognition of the limitations of institutions and men, be written somehow into every political doctrine and every theology of international relations? I believe profoundly that this is the case and no amount of rhetoric about new problems and more contemporary approaches can change this enduring fact. Incidentally, I have the sense that John Bennett perceives this, while some of his younger followers caught up in the challenge of a new theology may not yet understand it as fully as he does.

Finally, must not idealism continue to be the broad and overarching framework that inspires each emergent theology? Is it not the "higher thought" that can lead men to the stars? Is not the ultimate task of theology that of blending idealism and responsibility, of glorifying and humbling mankind, and of channeling and examining human aspirations? Must not idealism be the molder of the dreams of all men whatever the limits of human achievement?

There is need then for the old and the new, the inspirational and the practical, and the creeds that are relevant for the present and for all time. Theology which has addressed itself to the stark issues of international relations must learn from the John Bennetts and Reinhold Niebuhrs of our time who have had the courage to take hold of many strains of thought in order to meet many versions of one problem. What is the nature of man and how can he live with his neighbor whatever the context of the challenges that confront him?

❖ ❖ ❖ *Robert Wood Lynn, following his graduation from Princeton*
University and Yale Divinity School, served for a number of
years as assistant minister of Montview Boulevard Presby-
terian Church in Denver, interrupting his ministry there to
do graduate study at Union Theological Seminary. In 1959
he was called back to the Seminary, where he became Dean
of the Auburn Program in 1960, received his Th.D. degree
two years later, and in 1965 was made Auburn Professor of
Religious Education and Church and Community. Author of
many articles and chapters, he has written Protestant Strategies in Education *(1965). He has served as chairman of the*
Committee on Church and Public Education of the Board of
Christian Education of the United Presbyterian Church and
as president of the board of directors of Christianity and
Crisis *and consulting editor of* Colloquy.

In tracing the change in Protestant concern for the public
school as the defender of a nonsectarian public faith to the
emergence of a pluralistic society devoted to secular values,
this essay suggests a new role for the concept of public benefit
as the touchstone by which both public and parochial educa-
tion may be measured.

8

THE ECLIPSE OF A PUBLIC:
PROTESTANT REFLECTIONS
ON RELIGION AND PUBLIC EDUCATION,
1940-1968

❖ ❖ ❖ *Robert W. Lynn*

THE MID-DECADES of the twentieth century have often been
described as "post" something else.[1] A futurologist, for example,
foresees the emergence of the "post-industrial society."[2] Or many a
theologian today speaks of "post-liberal" theology, of a "post-Christian" era, and even (in the most extravagant phrase of all) of a
"post-religious" age. These expressions are the telltale signs of an
interlude in which the present and the future are best understood
by references to a past, whether near or far. It is as though contemporary men, including the self-consciously *avant garde,* are
riding into the future facing backward.

The "post" character of our time becomes abundantly clear when
we review the controversy over religion in the public schools during
the last three decades. Here, as perhaps nowhere else in recent
American history, one can discern a paradigm of life in the present
interim: an old era is finished, though its power still lingers on;
meanwhile the shape of the new age is not yet clear. And so we live
between the times.

This essay will explore the meaning of that interim by retracing
the thinking of two generations of Protestant leaders about the
American public, its common faith and education.

I. THE LAST GENERATION, ITS LAST HURRAH

In 1948 the longtime editor of *The Christian Century,* Charles
Clayton Morrison, issued a rousing tract for the times—*Can Protestantism Win America?* His "call to arms" seemed to point to the

future. But in fact the book signaled the beginning of the end of a once-dominant perspective upon this nation. "Three major forces," Morrison announced in his opening sentence, "are now bidding for ascendancy in the cultural and spiritual life of America. These forces are Protestantism, Roman Catholicism and Secularism."[3]

His argument unfolded in a clear and uncomplicated fashion. (a) Secularism threatens the unity and vitality of the nation, even though it is not incarnated in any centralized organization. (b) The tightly knit power of Roman Catholicism is all too visible; as an alien influence it subverts the cause of both democracy and true religion. (c) Protestantism must acknowledge, however belatedly, its destiny in the grand work of preserving America as a religious democracy. Perhaps Morrison was asking, not "Can Protestantism win America?" but will America be true to itself as a Protestant land?

The book was a last hurrah for a vanishing America. Its author belonged to that generation whose formative years came near the turn of the century. The nation was still Protestant in spirit; the public school was the great engine of Americanization, the very embodiment of civic unity. Although Morrison and his contemporaries lived fully through the events of later decades, they continued to rely upon certain perceptions learned in the early 1900's. They constituted the "Last Generation" (as I shall describe them here) to maintain a nineteenth-century understanding of the American public. For the most part, that image of the public remained latent, lurking beneath the surface of their thinking about religion and education. But Morrison, always the shrewd journalist, knew his audience and could voice its deepest convictions. In his strident, polemical way Morrison made explicit what others could only feel or hint at. If one strips away his polemics, the essential convictions of a generation remain. So let me recast Morrison's argument into a slightly less contentious mold.

a. *The Instability of a Secular Society.* The concept of the "secular" has had a curious career in the religious thought of twentieth-century America. It has figured prominently in the thinking of each generation, though with astonishingly different meanings attached to it from decade to decade.

The "Last Generation," unlike the "worldly" theologians of the 1960's, was never enamored of the pieties of the "secular city." In fact, they looked upon the secular as a sign of weakness, not strength.

One of their spokesmen was Luther A. Weigle, then dean of Yale
Divinity School and a leading churchman in his time. Weigle was
always suspicious of the impact of secularization: the secular man
may enjoy a momentary sense of autonomy and self-sufficiency; but
gradually he becomes the prisoner of a reduced and limited order of
existence. The process of secularization, in the estimate of Weigle
and many of his peers, involves a subtle leveling of life. The heights
and depths of humanity tend to disappear, and what is left is a closed
mind and a suspicion of any sense of mystery. It is not surprising,
then, that Weigle viewed the growth of secularity and "the cheap-
ening of human interests"[4] as related characteristics of the twentieth
century.

The apparent social consequences of this development were even
more unsettling to the members of the "Last Generation." In their
judgment a purely secular society is a fragile creation, unstable and
subject to paralysis. It can survive only by living off its inheritance
from a religious past. A typical analysis along these lines was offered
by William C. Bower, one of Weigle's colleagues in the religious
education movement:

> With the disintegration of the older sanctions of religion the
> once accepted moral standards have tended to give way before
> the free expression of undisciplined impulses at the same time
> that society has lost much of its cohesiveness. One of the marks
> of a secularized society is its tendency to fall apart in the pursuit
> of highly specialized and unrelated interests.[5]

The moral was plain: if any public-spirited man cares about this
nation, he will fight every manifestation of secularity. For what is at
stake here goes far beyond any ecclesiastical self-interest or worries
about the future of the church. The issue, according to the "Last
Generation," is the existence of the American public. The public will
not survive apart from a common religious faith. By implication,
therefore, the secularist is finally the private man *par excellence,*
only matched in his irresponsibility by the sectarian churchman who
insists upon his own personal version of the public's faith.

b. *Religion, Not Sectarianism.* One of the staples in the rich diet
of American invective is the word "sectarian." It crops up in different places—in Supreme Court decisions (where it has long
played a mischievous role), in church pronouncements, in atheist

manifestos, and—not least—in the argument about religion and education. In the 1940's, for instance, the "Last Generation" constantly inveighed against the dangers of sectarianism. The sectarian impulse, it believed, is disruptive and divisive, whereas religion is unifying.

But *whose* religion? And who is sectarian? Interestingly enough, few of the participants in this controversy ever described their own position as "sectarian." (That seemed to be the prerogative of their opponents.) Charles C. Morrison and others claimed—in effect—that Protestantism is the guardian of the public's faith, while Roman Catholicism embodies the sectarian spirit. They looked upon Roman Catholics as strangers in a Protestant Zion—to be tolerated, of course, but also to be kept under close surveillance. Otherwise, so it was argued, the Catholics would once again employ the tactics by which they had gained so much in earlier years. One such ploy was described by the conservative Calvinist W. S. Fleming in his jaundiced account of the exclusion of the Bible from the public schools.

> How then did the Book go? It was in the schools by custom not by mandatory law. Alien minorities, one or two in a community, went quietly to the teacher and demanded that the Bible be dropped and the teachers . . . reluctantly obeyed. The deed was done while the majority were asleep. The Book that made our civilization left the schools as quietly as night follows day. *The Bible was not legislated out of the schools; it was quietly crowded out by alien influence and indifference.*[6]

These hints about the machinations of "alien minorities" were not lost upon the alert Protestant reader of the 1940's. The code phrase —"alien minorities"—could be quickly translated as "Roman Catholics" and/or "Jews" (much as the expression "law and order" came to symbolize in the late 1960's the whites' fear of black Americans).

Not many of the other spokesmen for the "Last Generation" were as crude as Fleming. But even the most liberal among them were apprehensive about any new "concessions" (a revealing word in this context) to the minorities. The virtues of pluralism were not widely celebrated in the 1940's. For the most part the "Last Generation" accepted religious diversity as an inevitable fact of life in the twentieth century, but not as an automatically desirable state of affairs. Their emphasis was rather upon the majority and its rightful claims.

And if they did argue over these matters, they did so precisely at the point of defining the religious complexion of the majority.

Thus, while Luther A. Weigle granted the freedom of parents "to withdraw their children from the period of Bible reading and prayer,"[7] he warned against any more imbalance between minority and majority. "But to go farther and to divest the public schools completely of religious faith, to meet the scruples of the pagan few, is to coerce the conscience of the many for whom religion is an essential part of education."[8] Note that Weigle mentioned only one minority, "the pagan few." Everyone else, including the Jews and Roman Catholics, belonged to the American majority. In that respect he differed from Fleming, Morrison, and others who pleaded unabashedly for Protestant hegemony. The triumph of Protestantism was not his cause. Instead, he hoped to maintain a long tradition that antedated the spawning of the sectarian mentality in the nineteenth century. "The foundations of America," Weigle wrote in 1940, "were laid in that stern yet abiding and hopeful faith that is our heritage from the Hebrew prophets and from Jesus Christ."[9] In those beginnings lies America's true unity. Without that "stern yet abiding faith," America cannot be itself.

In the 1940's this version of the public faith seemed hopelessly "sectarian" to some of Weigle's critics. Today, a scant two decades later, it seems not so much sectarian as quaint and archaic, a voice from the distant past.

But let us listen again to that voice.

c. *The Public's Faith*: *"The Only Adequate Basis."* In 1948 the Supreme Court announced its decision in the controversial McCollum case. The Court's findings were limited and specific: a released-time program involving the use of public school property in a Midwestern town was deemed unconstitutional. Yet the case soon took on a symbolic meaning that stretched far beyond Champaign, Illinois. The "Last Generation," for instance, was alarmed and indignant; it believed that the high court was moving toward a coercive invasion of the rights of the majority. And so it chose "McCollum" as the battleground for its last major stand.

Their counterattacks were many, and varied greatly in effectiveness. The voice of this band of men can be clearly heard in the 1949 statement of the International Council of Religious Education, then the interdenominational agency for mainstream Protestantism:

Faith in God, the God of the Old and New Testaments, and faith in free men as His responsible creations have inspired our life and history from the early days of the nation. . . . This faith is embodied in our laws, documents and institutions.

We expect that the schools will expose our children to this point of view. We go further in our expectations. As far as the school can, in view of the religious diversity of our people, judicial opinions, and our American traditions, we expect it to teach this common religious tradition as *the only adequate basis* for the life of the school and the personal lives of teachers, students, and citizens in a free and responsible democracy.

There is nothing in our laws, nothing in our court decisions up to and including . . . the Champaign case, nothing in our traditions, which prevents the school, within its own program, from making provision for the religious interpretation of life.[10]

"The only adequate basis"—a strong claim, indeed. But anything less would have violated their conviction about the genius of the American experience. The America they loved was, to use a phrase of G. K. Chesterton, "the nation with the soul of a church."[11] This church had no satisfactory creed. The members of the "Last Generation" usually tumbled into difficulties when they tried to define its articles of belief.[12] That failure, however, never deterred them for long. They could still point to the scriptures of the common faith (the two Testaments in the Bible and the third testament of life, the Declaration of Independence) and their presence in everyday life, i.e., the religious texture of holidays and civic festivals, the "devotional" exercises in the schools, etc.

The thrust of their argument cut much more deeply than they ever made explicit. Its implications might be summarized as follows: the public's faith is the embodiment of the nation's memory and hope. If that faith is lost, then the country is cut off from its inner history. When an individual loses touch with his hopes and memories, he risks the danger of amnesia and eventual self-destruction. So does the public that neglects the renewal of its faith.

The "Last Generation" spent much of its time in the 1940's fighting off that danger. It held fast on two points:

1. The public school must be guarded as the *one* institution in and through which each new generation can be initiated into the common faith. This meant, of course, that there could be no state

aid for parochial schools. No compromise here was permissible. They even rejected the newly emerging theory of "child benefit," i.e., the state may provide certain "fringe" benefits to the child, but not grant direct aid to the private school.[13]

Their resistance was rooted, in part, in anti-Catholic prejudice. That much is surely obvious. But it was also a consequence of some deeply held convictions about the nature of the public. While they were apprehensive lest the Government aid the Roman Catholic Church in its presumed drive for prominence and power, they were even more concerned (according to their accounts) about the survival of America. In "the nation with the soul of a church" the public school had taken on a sacral character. And thus the defense of public education became an exercise in political ecclesiology. This interpretation helps to explain the devout tone so evident in their protective praising of the public school, and the absoluteness with which they rejected any hint of state grants for parochial schools. By its very nature as a "sectarian" institution, the Catholic school was ill-equipped to pass on the public faith, fully and freely expressed, to the coming generation.

2. The common faith can be taught in many ways through the public schools—and not least through the reading of the Bible and prayers in the classrooms. The "Last Generation" were aware of the controversial, somewhat soiled reputation of the so-called "devotional period." By 1940 a variety of critics looked upon these practices as empty rituals at best, and, at worst, concessions to unseemly clerical pressure. A few of the "Last Generation" acknowledged the inevitable; the most they could hope for was to find a *via media* between sectarian indoctrination and the policy of "no religion at all" in the schools. F. Ernest Johnson, for instance, advocated the alternative of an objective teaching about religion.[14] But a majority of Johnson's peers wanted something more than the study of religion. In this matter, Weigle, Fleming, and company never did accede to the charge that the state was being asked to do the church's work. On the contrary, they insisted, these "devotional" acts are undertaken precisely for the sake of the public and the nurture of its faith. For "the only adequate basis for the life of the school," in the judgment of the International Council of Religious Education, was a thorough grounding in America's "common religious tradition."

That statement proved to be the valedictory of the "Last Generation," a final hurrah for an America that is no more.

II. A PUBLIC IN ECLIPSE

Sometime in the 1950's a new twist on words quickly became popular across the country. The WASP was no longer just a summertime affliction; it had also come to signify the presence of a White Anglo-Saxon Protestant. Behind the momentary cleverness of this wordplay lay a common awareness, voiced by Norman Podhoretz in retrospect years later. In looking back upon his time at Columbia University in the late 1940's, he commented:

> When I was in college, the term WASP had not yet come into currency—which is to say that the realization had not yet become widespread that white Americans of Anglo-Saxon Protestant background are an ethnic group like any other, that their characteristic qualities are by no means self-evidently superior to those of the other groups, and that neither their earlier arrival nor their majority status entitles them to exclusive possession of the national identity.[15]

That "realization" did come in the 1950's and early 1960's. Perhaps it hit the white Protestant hardest of all. It was, ironically enough, the WASP himself who often invoked the term—sometimes as a form of self-mockery, occasionally as a confession of guilt, and almost inevitably, whether intended or not, as expressive of a new historical self-consciousness. He could no longer easily assume a "majority status" or "the exclusive possession of national identity." Those days of bland unconsciousness were gone forever. The Protestant America his forefathers had revered now seemed increasingly remote and irrelevant. By the mid-1960's the conventional wisdom of mainstream Protestantism embodied a "no" to each "yes" of the "Last Generation."

a. *The Public Faith: Not Much "Faith," Not Very "Public."* The public faith so generously affirmed by the "Last Generation" came under sharp attack in the 1950's. And no wonder. That decade turned into an open season for theological satire. Although the Niebuhr brothers, Paul Tillich, and other earlier neo-orthodox theologians had criticized the aberrations of "culture-religion," it was their students or disciples who became the vocal critics of "religion in general" during the Eisenhower years. The rising generation entertained some negative thoughts about the "positive thinking" of Norman Vincent Peale, worried about the new culture faith—the

American way of life—and lampooned Congressional prayer break-
fasts in Washington and other such manifestations of piety along the
Potomac.

Probably its easiest target was the then current fashion of
thought in public school circles. In the early 1950's a prestigious
group (including Dwight D. Eisenhower and James B. Conant)
joined together to affirm the importance of "moral and spiritual
values." Their report—*Moral and Spiritual Values in the Public
Schools*[16]—inspired a host of imitative and even less distinguished
efforts.

Here are two illustrations from just one state: in 1954 the New
York Board of Regents proclaimed that the times "call for the
teaching of 'Piety and Virtue' in the schools, and of that dependence
upon Almighty God so clearly recognized in the Declaration of Independence, the Constitution of the United States . . . and in the
pronouncements of the great leaders of our country."[17] One year
later the superintendents of the New York City school system issued
a guiding statement for teachers in that most heterogeneous of urban
areas. They began by saying: "The American people are, characteristically, a religious people who derive their accepted moral and
spiritual values from religion. These values are inherent in the He-
braic-Christian tradition. They presuppose the existence of a Supreme Being."[18] Among other recommendations, they suggested
"that the program of the public schools must reinforce the program
of the home and church in strengthening belief in God."[19]

This version of the public's faith did not go unchallenged. In the
estimate of its Protestant critics, it reflected neither the true quality
of faith nor the diversity of the public. "Faith in God," wrote William Lee Miller, "should be a source not only of support but also of
criticism of conventional morality and patriotism."[20] But instead the
proponents of "moral and spiritual values" tended to use religion as
a narcotic. Their affirmations were kept vague and vaporous; nobody's ox was gored and no group's interest was threatened. It was
a painless moral dentistry of the most appealing sort: such a faith
could help America—in the satirical estimate of Miller—"answer
juvenile delinquency, give security against Communism, create a
moral fiber for the nation. Religion is recommended because, like
Chesterfields, it satisfies."[21] The same superficiality was evident,
according to these theologians, in the claim that religion could unify
America. This kind of civic faith would lead only to a bogus unity.
Any appeal to a common core of moral and spiritual values tends to

flatten out significant religious differences between Americans. It makes them appear equally religious—and equally dull. "Where everybody is 'religious' nobody is religious."[22] Such were the dangers of popular religion.

And so this new generation was inclined to stress the actual religious diversity of Americans more than the old ideal of unity. The "Last Generation's" vision of the public faith was fading fast. Its eclipse was not far off.

b. *Beyond Sectarianism*: *A Pluralistic Society*. In the year of John F. Kennedy's election to the Presidency, John Courtney Murray, the Jesuit theologian, published his long-awaited book, *We Hold These Truths*. Both events signified, in quite different modes, a Catholic coming of age in America. In a strange way that perhaps he did not even understand at the time, Murray became the spokesman for an emerging consensus when he wrote: "American society is neither vaguely Protestant nor purely secular. The religion of America is not 'democracy,' nor is it some generalized faith in 'values.' Religion in America has a form, a precisely defined form, a pluralistically structured form. This is the fact."[23]

That, indeed, was the "fact." No one, to the best of my knowledge, ever successfully disputed his analysis. The old formula—"religion, not sectarianism"—was quietly disappearing from main-line Protestant reflections about the public schools. And in its place was a new reliance upon dialogue, a willingness to lay down the old arms and take up the argument.

This change, of course, did not happen all at once. The dialogue moved in a halting and uncertain manner during the 1950's. Perhaps one turning point came in May, 1958, when the Fund for the Republic, a "spin-off" from the Ford Foundation, sponsored a week-long conference about "Religion in a Free Society." Almost one hundred persons of different religious persuasions gathered, as John Cogley said later, "to talk candidly about a number of matters that are too often whispered about behind locked sectarian doors."[24] The ensuing talk was candid beyond all expectations. To wit: shortly after Will Herberg had stressed the public function of the so-called "private schools,"[25] the Protestant historian James Hastings Nichols replied with a countercharge that reverberated across the country for months afterward. Catholic schooling, he said, "is as 'private' as education can be. It is not merely separated from public review and criticism, but is separated by a certain sacrosanct halo. . . . Roman

Catholic controlled education is censored education, and part of a general strategy to establish enclaves of concentrated clerical political power."[26]

This exchange, however acerbic, was an important beginning. For one thing, it helped (along with other forces) to nudge the old dispute about religion and education off dead center. Instead of simply rehearsing tired arguments about the "wall of separation," religious freedom and the intent of the Founding Fathers, Herberg and Nichols pointed to the presence of the public as the crucial factor in the making of policy decisions. In effect, both men were asking the same questions—When, if ever, does a "private" school accomplish the public's work? What does "public control" mean? These issues would become even more important in the coming decade. Thus the conference represented a major step forward. Its significance lay, not so much in points scored in a debating match or in minds changed, as in the growing sense that dialogue was a possibility at last.

The ecumenical conversation also gained momentum when a few leaders managed to venture beyond the entrenched positions of their respective faith communities. John C. Bennett was foremost among these pioneers; his willingness to hear Catholic pleas for some state aid to parochial schools put him almost ten years ahead of his fellow churchmen. In the 1950's—well before the Vatican II Council and the era of good feeling engendered by Pope John—there was remarkably little Protestant sympathy for the plight of the Catholic schools. Even the much-lauded and presumably "liberal" Presbyterian statement on "The Church and the Public Schools" took a hard line against any kind of governmental assistance for religious schools:

> We . . . are unalterably opposed to the support of independent or parochial schools through the use of public funds. . . . We know full well that parochial schools, avowedly sectarian, are not amenable to the control of the community from which they seek support. There is a widespread and aggressive movement that asserts that the parochial school is really a part of public education. This contention confuses the public and is contrary to the fact that parochial schools and public schools are erected upon utterly different foundations. . . .
>
> We are opposed to the indirect use of public monies for parochial schools even though they are expended under the legal category of "welfare funds."[27]

Bennett was restless with this sort of absolutism, for it did not—in his judgment—illumine the ethical dilemma actually facing the American people. To ignore the parochial schools' share in the education of the public is unfair and morally myopic. "Can Protestants," he asked, "continue to deny that there is any basis for the Catholic claim that there is injustice in their double burden of expense for education?"[28] Yet if extensive direct aid is given to the Catholic schools, "there is the danger . . . that the whole public school system might soon be weakened and the educational resources of the community dissipated."[29] Bennett's response in this situation was to search for viable compromises. Thus he became the first major Protestant spokesman to stress the "child benefit" principle and among the first to anticipate the option of "shared time" (although he used another label).[30] In doing so, he marked out the position that would be later occupied by an ecumenical coalition in the next decade.

In the early 1960's a new force began to be visible in the politics of American education. It was a strange assortment of old opponents who had now become temporary allies. The shape of this coalition was first apparent in the flurry of interest over "shared time," or the plan for dual enrollment as it was called later in the decade. The supporters of this option ranged across the religious spectrum—many Catholics and Protestants and some Jews. The coalition came to life again in the mid-1960's during the fight over President Johnson's federal aid to education bill. A deadlock born out of years of bitter religious strife and political controversy was finally broken when the Elementary and Secondary Education Act of 1965 became the law of the land, the first of its kind after a long history of failures. The sources of this legislative triumph were multiple: the momentary euphoria induced by enthusiasm over the "Great Society"; a powerful Congressional majority that was committed to some form of general aid for American schools; and—not least—the shattering of the stalemate on the church-state frontier.

For years Catholics had exercised a *de facto* veto over any federal aid bills that did not include some benefits, direct or indirect, for the parochial schools. Likewise the non-Catholics were watchful lest any possible governmental funds be diverted from the public schools. But in 1965 a mild truce was declared. Some spokesmen for American Protestantism testified before Congress on behalf of a wider range of benefits for students in the nonpublic schools. Their Catholic counterparts, meanwhile, did not push their claims too far. Both forces could agree upon some expressions of the "child benefit" theory. The resulting "ecumenical chorale," as *The New York Times* called it,[31] smoothed the way for a historic piece of legislation.

Few knowledgeable observers in the early 1960's would have dared predict this outcome. And it would have been unthinkable to the "Last Generation" several decades earlier. The intervening years had wrought a profound alteration of the American religious scene, a set of changes that cannot be attributed to any one man or group. A variety of forces, including the ecumenical dialogue, had pushed American Protestants onto new terrain where most of the familiar landmarks were missing. Those who still clung to the outlook of the "Last Generation" now began, strangely enough, to feel like aliens and exiles in a foreign land.

c. *"The Liberating Irritant of Secularization."* Another blow to the "Last Generation's" image of the public and its faith had come earlier in the 1960's. The United States Supreme Court in 1962 ruled that the Regents' prayer, a brief and bland invocation for use in New York State classrooms, was unconstitutional.[32] One year later, in the midst of a storm of protest over the Regents' Prayer case, the Court declared that the practice of Bible-reading and the recitation of the Lord's Prayer in the public school were also unconstitutional.[33] Both decisions stirred up a tumultuous controversy that is still alive in some parts of the country.

The theologians returned a split verdict on the Court's work. The first response of a minority was to deplore these decisions as another evidence of the triumph of "secularism." "The Supreme Court," Bishop James A. Pike said after the Regents' Prayer ruling, "has just deconsecrated the nation."[34] The effect of the decision was the establishment of a state religion "of secularism."[35] There were some Protestants and a fair number of older Catholics who reached the same conclusion.[36] But the majority of the theologians, especially the younger ones, were not overly impressed by this accusation. The charge of "secularism" had been used so often and so carelessly during the 1940's and 1950's[37] that it had begun to lose its bite.

That was only part of the story. There was also a "generational gap" in the making. If the "Last Generation" fought "secularism" as the enemy of the American public, the group of theologians who rose to prominence in the Kennedy years accepted "secularization" as a newfound ally. "Our task," wrote Harvey Cox, "should be to nourish the secularization process, to prevent it from hardening into a rigid world-view. . . . Furthermore, we should be constantly on the look-out for movements which attempt to thwart and reverse the liberating irritant of secularization."[38] The work of the Court seemed to be a superb illustration of the "liberating irritant of secularization" at work. Where else in America during the early 1960's could one have found a better example of liberation from a dead past? The secular theologians cheerfully affirmed what Bishop Pike at that time deplored. In their view the nation had been "deconsecrated" for some time; the Court was simply removing the last vestiges of an outmoded public piety.

By the end of the decade there were only a few major theologians left who would quarrel seriously with the Court's action. Indeed, the current tendency is to accept those decisions as symbolic of a cleft in history. The years of 1962 and 1963, it is often said, mark another turning point in the American experience, the end of one period and the beginning of another. No matter how the present era is described—whether it is defined as "post-Christian or "post-religious"—the felt reality is usually the same: the past is gone. The thrust of secularization has pushed America beyond the point of no return.

In this "post" time most Protestant theologians have exhibited a curious ambivalence toward the past. On the one hand, they warn against the dangers of nostalgia—the temptation, for example, to attempt retreat to the privileges of an earlier day when Protestants were the creators of the public's faith. The cultic acts of Bible-reading and prayers are gone, once and for all. And if perchance the school's study of religion takes on the "devotional" flavor of those acts, then the worst suspicion of its critics will be confirmed.[39] In short, we must be free from the past.

For the most part, however, the theologians appear to be captives of that past. At least their comments about religion and education do not venture much beyond a strident "no" to the practices of a bygone era. The character of "post" thinking on this topic has been *critical* rather than *formative*. This type of theological reflection was relevant as long as there was any force powerful and significant enough to criticize. The "no" lived off the power of the prior "yes." But when the power of those earlier affirmations faded—as is surely true in the case of the "Last Generation's" vision of the American public—then the currently fashionable "no" loses its power and meaning. It becomes, instead, a cry of impotence by those who now feel stranded in an interim.

III. The Public and Its Problems

John Dewey, the last great philosopher of the "public," spoke wistfully about the seeming "eclipse of the public."[40] "If a public exists, it is surely as uncertain about its own whereabouts as philosophers since Hume have been about the residence and make-up of the self."[41] This observation about life in the 1920's applies equally well today. Though contemporary man speaks constantly of the public, he is seldom able to be precise concerning its whereabouts. There are some thinkers who would gladly ban the notion itself from discourse and thought. But I doubt that such radical surgery will ever work for very long. The notion of the public reflects something deeper—an ineradicable, unavoidable reality. In this essay I have traced the eclipse of *a* public (and its spokesmen, the "Last Generation") but the public remains. If Christian theologians hope to speak a formative word on the topic of religion and education, they will have to wrestle once again with this root mystery.

The challenge of that task is manifold. By way of conclusion, let me suggest two examples. The first is the enduring controversy over state aid to church-sponsored schools. For all of the recent gains in ecumenical understanding, there are still significant, unresolved differences over this matter. The center of the problem has shifted from the old question—Should aid be granted at all?—to a new query—What constraints should govern the flow of governmental funds to the nonpublic schools? Of course there is no single, uniform answer, one that will fit every situation. Doubtless some observers will continue to insist upon the "child benefit" theory. My own guess is that this interpretation will grow increasingly strained as it is stretched to meet a multitude of emerging complexities. In its place will come a different legal doctrine. For want of a better term, it might be called the theory of "public benefit," i.e., the government can direct aid to the nonpublic school if it performs a public function. If that is the shape of the future, then Americans of all persuasions will face novel and disturbing questions. When does a school meet its public responsibility? Can a nonpublic school be, in fact, the public's school? These are some of the issues facing America in the days ahead. Will theologians have anything to say?

Second, the problem of the public's faith is still very much with us, even as we reject every extant version of that faith. This is a difficult admission to make, especially after a numbing exposure to the obituaries of civil religion[42] that have appeared in the last decade.

But I think these necrological accounts are premature. There is still life in some of the concerns that moved the "Last Generation" to its affirmations. Ironically, it was the chief celebrant of "secular city," Harvey Cox, who several years ago hinted at a renewal of an old agenda:

> We do not want to elevate values to a religious status, nor do we want to substitute for traditional religions some synthetic religion such as Americanism. Still, we realize that when we rely as a society on the values which safeguard pluralism but do not nurture the symbolic affirmations in which they are anchored we have no evidence that the values themselves will continue to flourish. Our commitments to pluralism and to secular education thus seem in some measure contradictory.[43]

Can these commitments be reconciled? How can a nation achieve civic unity at a time when its crisis is not pluralism, but *caste*?[44] These are the questions of the interim—and indeed, the future. For if, as John Dewey wrote years ago, the "philosophers since Hume" have been searching for the self, so will responsible men in the decades ahead continue the ancient quest for an understanding of the public.

NOTES

1. Peter F. Drucker uses the phrase "'post' something else" in a slightly different context in his book *Landmarks of Tomorrow* (Harper & Row, Publishers, Inc., 1959), p. x.

2. Daniel Bell, in Herman F. Kahn and Anthony J. Wiener, *The Year 2000* (The Macmillan Company, 1967), p. xxvii.

3. Charles Clayton Morrison, *Can Protestantism Win America?* (Harper & Brothers, 1948), p. 1.

4. Luther A. Weigle, "Public Education and Religion," *Religious Education*, Vol. XXXV, No. 2 (April–June, 1940), p. 70.

5. William Clayton Bower, *Church and State in Education* (The University of Chicago Press, 1944), p. 17.

6. W. S. Fleming, *God in Our Public Schools* (The National Reform Association, 1942), pp. 44–45.

7. Weigle, "Public Education and Religion," *loc. cit.*, p. 74.

8. *Ibid.*

9. *Ibid.*, p. 70.

10. Cited by Nevin C. Harner, "A Protestant Educator's View," in F. Ernest Johnson (ed.), *American Education and Religion* (The Institute for Religious and Social Studies, 1952), p. 88. Italics supplied. See also p. 12 in the same volume.

11. Cited by Sidney E. Mead, "The 'Nation with the Soul of a Church,'" *Church History*, Vol. XXXVI, No. 3 (Sept., 1967), p. 262.

12. For example, Luther A. Weigle attempted to locate the public faith in the core of beliefs held in common by the religious majority. See Weigle, "Public Education and Religion," *loc. cit.*, p. 71. His resolution of the problem satisfied no one—except, perhaps, a few like-minded Protestants.

13. The advocates of this position built their case upon an appeal to the majority opinions in two Supreme Court cases: *Cochran* v. *Board of Education* (1930) and *Everson* v. *Board of Education* (1947).

14. Johnson was chairman of the committee that produced the statement, *The Relation of Religion to Public Education* (American Council on Education Studies, Series I, Reports of Committees and Conferences, Vol. XI, No. 26 [April, 1947]).

15. Norman Podhoretz, *Making It* (Random House, Inc., 1967), p. 49.

16. *Moral and Spiritual Values in the Public Schools* (Educational Policies Commission, National Educational Association and the American Association of School Administrators, 1951).

17. Cited by William Lee Miller, "The Fight Over America's Fourth 'R'," *The Reporter*, Vol. XIV, No. 6 (March 22, 1956), p. 20.

18. "Moral and Spiritual Values and the Schools," *The New York Post*, Nov. 13, 1955, p. 4M.

19. *Ibid.*

20. William Lee Miller, "The Fight Over America's Fourth 'R'," *loc. cit.*, p. 24.

21. *Ibid.*, pp. 23–24.

22. *Ibid.*, p. 22.

23. John Courtney Murray, S.J., *We Hold These Truths: Catholic Reflections on the American Proposition* (Sheed & Ward, Inc., 1960), p. 144.

24. John Cogley (ed.), *Religion in America: Original Essays on Religion in a Free Society* (Meridian Books, Inc., 1958), p. 7.

25. Will Herberg, "Religion, Democracy and Public Education," in Cogley (ed.), *op. cit.*, pp. 125–126.

26. James Hastings Nichols, "Religion and Education in a Free Society," in Cogley (ed.), *op. cit.*, pp. 162–163.

27. "The Church and the Public Schools: A Statement of the Official Position of the Presbyterian Church in the United States of America

Adopted by the 169th General Assembly," *Social Progress*, Vol. XLVII, No. 11 (July, 1957), pp. 19–20.

28. John C. Bennett, *Christians and the State* (Charles Scribner's Sons, 1958), p. 248.

29. *Ibid.*

30. Bennett said, "It might be possible to persuade Catholics in some communities to substitute such part-time parochial schools for full-time parochial schools with advantages to the community" (*ibid.*, p. 243).

31. Cited in "New Opportunity for Education," *Christianity and Crisis*, Vol. XXV, No. 3 (March 8, 1965), p. 31.

32. *Engel v. Vitale*, 370 U.S. 421 (1962).

33. *Abington School District* v. *Schempp* and *Murray* v. *Curlett*, 374 U.S. 203 (1963).

34. *The New York Times*, July 14, 1962, p. 9.

35. *Ibid.*

36. For a fair cross section of opinion of the court's decisions, see "Symposium: Religion in the Public Schools," *Religious Education*, Vol. LIX, No. 6 (Nov.–Dec., 1964), pp. 443 ff.

37. Earlier in the 1950's Edwin E. Aubrey had tried to warn against the indiscriminate employment of this term—but to little avail. See Edwin E. Aubrey, *Secularism a Myth* (Harper & Brothers, 1954), pp. 11, 17 ff.

38. Harvey Cox, *The Secular City* (The Macmillan Company, 1965), p. 36. In his reference to a "hardening world-view," Cox was alluding to the distinction between secularism and secularization. This distinction enabled the theologians of the 1960's to be more sophisticated in their analysis than were the members of the "Last Generation." Martin Marty, for instance, made good sense when he wrote: "A neutral secularity . . . may state that it is legally necessary in a modern pluralistic state *not* to permit prayers in public schools. The deadening corollary may be the logical deduction that the God once prayed to is silent or dead. But actually the practice of the state is not to pass this judgment; it makes no comment on God's existence or activity but only on the legality of imposing a spiritual climate on all school children." (Martin E. Marty, *Varieties of Unbelief*, p. 146; Holt, Rinehart and Winston, Inc., 1964).

39. The alert, non-Christian critic has a right to be skeptical. The option of teaching about religion has caught the fancy of large numbers of Protestant and Catholic churchmen across the country. For instance, local and state councils of churches have focused upon the advocacy of this plan as one of their "public" services. Why this interest? some critics ask. The conventional response: our true concern is for knowledge, not faith, religious literacy rather than civil irreligion. Sometimes there is a disingenuous quality about these protestations of freedom from bias

and self-interest. Why is this form of knowledge so significant? What educational rationale supports the claim that the subject of religion is more significant than, let us say, the study of "black history" or the investigation of America's difficulties at home and abroad? These are difficult questions to answer in any convincing way. The churchmen must disavow ecclesiastical self-concern; they cannot appeal to the old rationale that the education of the public depends upon this sort of instruction. Moreover, there is no clear-cut educational reason why teaching about religion is any more important than many other worthy subjects of study. In the absence of a compelling response to these queries, a critic may understandably wonder out loud if the current preoccupation with the study of religion is not, in fact, a covert effort on the part of certain groups to gain special treatment.

For an excellent account of a Jewish perspective on these issues, see Eugene B. Borowitz, "Judaism and the Secular State," in Theodore R. Sizer (ed.), *Religion and Public Education* (Houghton Mifflin Company, 1967), pp. 277–283.

40. John Dewey, *The Public and Its Problems* (Henry Holt & Company, Inc., 1927), pp. 110 ff.

41. *Ibid.*, p. 117.

42. In recent years several interpreters have returned to the theme of "civil religion." The work of Robert N. Bellah is of particular interest here. See Robert N. Bellah, "Civil Religion in America," *Daedalus*, Vol. XCVI, No. 1 (Winter, 1967), pp. 1–21. Bellah's vision of the public's faith is to be distinguished from the "nationalistic" or "idolatrous" forms of civil religion as criticized by Will Herberg.

43. Harvey Cox, "The Relationship Between Religion and Education," in Sizer (ed.), *op. cit.*, p. 100.

44. The harsh, intractable reality of the division of America into white and black castes should not be confused with the "softer" religious differences so often praised in the usual celebration of American pluralism.

❖ ❖ ❖ *James Alfred Martin, Jr., has focused his career on the role of religion in higher education. After graduation from Wake Forest College he completed his M.A. at Duke University and his Ph.D. at Columbia University. His major teaching posts have been as Professor of Religion at Amherst College (1946–1960), Danforth Professor of Religion in Higher Education, Union Theological Seminary (1960–1967), and Professor of Religion, Columbia University. He is chairman of the Department of Religion at Columbia and serves as Adjunct Professor of the Philosophy of Religion at Union Seminary. He is past president of the Society for Religion in Higher Education. Among his books are* Fact, Fiction, and Faith *(1960) and* The New Dialogue Between Philosophy and Theology *(1966).*

The important but always complex interrelationships between religion and higher education are even more problematic in a time when both are being subjected to sweeping changes. Professor Martin explores the dimensions of these transformations.

9

JERUSALEM
AND ATHENS
IN TRANSITION

❖ ❖ ❖ *J. Alfred Martin, Jr.*

Gოდ IS DEAD." "The university must be destroyed." Each of these
assertions has been heard in our time. The first has come
from some theologians committed to Christian faith. The second
has come from some students and others committed to higher education. At first glance the slogans might seem unrelated—for God and
the university are not necessarily inseparable. But at second glance
these slogans are similar. Both are used with a variety of meanings.
Both express preliminary negation as prelude to, and prerequisite
for, subsequent constructive affirmation. They are motivated by
hope, and by serious concern for authenticity. One expresses concern
for a theology relevant to the demands of modern thought; the other,
for higher education relevant to modern society.

The "God question" and the "university question," therefore, may
be more closely related, even in these modern secularized and negative forms, than we first suppose. While most theologians have taken
a critical view of the "death of God" movement, many have realized
that it symbolizes the centrality of the "God question" for current
theological discussion. While most educators have feared the demand to destroy the university, many have said that the recent un-
rest on campuses reveals a genuine need for radical reappraisal and
restructuring of programs of higher education. Thus, while Jerusalem and Athens may not lose their identity in the secular city, both
are clearly in transition and the relation between them is changing.

The citizens of Jerusalem and the citizens of Athens are both
aware of new complexity. In Jerusalem, theology has lost its self-
confidence; in Athens, reason has lost its assumption of omnipo-

tence. Cultural change has confounded, but also encouraged, both. Some would say that it is no longer fruitful to generalize about either theology or higher education, or about the relationships between them. Others would say that, while reflection about higher education may well, and increasingly does, go on without any reference to theological concerns or dimensions, no one who still takes theology seriously can avoid careful appraisal of the relations of theology to the multiple factors and issues encompassed in the structures, foci, and procedures of higher education. It is clear that there are no neat causal relations between theological movements and trends in higher education. It may be helpful, nevertheless, to trace briefly some major developments in theology since World War II; some emerging problems and movements in higher education in this period; and some attempts by theologians to relate theological conviction to educational policy. In the light of this review, we may discern some next steps for theology in relation to higher education in the immediate future.

The dominant theology of Western Protestantism during and immediately after World War II was the Theology of Crisis. While this theology expressed a number of central convictions, its dominant theme was an emphasis on divine transcendence. As political and intellectual goals formed by the Enlightenment and liberalism fell prey to political forces of unsuspected demonic character, and to intellectual critiques stemming from radically different assumptions, theologians sought anchorage if not refuge in a reality alleged to transcend political and intellectual relativities. This reality, it was said, is the source of judgment on cultural idolatries, and the source of salvation within, if not from, these idolatries. Theology was understood to be systematic reflection on this transcendence as set forth in the Bible and celebrated in the life of the church. It was thought that theology thus secured could provide the basis for incisive comment on all human enterprises not thus secured.

Not many theologians on the Continent could go as far as Karl Barth in systematically working out the grounds for and implications of alleged theological autonomy, but most saw their task as responding to the challenge posed by him. In Britain and the United States few could follow Barth all the way, but many could sympathize with his criticism of previous theological accommodations to culture and of the dubious grounds of liberal optimism. For a variety of reasons a new note of realism appeared in the work of such men as Reinhold Niebuhr and John Bennett, and "Christian realism" provided the framework for trenchant social analyses applauded by "secularists" and theologians alike. Such theology seemed to have a relevant word for an era of social turmoil and war.

The social categories of conflict, however, proved inadequate for orientation in a world of peace or cold war. Postwar theological reflection probed more intensively the problems of individual existence and meaning, and various forms of existentialist thought were appropriated for theological articulation. The traditional sources of authority were demythologized, and the whole idea of theological "system" became increasingly suspect. Common cause was found with others who were seeking and affirming individual meaning, and were expressing conviction about individual meaning in a variety of new social allegiances. Finally, in the recent past, the search for theological authenticity in the causes of social justice, revolutionary or evolutionary, has led many to a theological stance at least superficially similar to the social liberalism of the prewar era. John Bennett remarked, at the conclusion of a lecture by a contemporary young theologian marked by social passion and hopeful optimism, "I increasingly have the feeling that this is where I came in!"

After World War II there was extensive analysis of the failure of prewar university structures and programs to prevent global debacle. Attention was focused first on the nature and role of university education in the defeated Axis powers, and part of the blame for Axis aggression was placed at the doors of universities. The vaunted aloofness of German scholarship and scholars from political and social stresses and movements was said to have turned an illusory neutrality into an abandonment of responsibility. Scientific objectivity had been unable to withstand the pressures of political fanaticism. Restriction of university education to an elite had deprived the masses of appropriate critical judgment. Emphasis on "pure" scholarship had led to sterility in the humanities and morally vulnerable research and technology in the sciences. In Japan, the imperial universities which had emerged from the imperial reforms of the late nineteenth and early twentieth centuries had linked educational endeavor to nationalistic aims and placed scholarship at the disposal of demagoguery.

Similar, if less drastic, analyses claimed the attention of British and American educators. In Britain, the dominance of the Oxford and Cambridge patterns of residential colleges for the education of an elite was challenged, but at the same time the utilitarian aims associated with the newer "red brick" institutions were severely questioned. Robert Hutchins and others in the United States denounced the "service station" model for mass university education, and programs committed to a more classical curriculum and purpose were undertaken. There was widespread interest in "general education" of a cross-disciplinary character, to provide ground and direction for increasing specialization in inquiry and more responsible and critical participation in the processes of social change. Modified "Great Books" courses appeared in many revised curricula, and natural and social scientists sought ways to make their disciplines integral parts of a humanistic enterprise. Emphasis on an ordered educational experience replaced the "free elective" emphasis of the prewar era.

All these movements were soon affected by the necessity to expand the resources of higher education for a rapidly expanding university population. The technical demands of postwar reconstruction and economic development further accentuated the technological orientation of many institutions of higher learning. The military-industrial demands of the cold war, and of the Korean and Vietnam conflicts, increasingly determined the directions of university research. Emphasis on liberal general education was eclipsed in practice by the predominantly practical concerns of students and supporting agencies.

While state universities in America, and new universities in Britain, sought to meet increasing demands for higher education, the largest relative increase in numbers of people involved in some form of higher education was in the so-called "developing" countries. Russia was committed to widely available education for scientific, economic, and cultural development before the war; after the war, university systems in countries of "the Soviet bloc" were reformed along ideological lines to spur economic and political change. Similar developments were launched in China after the Marxist takeover there, until internal divisions over ideology and policy seriously threatened all educational work. Inherited systems of higher education in former colonial cultures of Asia and Africa proved inadequate to the needs of economic growth. The British system dominant in India had been designed to train an elite group of Indian civil servants. Its emphasis on the Western humanities seriously limited its relevance to postwar needs for economic planning and reform in an independent country with its own significant cultural heritage.

The confluence of these theological and educational trends was marked by new efforts toward systematic consideration of the relation of theology to higher education. In Britain and America the work of such men as Sir Walter Moberly,[1] Arnold Nash,[2] John Coleman,[3] and Alexander Miller[4] indicated a new awareness of the significance of the university for the church, and of theology for critical appraisal of university structures and programs. The history of the relation of theology to university movements was reexamined and reappraised by these men, and by historians such as E. Harris Harbison[5] and Jaroslav Pelikan.[6] There was renewed appreciation of the extent to which seminal theological movements have been products of university study and debate. At the same time, the traditional insistence on the relative autonomy of *Studium, Imperium,* and *Sacerdotum* was underscored in the work of church historians such as George Williams.[7] A new era of extensive discussion of the relation of theology to higher education was launched.

In this discussion, some of the theological themes noted above were expressed in views of the character of higher education. The emphasis on divine transcendence, and on the role of finite vision and rationalized self-interest in all affairs of men, led to trenchant criticism of claims for purely neutral objectivity in scholarship. It was asserted in many quarters that naïveté concerning the possibilities of objectivity had led many educators to espouse unexamined goals actually grounded in a liberal, humanistic world view. Much of the discussion about the relevance of insights from Christian theology to a more critically mature academic enterprise centered on the role of "presuppositions" in inquiry. The selection of fields for scholarly attention, the choice of methods for examining these fields, and the relation of inquiry to social goals all were said to rest on basic starting points, "givens," or matters taken for granted (or taken as granted). Some used the term "faith" to indicate the implicit or explicit assumptions of inquiry and its goals. There was much discussion of "conflicting faith principles" in scholarly endeavor, and a call to make explicit the assumptions underlying varying views of education.

Analyses of this sort were one factor in the development in the postwar decade of a number of programs of theological and religious studies in colleges and universities. In many instances the rationale for these was—in addition to the general cultural significance of theological and ecclesiastical phenomena—the view that Christian faith should receive a "fair hearing" as a "live option" among available world views. Courses of study were adapted from theological seminary curricula. The fact of religious pluralism was recognized, especially in some state universities, by attempting to provide "equal coverage" for Catholic, Protestant, and Jewish traditions, as expounded by men committed to these traditions.

This theological self-consciousness was reflected also in the structures and programs of extracurricular religious activities. Campus ministers and student religious groups turned with new interest to theological study, and to an awareness of the interrelations of study, work, and worship in the life of the Christian scholar. The vocation of the Christian student was widely discussed, and the university as a forum for Christian witness was freshly examined. Groups of "lay scholars" and "Life and Work" communities committed to theological and devotional discipline appeared in many quarters. At the same time, Christian faculty members interested in the "theological renaissance" devoted increased attention to theological appraisal of their vocation. The Faculty Christian Fellowship was formed in the United States, while similar groups came into being around the world, under the auspices of the World Student Christian Federation. A quarterly, *The Christian Scholar,* was founded as a medium for discussion of theological and interdisciplinary concerns, and a series of monographs expressing views of the relation of theological insights to the work of various academic disciplines appeared.

At the same time there was reexamination of the rationale for and purposes of church-supported higher education. Associations of church-related colleges were formed, and some new church-related colleges with theologically grounded experimental curricula were established. Avowedly evangelical purposes, however, were abjured. The case for the Christian college was usually made in terms of assuring a "fair hearing" for the Christian faith among other options, and in terms of concern for "the whole student" in a community made sensitive to human needs by Christian conviction. More recently an extensive study of the character and resources of, and future prospects for, church-related colleges in the United States has precipitated additional informed discussion.[8]

In developing countries such as India, Christian educators are now seeking to specify the distinctive contributions Christian colleges can make to the educational needs and resources of their cultures. It is widely agreed that there is no need for church-related institutions that merely duplicate, with varying effectiveness, the work of state-supported and other institutions. Discussion of these issues is increasingly ecumenical and cross-cultural in orientation, though it must be noted that in cultures where Christians are a very small minority of the population there is a lingering "ghetto psychology" in some considerations of educational programs and goals.

Theological education itself—that is, education for the professional ministries of the church and for theological scholarship under church auspices—showed new vitality in the first postwar decades. There was a significant increase in enrollments in theological seminaries, and some increase in numbers of candidates for the ministry. Many able young men and women, grappling with the problems of identity and commitment in the postwar world, were attracted by the insights exhibited in the "theological renaissance" to engage in theological study, without clear commitment to church vocations. For many, the work of theologians such as Barth, Brunner, and Tillich and the social insights of Christian realists such as John Bennett and Reinhold Niebuhr were stimulating and suggestive. There was also a new wave of interest in the Biblical foundations of Christian thought, and in the "Biblical theology" prominent in theological discussion.

The concern for exploring the relation of theology to other disciplines, noted above, carried over into the seminaries. It was marked by the establishment of a number of chairs and programs of the "Religion and, or in—" or "Theology and—" variety: "Religion and: Literature . . . Science . . . Psychology . . . Drama . . ."; "Religion in . . . Higher Education"; "Theology and the Arts . . . Society . . . Culture." It was said by some that theological seminaries must become, in effect, "theological universities," where the theological foundations and implications of all academic disciplines are explored and articulated. A variety of programs with a variety of rationales have functioned under these various rubrics. Some of them have expressed a concern for "relevance"; others have stressed the importance of "thinking theologically about . . ." (usually the "whole problem of . . . ," which may mean a complex of unsorted problems).

The concern for "relevance," and for a theology shaped by and responsive to the needs of society, was also expressed in the development of a number of programs designed to immerse students of theology in the frontier problems of social change and psychological understanding. "Clinical training" programs in mental and other hospitals, or in industrial and agricultural enterprises, increasingly became standard elements of theological education. New and imaginative approaches to ministry in the inner city claimed the interest and allegiance of increasing numbers of able and sensitive students.

At the same time, the validity and relevance of many traditional forms of "parish ministry" were seriously questioned, and decreasing numbers of students elected to "go into parish work." As a result, some institutions sought to devise more imaginative and challenging field education programs involving students in a variety of parish situations, with trained leadership coordinating the field experience with the more traditional "academics" of the seminary. Theological education, in brief, steadily developed a concern for "the world": for more intelligent understanding of social forces and institutions, and for more imaginative and innovative work on the frontiers of social change. This movement "from the cloister to the world" has now come to the point where the validity of the cloister itself is radically questioned.

The questioning has been most insistent if not strident in the work of the so-called "radical theologians." They have said that a major reason for the previous isolation of the cloister from the world, or for unproductive relations between the two, has been the perpetuation in modern theology of untenable ideas of transcendence. The popular slogan for expressing this conviction has been the "death of God." Those who have proclaimed the divine demise have had in mind many things, but in any case, many would say that the view of radical transcendence associated with Barth means in effect a dispensable transcendence. Scientific consciousness, psychological maturity, and cultural "coming of age" render irrelevant all previous formulations of divine transcendence, according to the radical theologians. Thus a major assumption of much postwar theological reflection on higher education has been radically challenged.

Yet denial of previous articulations of transcendence has not led all contemporary theologians to dispense entirely with the category. The situation was nicely expressed in a *New York Times* headline in the spring of 1968 that affirmed: "Death of God Gives Way to Theology of Hope." At the heart of all religion, it is said, is some reference to that which "is not . . . as other things are . . . or is no longer . . . or is not yet." In many quarters at the present time it is said that the "other" of Christian allegiance and devotion, the "unseen," is the not-yet-seen. It is the *future* which is transcendent. An influential expression of this theme is Jürgen Moltmann's *Theology of Hope*,[9] with echoes in the Roman Catholic Leslie Dewart's *The Future of Belief*.[10] It is affirmed that resurrection and eschatology, rather than Fall and justification should be at the center of theological discussion. The Biblical vision of history is of history always on the move, toward Messianic fulfillment. The church is always the "exodus church." Christianity affirms that the future belongs to the crucified-risen Christ, and Christian action must be predicated on that affirmation. Openness to the possibilities of radically new structures in the present, which may lead to an otherwise unattainable future, must replace the cautious liberalism of Christian realism. Hopeful belief is itself an important factor in the processes of social change.

There are many problems in these recent expressions of the locus of Christian belief in "the future." There is the question of empirical base: the empirical base in previous historical events, including Biblical events (the "crucified-risen Christ"), and the empirical grounds for hope discernible in actual social processes at present. Moltmann seems evasive regarding the former, apart from renewed appeal to an existential sense of dissatisfaction, longing and not-yetness—or, more radically, appeal to a sociology of knowledge which would make the "givenness" of the resurrection the controlling "datum" in arriving at criteria of historical possibility. Dewart, Harvey Cox, Richard Shaull, and others who in varying ways and on varying grounds would accent the future as a basis of radical criticism of and change from the present might seem to Christian realists to be insufficiently aware of the need for careful examination of the actual structures of the present, and for careful development of viable procedures for social change.

Other theologians have found a more viable basis for hope, leading to creative innovation, in the evolutionary processes of reality, both nonhuman and human. Pierre Teilhard de Chardin—though his vision of an evolving history about to achieve a new level of "hominisation" is subject to scientific, philosophical, and theological criticism signals a new interest in and appropriation of the theme of evolution. At the same time a growing number of theologians, including Daniel Day Williams, Schubert Ogden, and John Cobb, find in the process philosophy of Alfred North Whitehead a vision of organic cosmic development which points to empirical substance for Christian hope without Utopian pretensions and which affirms the immanence of God in the world, and of the world in God, without abandoning an affirmation of divine transcendence.

No theological system or outlook dominates current discussion. Central to current discussion is the question whether a theological *system,* with systematic implications for higher learning or anything else, is any longer possible. Some radical theologians say that theology must henceforth be piecemeal and impressionistic. Perhaps so. If so, theology may eventually disappear. Others are saying that what is now emerging is a new "Christian humanism." Perhaps so. If so, what is to be distinctively Christian about it?

While radical theologians have posed problems for theology by proclaiming the death of God, radical educators have demanded the "death" of existing university structures as a necessary first step toward the creation of a system of higher education more worthy of man and relevant to the modern age. Those who are calling most insistently for radical change in university life are the students, with support from many younger and a few older faculty, some innovative administrators, and a variety of off-campus social critics. The student revolt in the universities seems thus far to be either nonideological or expressive of such various and shifting ideologies that it tends to be unsystematic and nonprogrammatic. What protesting students are saying is that they do not like the *status quo;* they find it inhumane and uninspiring. Why they find it so, and what might make the situation otherwise, they either find it hard to say, or say in so many different ways that others find it hard to know what they are talking about.

Specific targets of university protest vary from country to country. In China they reflect internal party strife. In Japan they reflect political criticism coupled with frustration over the high selectivity and competitiveness of Japanese university admissions systems. In India students tend to demand more leniency in application of educational standards, rather than basic reform of university training designed to make it both more rigorous and more relevant to indigenous problems of social development. In Eastern Europe they demand more freedom and flexibility in the various expressions of Marxist political organization. In Western Europe they demand more adequate facilities, more attention to individual development, and a greater role for students in determining and implementing university affairs. There and in Britain they ask also for more imaginative and relevant curricula and examination procedures. In the United States they call for greater sensitivity of universities to problems of social justice, greater student power in university affairs, freedom in social conduct, and more challenging and relevant curricula and teaching procedures.

It is natural that many who have been influenced by or are exponents of radical theology should identify themselves with the causes of radical student protest. A volume written by campus ministers related to Columbia University, in a year of traumatic student protest there, is entitled *Never Trust a God Over 30*.[11] Many who theologize professionally about higher education today emphasize the values of a richer and less inhibited "humanity" as the goal demanded by the gospel for university experience. Student religious leaders and groups move from picket lines in behalf of racial justice and world peace to picket lines in behalf of university reform or revolution. The eschatological vision of a future just society focuses on a future new university. In both, it is affirmed, individuals should be free to realize their distinctive worth through a variety of life-styles. The Kingdom of God should come in Athens as well as in Jerusalem.

Reflection on these theological themes involves little of the systematic study of the larger tradition of Christian theology which was associated with the postwar theological renaissance. Celebration of the faith tends to be innovative, experimental, and open to new materials and media. If personal disciplines are undertaken, they are purely voluntary and individualistic. The common concerns so far transcend traditional ecclesiastical divisions that most of the structures of "ecumenism" seem outmoded and irrelevant. There is a new interest in philosophical, psychological, and aesthetic expressions of Eastern religious traditions, and in the charismatic phenomena of left-wing and sectarian movements in Christianity.

On the curricular level there is a lively concern to relate classroom studies to the problems of society, and to bridge the gap between the on-campus and the off-campus experiences of socially concerned and culturally aware students. The ancient educational insight into the relation of interest to "readiness" in learning is being reaffirmed, and the role of the university as social critic and reformer as well as supplier of socially needed knowledge and skills is once again stressed.

What is the interplay between contemporary ferment in theology and the ferment in the university? Do they reinforce each other, or work at cross-purposes? Can they be constructively related or do they herald the dawn of new division? How does the loss (or redefinition) of transcendence in theology relate to the ferment in the universities in which there is uncertainty as to how the present inadequacies may be overcome?

A new *humanism* may be emerging from both current theological debate and current discussion of the purposes and processes of higher education. Perhaps the theologians of hope, who have tried to preserve Christian nuances in this new humanism by insisting on the "transcendence of the future," will conclude that there is a more viable philosophical base for their vision in a naturalistic humanism than in a pseudo-transcendent eschatology. The authority of the transcendent to which they appeal may be the authority of the ideal, but an ideal whose roots are in nature, including human nature and its imaginative capacities. In such a framework the call for a genuinely open future, in which the issues are not settled, but in which intelligent and courageous human action obedient to the authority of the ideal as ideal may largely determine the outcome, may be heard with new sympathy.

Likewise, a new realism may emerge in the university. There seems to be movement on the part of some of its members away from trust in easy answers to the university's ills. It remains to be seen whether increased student power will bring increased student responsibility and wisdom in dealing with the detailed work of academic governance, support, and operation. The current wave of enthusiasm for university reform may result in greater understanding of the many factors that constitute the university tradition, and of the delicate and difficult task of bringing a variety of legitimate academic interest groups into constructive harmony. In this process, the insights of Christian realism into the polar dangers of anarchy and tyranny, and into the deceptive self-righteousness of total allegiance to limited causes, may once again prove relevant.

The new humanism that may be emerging from theology and the new realism that may be emerging in the university could work together to probe the rich experience of cultural traditions. Though contemporary society may be radically different in both its perils and its possibilities from all previous societies, some aspirations and achievements of the human spirit are of perennial significance. A theology that has freed itself from bondage to descriptions of transcendence in the particularistic modes of one tradition can share in the purposes of a university that seeks to explore the complex variety of cultural heritage and cultural aims in all branches of learning.

No curriculum designed to explore such an extensive set of concerns could leave out either natural science, social science, or the humanities. The "general education" movement was correct in affirming this, and much of the appropriate demand by students for more relevant and humane education may be met by renewed and more imaginative attention to the goals, if not the previous structures, of the "general education" movement. It should be clear by now that these goals must be pursued with full awareness of varieties of cultural heritage and cultural aims. The world of the university is increasingly in fact what it has long been in theory: the world of universal culture.

These reflections are relevant to consideration of the rationale for and role of the study of religion in universities. Insistence on the study of Christian theology alongside other religious "options" in a "free marketplace of ideas" must be qualified and amended by more appropriate academic reasons for the study of any subject matter. Religious ideas, practices, and institutions are cultural facts. A university can be neither informer nor critic of society when it does not examine religious phenomena in their integrity, employing all appropriate methods and clusters of methods of study. The purpose of university study of religion is not to exhibit "faith options" for life commitments but to achieve critical understanding of the data of religions in all their complex relations to ideational and social structures. It will thus employ historical, psychological, philosophical, sociological, and other approaches to understanding. Its priorities will not be those of religious communities as such, though it will seek to understand religious communities and their priorities. Universities must not shirk the task of objective study of religion because of either the complexity of the enterprise or the sensitivity of religious communities. The methodological problems involved in the delineation and understanding of religious phenomena reflect a wide range of methodological issues that are crucial to the definition and practice of inquiry as such. The freedom of universities to examine critically all cultural phenomena, including religious phenomena, is integral to the validity and health of the university enterprise. Thus it may be said that what a university does about the study of religion is one of the most significant indications of the extent of its autonomy and of the sophistication of its methodological awareness.

When the study of religion is appropriately grounded in academically sound principles, it will be seen that Christian theology is indeed a significant and appropriate object of study. It is significant as the ideational expression of a specific religious tradition responding to specific intellectual and cultural forces. Most religious traditions have developed systems of intellectual articulation as well as ethical views and cultic practices. These articulations must be understood if the traditions are to be understood. To the extent that religious traditions have influenced cultures, the cultures cannot be understood without careful and critical attention to all aspects of the relevant religious traditions, including the intellectual aspect. When Christian theology is seen in the context of the history of religions and of ideas it is seen to be a distinctive product of the merging of certain Semitic and Hellenistic motifs and thought habits. The concept of "theology" as understood by Christians is indigenous to this one religious tradition, with some corollaries in the Jewish and Islamic traditions. University study of theology, in the context of the history, philosophy, and sociology of religions, may help both to place Christian theology in the spectrum of systems of religious ideas and to underscore its significance and its integrity. The university's rationale for attending to it is the same as its rationale for attending to ideational expressions of Buddhism, Hinduism, and other religious movements. Methods of approach should be basically the same in each case, with adaptations responsive to the character of the phenomena themselves.

In the immediate postwar discussion of the relation of Christian theology to higher education, the phrase "Let the university be the university" was widely used. Perhaps we are just now coming to some understanding of what this means with respect to university study of religion, including theology, in relation to church-sponsored study of theology for the purpose not only of understanding but also of celebrating and commending the Christian faith. The latter is the task of the theological seminary as an educational agency, and ideally the "intellectual conscience," of the church. Theological education of and for the church must be based on a better understanding of the relation of the work of the university to the work of the seminary, and on a greater sense of the importance, dignity, and autonomy of the enterprise of theological education as such. Theological education must, in brief, become appropriately and self-consciously *professional*. This affirmation is made quite apart from the theological issues of ordination or discussion of roles of clergy and laity in the work of the church. The work of the church requires individuals who are critically informed of the sources of the Christian tradition and its distinctive ideational and institutional expressions through the ages; critically informed of the structures and problems of contemporary society in relation to the faith and work of the church; and carefully nurtured in the devotional roots of Christian formation and commitment. Theological education must reflect the convergence of theory and practice, and of knowledge and concern, which characterizes other forms of professional education in appropriately varying ways.

Because theological education requires access to the study of religious phenomena in all their complexity, and to the study of structures of contemporary society in all their complexity, it should be carried on in liaison with the university study of religion and should draw on university resources in all relevant areas. It would be both presumptuous and inexpedient for theological seminaries to attempt duplication of university programs for study of religion, just as it would be academically inappropriate for universities to model their curricula of religious studies on the curricula of theological seminaries. A working partnership is needed, in which each respects the integrity, and appropriately utilizes the resources, of the other.

Can universities appropriately utilize the resources of theological seminaries in their programs for study of religion? Yes, they not only can but should, so long as they fully understand what they are doing, and why. Christian theology, we have said, is the intellectual expression of a specific community of faith, and it is complexly and distinctively related to the life of worship and social witness in that community. The study of theology in a professional school, committed by design to examination of all aspects of the life and ongoing witness of the religious community which has nurtured and is responsible to its theological formulations, may exhibit an academically appropriate sense of the complexity of the relation of theory to practice, and of commitment to understanding, in any religious tradition. Ideally, university study of all religious traditions should take full account of the concrete relations of intellectual expressions to the cultic life and social practice of each tradition *in situ*. Increasingly, "field studies" involving anthropological and sociological as well as philosophical and historical approaches to living religious traditions in their most vital cultural settings are being developed. There are good reasons for universities in America to utilize the resources of Christian theological seminaries for some forms of understanding of the intellectual expressions of the Christian tradition—and to utilize the resources of Jewish and other professional theological schools for comparable understanding of other traditions; and for universities in India to draw on Hindu-sponsored study in practice, and universities in Japan to draw on Buddhist-sponsored study in practice.

The basic purposes of universities and the basic purposes of professional schools of theology are complementary and compatible, but they are not the same. Recognition of the differences—hard-won and painfully arrived at in many instances—need not lead to the disparagement by either of the work of the other, or to aloofness springing from hypersensitivity to past mistakes and present perils of misunderstanding and confusion of aims. But, if each should respect the other, neither should attempt to imitate the other or feel that its distinctive task is inherently superior or inferior to that of the other.

A mature theological view of higher education today will not simply "let the university be the university." It will *insist* on the university's being the university and will affirm the integrity of the university's pluralistic means of pursuing knowledge in all areas. There must be less self-conscious (if not presumptuous) "theologizing" about "presuppositions" and "value commitments," and more rigorous and productive participation in the work of the university itself. Those who are concerned for relevant theology and effective theological education must keep abreast of developments in the university world and the growing edges of discussion of higher education. This may best be accomplished in the future through participation in and utilization of university-sponsored reflection on higher education, through departments and institutes, rather than through seminary-based programs of study of "Religion in Higher Education." Jerusalem does not need to become Athens in order to gain the respect of Athenians, and Athens need not fear or disdain the mission of Jerusalem in the enterprise of thought and action needed for a more humane society. Both Jerusalem and Athens are clearly in transition; indeed, both are besieged in many quarters by those who would do them in. If they can make common cause based on mutual understanding and respect—and if they can see that Moscow and Benares and Kyoto are also significantly involved in their common venture, they may contribute constructively to the urgent task of new delineation and achievement of human good.

NOTES

1. Walter H. Moberly, *The Crisis in the University* (The Macmillan Company, 1950).

2. Arnold S. Nash, *The University and the Modern World* (The Macmillan Company, 1943).

3. A. John Coleman, *The Task of the Christian in the University* (Association Press, 1947).

4. Alexander Miller, *Faith and Learning* (Association Press, 1960).

5. E. Harris Harbison, *The Christian Scholar in the Age of the Reformation* (Charles Scribner's Sons, 1956).

6. Jaroslav Pelikan, *The Christian Intellectual* (Harper & Row, Publishers, Inc., 1966).

7. George H. Williams, *The Theological Idea of the University* (The Commission on Higher Education, National Council of the Churches of Christ, 1958).

8. Danforth Foundation, Commission on Church Colleges and Universities, *Church-sponsored Higher Education in the United States* (American Council on Education, 1966).

9. Jürgen Moltmann, *The Theology of Hope,* tr. by James W. Leitch (Harper & Row, Publishers, Inc., 1967).

10. Leslie Dewart, *The Future of Belief: Theism in a World Come of Age* (Herder & Herder, Inc., 1966).

11. Albert H. Friedlander (ed.), *Never Trust a God Over 30* (McGraw-Hill Book Company, Inc., 1967).

PART THREE

*The Person and Thought
of John Coleman Bennett*

❖ ❖ ❖ *Reinhold Niebuhr, Charles A. Briggs Graduate Professor Emeritus of Ethics and Theology at Union Theological Seminary, is one of the most provocative thinkers of the twentieth century. Educated at Elmhurst College, Eden Theological Seminary, and Yale Divinity School (B.D., 1914; M.A., 1915), he was pastor at Bethel Evangelical Church in Detroit for thirteen years. From 1928 to his retirement in 1960 he taught at Union Theological Seminary, serving also terms as Dean of the Faculty and as Vice-President. He has engaged in a multitude of religious and social activities that have made his name familiar throughout the world in religious, educational, and political circles. Among his many books are* Moral Man and Immoral Society *(1932);* The Nature and Destiny of Man *(the Gifford Lectures, published in two volumes, 1941 and 1943);* The Structure of Nations and Empires *(1959), the outgrowth of a year with the Institute of Advanced Studies at Princeton. Dr. Niebuhr has been honored in many ways: eighteen honorary doctorates and, in 1964, the Presidential Medal of Freedom.*

Dr. Niebuhr and Dr. Bennett have been friends and colleagues for many decades; one of their most fruitful partnerships has been on the editorial board of Christianity and Crisis. *In this very personal tribute, Dr. Niebuhr salutes his longtime associate.*

10

JOHN COLEMAN BENNETT:
THEOLOGIAN,
CHURCHMAN,
AND EDUCATOR

✧ ✧ ✧ *Reinhold Niebuhr*

I DESIRE to make my contribution to this *Festschrift* a tribute to John Bennett's achievement as President of Union Seminary. He showed himself as a leader both of the faculty and of the student body of the institution. Among the latter he maintained a high morale during the difficulties of the student antiwar and antidraft demonstrations and the upheaval in Columbia University that resulted in a student strike. In both of these crises, the president of the seminary preserved a high morale and mutual understanding between the students, the faculty, and the board of the seminary. This achievement revealed a high order of statesmanship, involving the special graces of his modesty, his integrity, and his compassion.

John Bennett has also been an ecumenical leader, and here there must be distinguished the earlier ecumenical project of the non-Roman churches, Protestant and Orthodox—and the later more modern and exciting ecumenical enterprise, involving the relations between Christians and Jews, and also between Protestant and Catholic Christians. President Bennett's contribution to the ecumenical movement that culminated in the World Council of Churches is preserved in volumes published in connection with the Conference on Church, Community, and State at Oxford in 1937 and in preparation for the First Assembly of the World Council of Churches in Amsterdam in 1948. His essay in the Oxford volume was entitled "The Causes of Social Evil"; that in the pre-Amsterdam volume on the general theme of the church and the disorder of society was captioned "The Involvement of the Church." In both volumes, Bennett shares the enterprise with such figures of yesterday as Dr. Temple, the Archbishop of Canterbury.

The second chapter in ecumenical leadership began when President Bennett invited the distinguished Jewish theologian, Dr. Abraham Heschel, to be the Fosdick Visiting Professor at Union Seminary. Needless to say, Dr. Heschel captivated not only his classes at Union but also groups of alumni and others all over the country which, as the Fosdick Professor, Dr. Heschel visited in the second semester of the school year. The ecumenical enterprise was advanced farther in the most recent past and present when he arranged an interchange of faculty and students with Fordham University, a Jesuit institution. As an occasional leader of a semester seminar, I can give personal testimony to the creative effect of having classes in which Protestant and Catholic students are present and are free to ask pointed questions about both medieval Catholicism and the Reformation, and in which the differences and similarities of both communities of faith are discussed. In the realms of industrial and racial justice, the Protestant students well may have been surprised by the discovery of a Catholic virtue in these realms of collective morality. One assumes and hopes that Catholic students also, for the first time, may have understood why the Catholic position on birth control is not an agreed moral standard, not only in the Christian churches, but in modern culture generally. The "population explosion" challenges everyone. The high birth rate in nontechnical cultures tends to negate the desperate ambition of these nations to lift their people out of the morass of poverty and undernourishment.

President Bennett's Protestant-Catholic venture in ecumenical partnership now involves a new dimension. There have been negotiations to have the renowned Jesuit Seminary at Woodstock, Maryland, move to New York and establish academic relations with Union and Columbia University. Also, his friendly relations with the Jews have been expressed in the comradeship between Dr. Bennett and Dr. Heschel in the creation of a National Emergency Committee, Clergymen and Laymen Concerned About Vietnam.

While I accept my assignment from the editors to give an analysis of what is regarded as the crowning glory of a distinguished theological career, I cannot forgo the opportunity of recording the history of a precious partnership and friendship in the common field of Christian social ethics and theology. When I came to Union in 1928, Dr. Bennett's predecessor, Dr. Van Dusen, then an instructor there, advised me that a young colleague, John Bennett, was uncommonly endowed with wisdom and common sense; and I would do well to ask his advice on any problem I found difficult. I took Dr. Van Dusen's advice, and thus began a partnership in the seminary, interrupted only by Bennett's terms of service at Auburn Seminary and The Pacific School of Religion. We worked together on the journal *Christianity and Crisis,* of which we became coeditors until my retirement at the twenty-fifth anniversary of the journal. All this time, I followed Dr. Van Dusen's advice. I consulted with Dr. Bennett in all difficult academic and journalistic problems, and I believe that in all these issues we achieved an essential accord.

Many of my distinguished colleagues are dealing in this volume with various aspects of Dr. Bennett's theology and ethics. I therefore must risk competing with them, or perhaps gleaning after the reapers of the harvest, in giving a superficial overall account of our common preoccupation with the social dimension of the Christian faith. This field is commonly, but erroneously, defined as "the Social Gospel." The definition is erroneous because there is only one gospel. This gospel promises forgiveness of our sins, but also enjoins our responsibility for the welfare of the neighbor. In the endless complexities of a technical age the love of the neighbor must be expressed in the "nicely calculated less and more" of justice. The final glory and predicament of this technical age is that it must preserve a precarious nuclear peace by a "balance of terror" between the two great imperial nations of our age.

Dr. Bennett's contribution to the consideration of these insoluble problems, for which we can only venture proximate solutions, is recorded in many volumes, which will be analyzed more adequately by my colleagues. I can report only that he has achieved a consistent approach in which common sense and religious sensitivity are blended. Whether he is writing about "Nuclear Weapons and the Conflict of Conscience," or "Christianity and Communism Today," or "Foreign Policy in Christian Perspective," he consistently tries to formulate the problem in order to avoid the almost universal self-righteousness of the participants, whether informed by the communist utopian creed or by the nostalgic innocence of our own nation. A historian has dubbed the U.S.A. a "Redeemer Nation"; and from Jefferson to Lincoln and Woodrow Wilson, we have regarded our democracy as the only pure democracy, or, in Lincoln's phrase, "The Last Best Hope of Earth." We have not even betrayed scruples in the days of our imperial power that the virtues of our maturity may not be as they were in the days of our youth. Like Solomon of old, we may not be "so tender" when we are no longer "so young."

Whenever President Bennett views the responsibilities and predicaments of our technical collectivism, whether under democratic or communist auspices, he always reveals a cool and balanced view of the issues, whether of justice at home or of peace in a fearful nuclear balance of terror in which the contending parties are assessed with remarkable objectivity. This tendency is most clearly expressed in his volume *Christianity and Communism*. The other creative quality of his religious and social thought is revealed in his steady and unpolemical views both of the realities of our collective life, embodying both interest and power, and of the responsibilities of our individual consciences that must never be obscured even by the perplexing ambiguities of our technical and nuclear age. This quality is most clearly expressed in a volume that he edited entitled *Nuclear Weapons and the Conflict of Conscience*. The reader always is aware of this combination of common sense and religious sensitivity.

As an old man, who in his age regrets the polemical spirit of his youth, I wish I had profited a little earlier by noting the unpolemical genius of my—then young—friend, with whom I maintained a personal, academic, and journalistic partnership without friction for four decades. His unpolemical wisdom accounts for much of his success as a scholar. He always was fair to opinions with which he disagreed. It also explains his remarkable success as seminary president and ecumenical statesman.

❖ ❖ ❖ *Daniel Day Williams, distinguished theologian in his own right, has also made a special place for himself as a theological educator and as an interpreter of the thinking of his contemporaries. After graduating from the University of Denver, he earned an M.A. degree from the University of Chicago, a B.D. from Chicago Theological Seminary, and studied at Union Theological Seminary and Columbia University, which granted him the Ph.D. in 1940. He was ordained to the ministry and served a pastorate in Colorado Springs, he was Dean of the Chapel at Colorado College, and he taught theology at Chicago Theological Seminary and on the Federated Faculties of the University of Chicago before going to Union Seminary as Professor of Systematic Theology. Since 1959 he has occupied the Roosevelt chair. He has frequently held distinguished lectureships and has been active in the work of churches, learned societies, and civic affairs. In 1954–1955 Professor Williams was associated with H. Richard Niebuhr and James Gustafson in a survey of theological education in the United States and Canada and collaborated with them in volumes reporting that study. Among his books are* What Present-Day Theologians Are Thinking *(1952, rev. 1959, 1967) and* The Spirit and the Forms of Love *(1968).*

His study of John Bennett's theology draws attention to the wide range of theological insight in the thought of one who is especially known for his ethical and social teaching, but who has maintained a broad and balanced theological perspective.

11

THE THEOLOGY
OF
JOHN COLEMAN BENNETT

❖ ❖ ❖ *Daniel Day Williams*

I BELIEVE that this tendency to neglect the Jesus of history threatens Christianity with a great perversion. . . . Let another generation arise that is brought up from the beginning on this theology that neglects Jesus and we may expect to find Christianity a cult of salvation which has forgotten that, though salvation may not be earned by works, the most important test of its presence is ethical."
—*John C. Bennett,* Christian Realism[1]

John Bennett clearly belongs in the tradition of liberal Protestant Christianity, especially its American version. But his breadth of thought has earned him respect from a wide segment of theological opinion, both Protestant and Catholic. He has woven elements of empiricism, prophetic moral concern, freedom for doctrinal diversity, and attention to the practical-activistic side of Christian experience into a synthesis. He is one of those liberals who worked out a mature theological position chastened by disillusionment with overly optimistic views of history. He responded appreciatively, yet critically, to Karl Barth, and was led by Reinhold Niebuhr into a more realistic doctrine of man and of political ethics. His liberalism came face to face with the issues in the Christian response to Fascism and World War II, and was worked out in a broad ecumenical context as embodied in the Life and Work program of the World Council of Churches. In a personal essay written in 1939, reviewing how his mind had moved in a decade, John Bennett called himself "A Changed Liberal but Still a Liberal."[2]

Even though Bennett's theology may be described as "liberal," it must be interpreted in the context of a very complex theological position. The roots of Bennett's theology lie in the Biblical tradition of evangelical Christianity with its classic doctrines of justification by faith and salvation by grace. Bennett stands in the center of this tradition. Far from being parochially identified with one phase of American theological thought, he is both evangelical and catholic in the broadest sense of these two terms. He represents the mainstream of the Christian tradition, responding to the pressing demands of the twentieth century for concrete historical responsibility and adequate ethical and intellectual guidance.

Bennett's theologizing is done largely by dealing with concrete ethical issues. He exemplifies the concern to keep doctrinal reflection in a constant interplay with practical human action. But he does this within the tradition of the whole church, past and present. He draws upon a very wide range of Christian thinkers. He himself mentions those who have had the greatest influence upon him: Reinhold Niebuhr, Baron von Hügel, F. R. Tennant, Nicholas Berdyaev, and John Oman.[3]

If we are to understand John Bennett's theology, we must find the meaning of his kind of liberalism within the stance he takes in relation to the Biblical faith and tradition. In the autobiographical paper just mentioned he says that

> if we are to be empirical, we must realize that the experiment does not begin with us, that the surest way in which to arrive at religious truth is to select the company of people whose religious tradition has stood up in fair weather and foul through a long history, and which on the whole satisfies our own minds and speaks to the events of our own time. In other words, there is a loose sense in which the quest for religious truth should be regarded as the quest for the true church.[4]

Thus, an understanding of Bennett's judgment on theological issues and social ethical concerns involves attention to those themes in the tradition which enabled him to relate his thought to many theological positions and still preserve an integrity of outlook.

I. THEOLOGICAL METHOD

To characterize John Bennett's theological method requires critical attention to its controlling spirit. The key to Bennett's theology

is the principle of *balance*. In all his statements of theological
method, in his specific judgments on Christian doctrines, and in his
study of ethical principles, Bennett practices a way of finding the
truth through preserving intellectual and spiritual balance. He is
perhaps of all contemporary theologians the one least likely to plump
for some extreme or one-sided methodological principle or doctrinal
position. The concern for the true church and its message is for him
a concern for spiritual and moral sanity in which the truth is found
through weighing conflicting claims and in keeping open to every
view that may throw some light upon the final mysteries. This is not
a search for the "middle of the road." Often the truth as Bennett
sees it cuts strongly against certain positions. But he refuses to be
tied down to any one rigid type of doctrine about God or man.

  Balance in this sense might seem to be a characterological rather
than a theological principle. Certainly John Bennett has an extraordinarily sane, commonsense, and just temperament—as anyone
who has worked with him and discussed issues with him will testify.
But the concern for *balance* is for him not something temperamental.
It is a theological principle derived from what Christianity is and
what its message says about God and man. The search for balance in
the statements of truth is required, according to Bennett, by the
nature of man and his situation before God.

  Man is the sinner, estranged from God, subject to the perversities
of pride and idolatry; at the same time he is the good creature, made
in God's image, bearing the possibilities of creative life. A true perspective on man, therefore, must preserve the two sides of the human
situation. Man is God's good creation who spoils his own goodness
and can be restored to a sane and whole existence only through
God's gracious giving of what man needs. Bennett's theology is without qualification a theology of grace. Only grace can restore man to
his rightful mind. But grace restores that for which man is essentially created and which he never wholly loses. Therefore, the task of
theology is to keep its proper balance in setting forth its understanding of sin and salvation. It must refuse to let go, either of the
positive doctrine of man's goodness or of the realistic appraisal of
the depth, universality, and destructiveness of sin and evil.

  Bennett appeals directly to the principle of balance as he sets forth
his theological position. In *Christian Realism*, he says that the Christian conception of human nature "transcends our optimistic and
pessimistic fashions of thought. It makes full room for the truth in
both. . . . Christian thinkers are usually unable to do justice to the

balanced character of the Christian view." One-sided emphases have to be corrected. This can be done only from within the perspective of faith, for "what is not seen when you approach Christianity from the outside is that at the heart of it there is a balanced view of human life that constantly corrects one-sided aberrations. It should save us from sentimentalism and cynicism alike."[5]

Again he appeals to the principle of balance in his picture of Jesus, maintaining that "we discover in Jesus a balance of qualities which is not only unique but also supreme in its claim upon our reverence."[6] He finds a balance between love and aggressiveness in Jesus' dealing with evil and says that Jesus avoided the extremes of ascetic religion and of this-worldly religion, of Hinduism and Communism.[7]

Bennett observes that theology itself can lose balance, since its formulation "invariably becomes more one-sided than the realities of life."[8] Bennett is never antitheological, but there is a strong element in his attitude toward theology itself of the prophetic and humanistic protest against doctrinal systems that falsify or distort the realities of life. He goes behind theological system to appeal to the teaching of Jesus. This teaching gives balance, that is, sanity and authenticity, to the Christian understanding of life. Thus, "the teachings of Jesus do not take the place of theology, but they are an extremely important test of theological systems."[9]

The protest against deductive theology derives from the same demand to return to that deeper truth in the central Biblical experience which cannot be captured in theological formulas. "Just as the theologian who likes to recite his formulas concerning salvation by grace needs to be reminded that Jesus used as his test of discipleship responsiveness to human need, so the Church needs to have the words of Jesus sound forth to test every sacred institution: 'the Sabbath was made for man and not man for the Sabbath.' "[10]

This understanding of theology and the principle of balance that it involves is worked out in a theological method. What is revelation, how is it related to reason, what are the tests of truth in theology? John Bennett passed through several stages in seeking answers to these questions.

Until about 1930, Bennett held the view that a system of Christian doctrine was possible that would have two layers, a philosophical foundation and a superstructure of the special insight derived from the Christian revelation. This is the classic Thomistic pattern, and Bennett found it worked out in an even more satisfactory form

in William Temple's thought. He accepted Temple's view that the two layers were not quite so independent as the Thomists made them, since religious experience is part of the data for a philosophical doctrine of God. Bennett says that his confidence in this move toward a systematic integration of philosophy and theology was shaken by the realization that "in fact, the faith which was the core of the superstructure determined the choice of materials for the foundation."[11] Once this insight was gained, he realized he must accept Karl Barth's claim that revelation must bear its own criteria within itself or something else will be put in judgment over faith. He now came to the view that there is a Christian "circle of faith" which defines the perspective in which the Christian thinks, and the theologian must move within that circle. H. Richard Niebuhr's *The Meaning of Revelation,* also strongly influenced by Barth, reinforced this point most decisively for Bennett.[12]

The transition from the early confidence in an objective rational groundwork for theology to a position that stresses the centrality of faith for all Christian thought can be seen in *Social Salvation,* published in 1935. Here Bennett identifies four processes—creation, persuasion, judgment, and healing—as the work of God, but only through faith do we come to see these processes as the work of God. He discusses Henry Nelson Wieman's claim that since God is immanent in these processes, he can be directly discovered in experience. Bennett cannot accept this, and says "I do not speak dogmatically but it may well be true that we cannot know that [God is known in experiences] from the observation of the processes themselves." They might be regarded as just so many historical facts. Bennett holds that Wieman, by identifying the process of progressive integration as God, is "taking a jump of religious insight which is not justified by his theological method." Bennett believes that Wieman is right in making the jump (against John Dewey for example) but this "rightness of the move to God" is not a matter that can be proved from experience. "We can recognize these processes as the work of God *if we already believe in the existence of the Christian God.*"[13]

In *Social Salvation,* Bennett still looks to philosophy for some kind of support for Christian thought against the charge of wish-thinking. Belief in God can be "grounded" in a philosophy of religion such as that of E. W. Lyman or F. R. Tennant because such philosophy is "based upon man's whole experience of reality. It is confirmed by the intuitions of faith which come to those who are not mere spectators but who are loyal participants within the divine processes which we have described."[14]

Bennett seems here to waver between placing some confidence in a philosophical theism resting on general experience and holding the view that the intuitions of faith once given can be confirmed in such a philosophy. In *Christian Realism*, written six years after *Social Salvation*, he explicitly says he is inclined to put less reliance on philosophy[15] and makes this interesting confession concerning the nature of theology:

> To speak about God with any degree of adequacy one must be a poet or prophet or mystic. The prose of the theologian when he speaks of God is abstract and forbidding, but such prose is all that I can command. All our words are derived from experiences that are less than the experience of God for God is utterly unique and incomparable. Some mystics prefer negations when they speak of God but negations are as misleading as faltering attempts to say positively what God is and what God does.[16]

The conception of God in the Hebrew-Christian tradition is "no product of the academic mind. . . . Men came to it as they struggled with the problems of personal and social life, as they faced pain and death and national collapse."[17] It is within this historical process that revelation occurs. The possibility of the divine forgiveness "had gradually dawned upon men through the process of divine revelation and human response that we find in the Bible."[18] Revelation is thus the breaking through of the divine reality and truth into human awareness; but this awareness is of a reality that cannot be comprehended in a system. God is utterly unique and incomparable. Therefore the theologian must sometimes resort to paradox in his attempt to speak of God. For example, Bennett finds paradox necessary in speaking about divine forgiveness. The sinner has no claim upon it, and God is the upholder of the moral order. Yet he forgives.[19]

The necessity of paradox in speaking of God already had appeared in *Social Salvation*. On the one hand, God has a definite character that can be spoken about in analogy with personality, the highest reality we know. Bennett found this theme most profoundly developed by John Oman. On the other hand, God "cannot be judged by [any] human standards" and his nature cannot be "encompassed by any system of theology."[20] Theology must work mostly within the first perspective, but it must not forget the second. Here again is an illustration of balance in theological method.

Bennett rejects any simple identification of God with human rational ideals, or of theological method with a system created according to a formal principle. He gives us, rather, a theology of open-ended reflection upon themes that sound and recur throughout the life of the Christian people as they reflect upon their origins, their history, and their hopes in the ongoing encounter between God and man.

The principle of balance, while it is derived from the stance of the theologian within revelation and is ultimately given its criterion by faith itself, requires that the claim to revelation shall not be arbitrary. Hence, "we must continue to test all that we find in the light of the persistent facts of our experience."[21]

Bennett's theological method provides a broad place for continuing concentration on the evidence provided by experience. This is not a laboratory testing of hypotheses, but a pragmatic and ethical test of religious claims. This comes out clearly as Bennett deals with one of the topics that concerns him most, that is, the nature of evil. It also appears as he discusses the significance of social conditions for Christian judgments about human nature and human behavior. He insists that theological formulations of such themes as the fall, original sin, and human responsibility must be brought into relationship with the empirical analysis of historical reality. For example, Bennett begins his study of *Social Salvation* with two "case studies" on the relation of sin, moral responsibility, and social evil. One case is that of war, and the other is that of economic change. Again, in his contribution to the Oxford Conference volume on *Christian Faith and the Common Life,* Bennett chose to deal with the causes of social evil. He believes that Christians have too often fallen into vagueness and oversimplification in their diagnoses of particular social evils. One source of confusion is the tendency to reduce all evil to one root, sin. Such categories as "the demonic" or "autonomy" can be used as "catch-all explanations." Theologians should do more precise thinking, and this means for the most part more empirical thinking. Most theological discussion has obscured the necessity of a multiple attack on social problems.[22] Bennett also declares that empirical study goes to the roots of the problem of Christian hope:

It is my contention that one safeguard against this premature dogmatic pessimism is to remain longer than theological discussions usually remain within the area of specific social facts, and to seek to discover the roots of the particular social evils which have driven so many of us to this pessimism concerning the total human situation.[28]

We see then how pragmatic moral concern, empirical methods of investigation, and the perspective of faith all merge in Bennett's attack on theological problems.

We must still inquire about the ultimate criterion of truth. If the final determination of the perspective of Christian thought is within revelation received by faith, what are the limits of empirical data in determining our view of the meaning of experience? If we stress experience as giving theological insight, are we committed, after all, only to a natural theology that sets the limits within which revelation will be understood? John Bennett returned to these issues in an important theological paper written in 1955, fourteen years after *Christian Realism,* entitled "Are There Tests of Revelation?" This statement may be taken as the most adequate summing up of his view of the relation of revelation, reason, and experience.

He begins by recognizing the full weight of the position, taken by Barth and articulated in somewhat modified form by H. Richard Niebuhr, that there is a circle of faith defined by the acceptance of the Christian revelation. The norm for faith is given in revelation itself and is understood only within the experience of the community created by the revelation. But while he is willing to begin here, Bennett remains unsatisfied. He wants to find a wider range for Christian thought without losing its decisive and ultimate criterion. He appeals directly to his view of man in developing his methodological solution. He finds a dimension of transcendence in man's very understanding of his relativistic situation. We can enter into more than one circle of faith and thought through imagination. Moreover, there is an interaction between our minds and the points of view taken by others. Bennett discusses this interaction specifically with regard to faith and philosophy and suggests that it may be an acid test of the intellectual adequacy of a religion to be related to philosophies in order to illuminate them and to be illuminated by them while still transcending them.

Bennett seeks, therefore, some objective tests in human experience that can function significantly in dealing with any circle of faith and with the meeting of various faiths with one another. He appeals first to the growing body of tested knowledge, especially scientific knowledge. In addition to taking account of the facts, faith must show that it can enter into significant communication with the scientific and technological outlook. His next test is the fact of death. Here Bennett directs his argument especially against secular faiths such as Communist naturalism which do not have any way of understanding death. Thirdly, there is the many-sided fact of evil. Again he says this challenges the simple optimism of faiths which believe that the altering of certain social or economic conditions will remove all problems. Again, Bennett asserts that there is "a real moral order which can be discerned apart from revelation." And finally, there is the depth of the personal self, before which so many modern philosophies seem baffled.

These facts are "tests of revelation" only in the sense that they may lead to insights that are relevant to the Christian faith. They point toward it, but must also be interpreted and fulfilled by it. Bennett suggests that there are three circles of faith; first, that broad circle which is defined by Paul Tillich as encompassing all who have ultimate concern. A second circle is the theistic faith, with its recognition of the principle of personality as the key to ultimate reality. Thirdly, there is Christian faith. When we ask how these three circles are related Bennett says: "Perhaps what I am saying is no different from the common assertion that *general revelation* rather than *natural theology* is the sounder concept to be used in connection with this belief in God, which has a broader foundation than the Christian revelation."[24]

Here in Bennett's matured view of theological truth we find a balanced articulation of the dimensions of religious truth and their relationship to Christian faith. Bennett has not moved very far from his original program of holding together a philosophical foundation and a theological superstructure; but he has now put the position more guardedly and more subtly. He recognizes the interplay between faith and the ways we interpret experience. He keeps the way open for an approach to Christian truth through aspects of human experience that are available to all. And he holds that all claims to revelation, including the Christian claim, are responsible for integrating faith's assertions with inescapable aspects of human experience.

This method of relating Christian faith to the ethical and religious insight derived from experience outside the Christian circle has important implications for theological ethics. It enables Bennett to keep the Christian imperatives in an open and dialectical relationship with problems of human values and ethical norms without being caught either in a rigid natural law theory, on the one side, or in a dogmatic authoritarianism on the other.

II. GOD AND MAN

In dealing with specific doctrines, we find Bennett concerned with the identification of critical issues rather than with the elaboration of doctrine. The critical question for man is the problem of redemption. How can man find meaning in this tragic existence, especially in the face of the evil in the self? This, he says, is the most acute theoretical problem for theology, and for many it is the chief obstacle to the Christian life.[25] The problem of God is the problem of his Lordship, the moral order in history, and the identification of the saving divine activity. There is the joy mediated by the great and common things of life; but there is also the radical evil in human existence.[26]

It has already been pointed out that Bennett holds there are two sides to human language about God. There are the analogies drawn from experience, especially the personal analogy, but there is also God's transcendent mystery. "He shatters all our human plans, moralities, religions. He cannot be judged by human standards and His ways are beyond prediction."[27] God is not to be characterized as a Christian gentleman. Bennett finds the doctrine of the Trinity a framework in which the tension between God hidden and revealed and God transcendent and immanent can be held. "God the Father transcends human experience more than God the Son or God the Spirit."[28]

The problem of evil involves several issues. These include the origin of evil in the world (those factors which press upon man and lead him to destructive conflict and suffering), and the origin and presence of sin in man with his willful misuse of freedom. Bennett is characteristically concerned that theological statements about evil be kept in relation to the facts of experience. He is critical of the use of the idea of the fall to underline the fact of evil. He says this has some justification but that it leads to "theological fog." He opposes the tendency to revive the concept of the fall in the form of "myth." He believes that when the theologian gives an intelligible explanation of what the myth means, the myth is rendered unnecessary, though it may be useful pedagogically.[29]

On the issue of God's creation of a world with the possibility of evil in it, Bennett says in *Social Salvation* that evil is a "by-product of something which God did will and do."[30] The existence of evil "points to a limitation in the structure of things with which God has had to deal or to a limitation in His own nature."[31] There is really no way out of attributing the source of limitation to God himself. He returns to this problem in *Christian Realism* where he puts these points even more sharply: "God is no self-sufficient absolute whose realm is an eternity that is above the world of time and change, of struggle and suffering."[32] Bennett holds that we cannot admit a complete break between human ideals and God's character.

> To say that God completely transcends our moral standards is to exalt sheer power and to empty the idea of God of the moral content that is taken for granted in the Bible. God as revealed in Christ has a definite character to be understood in terms of goodness that does not transcend completely what men think of as goodness.[33]

Both human freedom and natural evil imply that there are structural limitations in the divine nature. God cannot create a world of moral persons unless they are left free to resist him. He cannot "create a world of persons" unless there is "a slow process of development which inevitably involves hazards and handicaps."[34] As to natural evil, such as the presence of disease germs, Bennett says all answers are speculative. Although much evil can be turned into good, and the cross stands as the supreme disclosure of this transmutation, there is still the evil that does not get so transformed when persons are unable to respond to this persuasive power. Bennett concludes that only "the horizons offered by immortality" suggest the "possibility that evil will finally be overcome by God."[35]

We have been dealing with the general problem of evil in God's world. The most difficult problem is the evil in the self, and especially that aspect of evil which makes the self subject to self centeredness and eventually to sin. Bennett speaks of sin only where there is freedom and explicit responsibility, but he is perplexed by the fact that so much of the structure of life involves great pressures toward sins both of appetite and of pride. Perhaps Bennett's empiricism leads him to seek some experiential explanation for the origin of sin. Here he follows F. R. Tennant's view that the self-centeredness of the infant or "pure little animal" is simply his normal constitution and that this drive for satisfaction is as necessary to future sanity and vigor as it is certain to bring pressure in the direction of a sinful use of freedom. When Bennett considers the question of why so many factors in life, such as inertia, stupidity, and the complexity of human problems, compound the evil consequences of sin, he observes that in the evolution both of the individual and of the race we have a "process of growth from the lowliest beginnings."[36]

Balance is the clue not only to Bennett's dealing with the problem of evil, but also to his view of man. Bennett believes that the Christian faith presents a profound picture of both the grandeur and the misery of the human situation. A somewhat personal remark reveals his unwillingness to be swept off his feet by either side of the mystery: "I cannot fail to be as much impressed by the goodness of people as I am by the evil in them; and even the evil seems more often to be weakness or moral inertia rather than unlimited pretension."[37]

The image of God in man includes man's capacity as a responsible, rational, creative being.[38] His nature includes impulses of generosity and self-giving, and he cannot will to do evil without self-deception. But Bennett never thinks of human goodness as something man achieves by himself. There is common grace as well as the grace that comes through the Christian revelation. Man is dependent upon God for all good, but man has worth.[39]

Bennett recognizes the depth, the universality, and the persistence of sin.[40] He sees man's initial tendency to self-centeredness reinforced by the circumstances of life, and this tendency to egoism becomes the chief root of the evil that enters the world through man. He agrees with Reinhold Niebuhr that the deepest roots of sin lie in the spirit. Pride and self-centeredness corrupt reason and even man's highest loyalties. Religious commitments may be disguised idolatries.

Every realm of life is subject to sinful distortion, but Bennett cautions against misuse of the doctrines of the fall, original sin, and total depravity. They rightly point to the universality of sin, but they must not be used to overwhelm the positive side with the negative. The fall is not a datable event in the past that places a burden of original sin upon man which he can do nothing about. Every man experiences the fall in his own being, and while this is a grim truth, it has the hopeful element that we are always on the threshold of a new freedom. There are degrees of the self-centeredness to which we are bound, and there are degrees both of sin and of ordinary goodness.[41]

A balanced view will keep in mind another polarity in man, the relation between the individual and the community. Bennett deals with this polarity in discussing the social dynamics of contemporary history where we see the tendency to absolutize individualistic theories of economic and political freedom on the one hand, and the tyranny of the new collectives in Fascism and Communism on the other. Christianity, he says, will always reject an extreme individualism. At the heart of the Christian ethic there is objective moral truth, and there is individual responsibility for the other person and for the common life. He points continually to the influence of social conditions on human behavior. The great evils of war, poverty, and economic exploitations are social evils that corrupt and destroy human beings. But in the end there is a sense in which Christian individualism must be given a high place, an individualism that, as Bennett says, is linked to a universalism which makes no distinctions of race or nationality among persons. The prophets defended the rights of individuals against the king. Similarly, Christians are concerned for the "marginal individual," the one in special need of being cared for and cared about.

Bennett develops this theme of Christian individualism in a significant direction by pointing out that the individual is responsible for more than one community. Indeed the individual is the point of intersection of many lines that run through family, vocational group, church, and nation. But God is the Lord of all humanity and must never be identified with the interests of any one group. So Bennett concludes: "It is this fact, that the individual is owned by no human group in spite of his varying degrees of responsibility to all human groups to which he belongs, which is the most distinctive mark of Christian individualism."[42]

With the issue of group loyalty we enter into a central theme of Bennett's theology. He identifies the absolute claims of the nation as one of two chief social evils. Such claims manifest sin at its most destructive level. The rise and fall of nations is a key source of insight into how God deals with human history. Bennett never identifies nationalism itself as evil, however. Honest elements of group love and loyalty belong to the nation. These can be exploited, but they are not in themselves evil. The evil comes when the nation arrogates to itself absolute authority and makes an absolute claim upon the loyalty of the person. "The absolute state with its claim to be the source of truth, the determiner of the purposes of society, and the judge of culture is an enemy of Christ in every age."[43] The claims of each nation to absolute sovereignty produce international anarchy and the intolerable destructiveness of modern war. As the prophets fought a continuing battle against Baalism and declared the judgment of God even upon his elect nation, so the Christian faith asserts the judgment and righteousness of God above every group and nation, including religious communities and churches.

The other major evil is the exploitation of the weak and poor by the powerful.

> The spectacle of a small number of people in every century appropriating because of their military, political or economic power, the chief sources of wealth and leaving the masses without the same access that they take for themselves to the means of health and to the opportunities to develop the possibilities within them is in the sight of God a great blasphemy.[44]

How then does the Lord of history deal with these offenses to the righteousness of his Kingdom? The first answer Bennett gives is that the judgment of God appears as the working of a moral order in history to bring punishment upon men for their blindness, sin, and arrogance. Here Bennett's ethical concern is directly linked with the theological doctrine of God's wrath and his punishment of evil. Bennett believes that "in the long run evil tends to destroy itself," and he sees in this fact one of God's ways of drawing men to himself.[45] "God . . . draws us and He punishes us."[46] Bennett thinks of the divine action as punishment but he does not assert that God intervenes in specific deeds to punish. God punishes by *not intervening* between our deeds and their consequences.[47] Bennett points to this theme in the teachings of Jesus and remarks that a study of Jesus' teachings shows that the reported sayings about judgment are much more numerous than those which stress the divine mercy.[48]

God has, however, another strategy, that of persuasion, and this culminates in his supreme self-revelation in Jesus. We shall discuss this side of the divine action in connection with Christology, although it should be remembered that Bennett finds elements of the divine mercy and gracious persuasion in all of life, not exclusively within the circle of Christian experience.

III. CHRISTOLOGY

There are two major motifs in Bennett's Christology.[49] The first is the concern to see Jesus as the revelation of God within the context of the whole of God's redemptive action. Jesus appears in a direct line with the great prophets of Israel, restating and sharpening both

the moral demand and the message of mercy. What God did in him
is in continuity with the whole movement of redemption. "The Jesus
of history is the center, but the center is not everything nor would all
else be meaningless without it."[50] This involves the possibility of
rational and empirical confirmation of the decision of faith that
responds to God's action in Jesus.[51]

The other motif is Bennett's insistence upon the significance of
the historical Jesus, his teachings, his deeds, and his personal quality
as the very center and criterion of the revelation. Perhaps here Bennett stands more against the stream of modern theologizing than at
any other point. In *Social Salvation,* he wrote, "Whatever our
Christological theory may be it is most dangerous to cut it loose from
the content of the personality and teachings of Jesus."[52] In *Christian
Realism,* he devotes an entire section to the issue created by skepticism about the possibility of knowledge of the historical Jesus. He
argues against this skepticism partly on the ground of historical
scholarship. "We may not know enough to write a biography of
Jesus, but we know enough about him to draw his portrait."[53] He
also analyzes Pauline and Johannine theology and argues em-
phatically that their understanding of God's redemptive action in
history is unintelligible apart from the actual man Jesus who lived
and taught and died and who was known in the resurrection. He
appeals also to the wisdom of the teaching of Jesus that is deeper
than any theological system. Jesus "saw most clearly the structure of
life."[54] While theologians may lose interest in the teaching of Jesus,
others discover its psychological soundness. Jesus' teaching never
permits us to forget the ethical demands of the gospel. Finally, Bennett appeals to the necessity for a norm to test the various experiences of the contemporary Christ. We all read our perspectives into
the picture of Jesus; so we must have that picture itself for the
correction of our subjectivity.

The extent to which Bennett preserves the liberal ethical protest
against "Christologies" as an escape from the prophetic side of the
gospel is manifest in this paragraph:

The "infant" at Christmas and the "victim" on Good Friday and
the risen Lord of Easter may easily become a part of the sanction
of whatever we may seek to preserve in the Church or in the
nation. But the Christ who says: "Love your enemies"; "Beware
of covetousness"; "Ye cannot serve God and mammon"; the Christ
who overturns the tables of the moneychangers; the Christ who

excoriates the proud and the self-righteous—that Christ is always needed to disturb what we seek to preserve in the Church and in the nation.[55]

It is interesting that Bennett here equates the misuse of the theme of atonement with sanctification of the established order and that he sees Jesus' teaching as protest against that order.

While the central emphases in Bennett's Christology are upon the continuity of God's redemptive action through all Biblical history, and the prophetic moral significance of the historical Jesus, Bennett holds to the centrality of the person and work of Christ in the movement of redemption. That work is God's unique work in him. While Bennett does not involve himself in the intricacies of the traditional Christological formulations, he makes clear his sympathies with the Antiochean type of Christology in which the union in the incarnation was a union of wills. "God drew this human will to Himself by the same means by which He draws others to Himself," but Jesus was fit to be the founder of the new religion.[56] His role in the historical process was at the center of the movement of redemption, and other Christlikeness usually depends directly upon him.

The resurrection has a central place in God's work in Christ. The resurrection means victory over death and the inauguration of the Christian movement. Its precise nature we probably can never know. Bennett says that the great moments in the history of the human spirit may be accompanied by extraordinary visions and states of consciousness. The visions of the resurrected Jesus are best understood as the means by which the earliest Christians became convinced of the continuing presence of the living Christ as the Spirit in the work that Jesus had begun.[57]

IV. REDEMPTION AND SALVATION

John Bennett uses the terms "salvation" and "redemption" synonymously. They are the Christian words for the total process of God's activity for the fulfillment of his Kingdom. Redemption has both an individual and a social dimension, and the two aspects are inseparable. We see this when we understand the social nature of human personality and the significance of personal responsibility that belongs to man.[58]

When we say Jesus Christ is the redeemer we acknowledge his

saving work in two senses. The first is expressed in the moral influence theory of the atonement in which Jesus is the center of the divine persuasion toward repentance and a new life. But, second, Jesus is objectively the center of God's creation of a new environment for humanity. Bennett follows Schleiermacher here in stressing the mediation of the Savior's influence through the church, a theme that becomes fundamental for Bennett's doctrine of the church.

In creating a new environment, the influence of Jesus preserves the essential ethical dimension. It gives the summons of the life of love for the neighbor, and of self-giving for the Kingdom of God. But none of this would represent salvation in Bennett's view if it were not set in the context of God's grace, which is forgiveness, mercy, and the offer of new possibilities to the sinner. Bennett's theology has its own unique quality, and we are near its center when we see the rigor of his insistence on the strenuousness of the ethical demand for man and society at the same time we see his recognition that salvation depends upon the divine forgiveness and the grace that seeks the lost. He says that

> Christianity has at its heart the promise that no matter how much we may become involved in disobedience, no matter how long our record of deliberate wrong-doing, it is always possible, if we are honest with ourselves and with God, to turn and be changed. We can begin again without a crippling sense of guilt and without thinking of ourselves as under condemnation.[59]

In this fusion of ethical imperative and the transethical resource of grace Bennett's theology exemplifies the balanced view of life that he believes Christian faith offers.

The movement toward blessedness is a process. The way is humility before God, gratitude for his grace, and the life of strenuous moral action in a history that presents difficult and sometimes tragic choices. The nature of the Christian hope for fulfillment of the movement of redemption is a critical problem, and Bennett gives considerable attention to it.

V. ESCHATOLOGY

The history of the mid-twentieth century raises critical problems for man's hopes, even the hope of survival on this planet. Bennett's theology has broken entirely with the optimistic notions of the elimination of evil that dominated some theological liberalism. For example, he poses sharp questions to a meliorism that claims to make everything right by making everything better. He asks, "What of the suffering along the way?" We have good reason to think that all future progress will be precarious.[60] In a world where "nothing is too terrible to be possible" what sustains moral effort?[61] Bennett rejects the notion that there must be assurance of perfection on earth. The basis of moral responsibility is obedience to the will of God.[62] But even a modest hope would give added incentive. His empirical temper leads him to a careful assessment of the dilemmas of historical movements toward peace and justice. He points out processes that represent the work of God but he also recognizes the ultimate questions posed by cosmic destruction, by the mystery of death itself, and by the ambiguities of human achievements. In a significant passage in *Social Salvation* he stresses the intrinsic worth of present experience. There is eternal meaning in the present, and there is a wisdom in accepting the immediate joys and tasks of life as containing the worth of life.[63] Amid all the grounds for hope that we find in the experience of God's use of tragedy and catastrophe for the good, of which the cross is the supreme symbol, there still is a mystery beyond which we cannot go. We have already noted that Bennett sees in immortality the symbol of the final hope that God will overcome all evil; but he does not make the worth of life or of Christian obedience depend upon any particular version of life beyond death.

VI. THE CHURCH

One aspect of the chastening of an earlier theological liberalism is the renewed concern with the distinctive character of the church and its centrality in the work of redemption. Bennett confesses that he had little interest in the church before 1930; but his later writing shows a sharp emphasis upon its unique character and its essential task.[64]

When Bennett speaks of the church he usually means the churches, the empirical communities in history that bear the name Christian. To be sure the true church is not coterminous with specific local churches. We can fix no sharp boundaries for the true church. But real communities of people in history mediate Christ to the world. "The local units are Churches in so far as they point beyond themselves to the Bible, to Christ, to the universal Church, to the Kingdom of God."[65]

Here again, while Bennett's ethical concern leads him to stress the moral failures of the church, he sees the ultimate significance of the church in terms that transcend ethical activism. The church's worship is an end in itself. The fellowship in the church is not just a means to world peace or social justice. It is a partial embodiment of the Kingdom of God.[66]

Bennett believes that the actual church is both our hope for salvation and its own worst enemy. The most important single fact about the church is that it points beyond itself to a judgment that it must accept upon its own life. "It may make Christ over into its own image, but Christ will in time shatter that image."[67] Bennett gives some attention to the structure of the church, but he is not too concerned with most of the issues about traditional polities and orders that have agitated so much of the ecumenical discussion. Rather, he emphasizes the need to perfect the "democratic character of any united Church."[68] He is for church union but "unity in itself is no panacea."[69]

Practical issues about the church's ministry and structure are largely focused for Bennett in the question of the freedom of the church, freedom for its prophetic message to be preached and heard and for social action to represent the pioneering edge of social concern. The social action of the church should not be limited to the majority opinion of its members at some point in time. Bennett takes a rather high view of the significance of an ordained ministry, which he justifies in part on practical, ethical grounds. In concrete situations, such as the struggle for racial justice, there are times when the ministry bears a special testimony to the character of the church against social forces that have allowed something other than the mind of Christ to be expressed.[70] Of course this does not mean that on some issues and at some times laymen may not be ethically far ahead of the clergy. Bennett places special emphasis upon the stand taken by minorities and remnants within the churches which have again created a basis for new life in the church in the twentieth century both in Europe and in Asia through the witness of martyrdom. There must be a realistic appraisal of the church as a sociological institution that reflects all the ambiguities of the common life; but it still bears its distinctive witness, teaches the gospel that condemns its own compromises, and nourishes the life of devotion that usually, through minorities, renews and redirects the life of the whole.[71]

We cannot leave this topic without mentioning John Bennett's statesmanlike appraisal of the Roman Catholic Church and its place in American society, his leadership in furthering Protestant-Catholic relations at many levels, and the validation of some of his earlier hopes for ecumenical understanding through the progressive movement in the Roman Catholic Church that is leading to a new and fruitful relationship between Catholics and Protestants almost everywhere.[72]

VII. The Christian Imperative and Ethical Principles

Theology and ethics are never separated for John Bennett. He has given his greatest attention in later years to specific ethical issues. He has done major work in interpreting Christian ethics in relation to social policy and in analyzing the relationship of Christianity and the state. To this latter theme he devoted his book *Christians and the State,* published in 1958.

Even an introduction to the content of Bennett's ethical thought would require a chapter as extensive as the present one. It is only possible here to point to the direction that his theology has taken in ethics, and to show how the foundations that he has laid down in his interpretation of Christian faith become resources for his thought on the complex ethical issues of human existence and Christian responsibility.

His ethical thought involves four polarities that are rooted in his theology:

First, there is the absoluteness of the Christian imperative to love, but understood in such a way as to give freedom for empirical appraisal of alternatives for moral decision and action. The positive ethical content of the Christian faith is the command to love even to the price of the cross. This means to seek the good of all God's children. Love so understood involves the special concern for the weak, the sinful, the needy. This gives to the Christian a basis of moral action that is distinctive in its quality. It is deeper than any rationalism. But to seek the good of the neighbor it is required to understand him and his situation as it really is in the full complexity of the history of groups and nations. Hence, Christian ethics must take account not only of what is good, but of what is possible, not only of men who are motivated by love, but of the fact that most men, Christians included, are motivated profoundly by self-interest. A responsible ethic is not a doctrinaire set of answers to every moral problem, but a search for the concrete guidance that is pertinent to the needs of the whole human family.[73]

Second, Bennett's doctrine of God's transcendence and immanence allows him, on the one hand, to assert the reality of a moral order in the world that cannot be violated with impunity and, on the other, to keep a freedom in articulating the demands of the moral order that avoids the absolutizing of a natural law which fixes detailed prescriptions too rigidly. The moral order is God's requirement for men to live together in peace and justice; but that order is related to the dynamic activity of man in history. Needs change, human responses change. A natural law theory which proposes to assert the eternal structure of human rights and ethical obligations is always in danger of being too rigidly conditioned by the culture in which it is expressed. Bennett believes that there is much in the tradition of natural law that a Christian ethic must maintain. There is a moral law that stands above even the law of the state. He seeks to articulate the main principles of that law, its requirement for universal justice, for free criticism, for equal opportunity for every new life. But Bennett rejects the view that specific systems of rights and duties can always be prescribed on the basis of natural law. Further, he points out that while the natural law is supposed to be accessible to human reason, the reinforcement of moral tradition, and in the case of the Christian, of Biblical faith, makes a very great difference in how "natural law" is understood and applied.[74]

Bennett's doctrine of a moral order prompts him to find ways in which Christians can join with others in seeking the common good even though Christians have presuppositions that transcend other ethical systems. Christianity does not have a monopoly on insight into social justice. Indeed Christians have had to learn many things from secular moralists and their protests. God's will for man can be partially discerned in all human experience even by those who do not recognize God's presence.[75]

Because he believes in an objective aspect of moral structures, Bennett is also able to steer between a pure situationism in ethics and a reliance on formal principles as adequate for moral guidance. Some of the situationists, emphasizing the context alone, have taken Bennett's affirmation of middle axioms as a residue of legalism that should be eliminated. But while the term "middle axioms" may seem to put too much stress on the finality of principles, Bennett's concern is that the achievement of broad social ethical policy as well as authentic personal decision requires some articulation of principles in the light of which action is taken. Middle axioms such as those which prescribe the right to education, health care, due process, and freedom of speech for every person do not tell us what to do in every concrete case; but Bennett holds that without such guidelines a viable ethic is impossible.[76]

In the third place, Bennett recognizes the absolute judgment of God upon all institutions and thus affirms that Christianity does not sanction one kind of government or social or economic order; and at the same time he can assert principles that lead to relative judgments against some types of social order and government and can affirm the necessity of defending and fulfilling certain kinds of political order. Specifically, this bears upon his analysis of the relationship of Christianity and democracy.

We cannot say, he holds, that there is one form of government that today is best suited for every people. But there are good reasons for supporting an essential democracy as the goal that can guide Christian judgment and action. Bennett gives three specific arguments for the Christian concern with democracy. First, the Christian faith upholds the dignity of all men before God; second, constitutional protections are necessary for the individual and for the minority against the majority; and, finally, universal suffrage provides a necessary check upon the interested power of every controlling group.[77] In a careful analysis of the issues involved in asserting the internal democratic tendency in Christianity, Bennett warns against the conclusion that this means it is the Christian's duty to establish a particular form of democratic institution immediately and everywhere. There are problems in democratic leadership, in economic arrangements, that may result in a too rapid equalizing of power and responsibility.[78] Bennett's critical and balanced view of the problems in the relation of the democratic-capitalist West to the communism of West and East is one area where his ethical and political sensitivity is superbly demonstrated.[79] All of this can be said while the Christian still allows "the democratic impulse to have the last word."[80]

Fourth and finally, Bennett's theology opens the way to a realistic analysis of the possibilities and limits of ethical action and especially of the ambiguities of concrete ethical decisions. Few writers on the problem of war show a more sensitive, humane, and Christian conscience than John Bennett; but he concludes that while absolute pacifism has a vocational significance and an important witness, it cannot be declared to be the only Christian way. In his autobiographical paper he remarks about being continually haunted by the sense that there is no choice in the international sphere that does not appear tragically evil.[81] With the passage of time he came to recognize even more fully such dilemmas as those created by the threat of atomic warfare.[82] The source of ultimate balance for the Christian, however, is not the assurance that there is one right thing to do, but is the call to responsibility and the trust in the working of God over and above the dimness of human insight. In *Social Salvation,* Bennett said, "There is no situation which is so bad that there is not a best thing to be done in it."[83] In later writing it is not clear that Bennett would even say there is always a best thing to be done, but he does say we can act in the light of our judgment as to what should be done, and in that freedom is the only relief there is from the fanaticism of identifying what we do with the will of God. Action within tragic choices can be undertaken in love even though it involves us in consequences, some of which we must recognize as evil, such as destruction in a war supported to resist tyranny. In discussing the ethical problems related to war Bennett disagrees with Reinhold Niebuhr that the perfection of love (agape) implies complete nonresistance. The restraint of evil may be required on the part of those who love, and is not just a concession to a lesser ideal.[84]

Thus the principle of balance that is required by man's situation before God appears within John Bennett's Christian ethics. For him the ethical life of the Christian requires a clarity about the ultimate nature of man's relationship to God with a knowledge of the two sides of God's action as judgment and as persuasion. There is a balance of moral command and outgoing compassion made incarnate in the teaching and life of Jesus and the promise of both moral empowerment and gracious forgiveness for those who walk in humility with God as they seek to do justly and to love mercy. His determination to resist the one-sidedness that besets theology has led John Bennett to an extraordinarily powerful and sensitive uniting of the polarities of Christian thought. Few theologians of our century have done so much to fuse the evangelical sense of grace with a humane and prophetic moral concern for a humanity in trouble. John Bennett has done this with freedom from dogmatism, openness to new insight, and a determination to remain close to experience in all its wonder and tragedy while probing the ultimate mystery of faith.

NOTES

1. John C. Bennett, *Christian Realism* (Charles Scribner's Sons, 1941), p. 124.

2. John C. Bennett, "A Changed Liberal—But Still a Liberal," *The Christian Century*, Vol. LVI, No. 6 (Feb. 8, 1939), pp. 179–181.

3. *Ibid.*, p. 179.

4. *Ibid.*

5. Bennett, *Christian Realism*, pp. 49–50.

6. *Ibid.*, pp. 118–119.

7. John C. Bennett, *Social Salvation: A Religious Approach to the Problems of Social Change* (Charles Scribner's Sons, 1935), p. 71.

8. Bennett, *Christian Realism*, p. 131.

9. *Ibid.*, p. 130.

10. *Ibid.*, p. 131.

11. John C. Bennett, "Are There Tests of Revelation?" *Theology Today*, Vol. XII, No. 1 (April, 1955), p. 68.

12. *Ibid.*, p. 70.

13. Bennett, *Social Salvation*, pp. 212–213. Italics by author.

14. *Ibid.*, p. 213.

15. Bennett, *Christian Realism*, p. 20.

16. *Ibid.*, p. 21.

17. *Ibid.*

18. *Ibid.*, p. 41.

19. *Ibid.*, p. 39.

20. Bennett, *Social Salvation*, pp. 184–185.

21. Bennett, *Christian Realism*, p. 20.

22. John C. Bennett, "The Causes of Social Evil," in *Christian Faith and the Common Life*, ed. by Nils H. Ehrenstrom *et al.*, in Oxford Conference Book, Vol. IV (Willett, Clark & Company, 1938).

23. *Ibid.*, p. 176.

24. Bennett, "Are There Tests of Revelation?" *loc. cit.*, p. 83.

25. Bennett, *Christian Realism*, p. 164.

26. Bennett, *Social Salvation*, p. 174.

27. *Ibid.*, p. 185.

28. *Ibid.*, p. 186.

29. *Ibid.*, pp. 35–36.

30. *Ibid.*, p. 195.

31. *Ibid.*, p. 194.

32. Bennett, *Christian Realism*, p. 31.

33. *Ibid.*, p. 173, n. 5.

34. *Ibid.*, pp. 173–174.

35. *Ibid.*, p. 184.

36. *Ibid.*, pp. 169–172.

37. *Ibid.*, p. 57.

38. *Ibid.*, Ch. 3. Perhaps the most concise statement of Bennett's doctrine of man is in his book *Christians and the State* (Charles Scribner's Sons, 1958), Ch. 5.

39. Bennett, *Christian Realism*, p. 54. Cf. Bennett, *Christians and the State*, p. 55.

40. Bennett, *Christian Realism*, p. 55. Cf. Bennett, *Christians and the State*, pp. 55–56.

41. Bennett, *Christian Realism*, p. 57. Cf. Bennett, *Christians and the State*, p. 55.

42. Bennett, *Christian Realism*, pp. 63–64.

43. Bennett, *Christians and the State*, p. 75.

44. Bennett, *Christian Realism*, pp. 84–85.

45. Bennett, *Social Salvation*, p. 160.

46. Bennett, *Christian Realism*, p. 72. Cf. p. 36.

47. *Ibid.*, p. 34.

48. *Ibid.*, p. 41, n.

49. *Ibid.*, pp. 116–137.

50. *Ibid.*, p. 133.

51. Bennett, "A Changed Liberal—But Still a Liberal," *loc. cit.*, p. 180.

52. Bennett, *Social Salvation*, p. 94.

53. Bennett, *Christian Realism*, p. 127.

54. *Ibid.*, p. 130.

55. *Ibid.*, p. 133.

56. *Ibid.*, p. 135.

57. *Ibid.*, pp. 119–120.

58. This is the theological ground of the imperative to change social institutions as well as individuals. "The individual soul is moulded by social conditions" to a considerable degree. See John C. Bennett, *Christian Ethics and Social Policy* (Charles Scribner's Sons, 1946), Ch. 1. This quotation is from p. 4.

59. Bennett, *Christian Realism*, p. 40.

60. Bennett, *Social Ethics*, p. 12.

61. Bennett, *Christian Realism*, p. 4.

62. *Ibid.*, p. 70.

63. Bennett, *Social Salvation,* pp. 172–177.

64. Bennett, "A Changed Liberal—But Still a Liberal," *loc. cit.,* p. 181.

65. Bennett, *Christian Realism,* p. 142.

66. Bennett, *Christian Ethics and Social Policy,* p. 104.

67. Bennett, *Christian Realism,* p. 143.

68. *Ibid.,* p. 157.

69. *Ibid.,* p. 155.

70. This point was forcefully made in a sermon preached in the Union Seminary Chapel during the early civil rights struggle.

71. Bennett, *Christian Realism,* p. 149.

72. On Roman Catholicism, see Bennett, *Christians and the State, passim;* and esp. Ch. 13 for the doctrine of the church which Bennett holds.

73. Bennett, *Christian Ethics and Social Policy,* Ch. 2.

74. For Bennett's discussion of natural law, see the concluding "Note" in *Christian Ethics and Social Policy* and *Christians and the State,* esp. Ch. 8.

75. Bennett, *Christian Ethics and Social Policy,* pp. 123–124.

76. *Ibid.,* pp. 77–83, 107. For critical discussion of this doctrine, see Paul L. Lehmann, *Ethics in a Christian Context* (Harper & Row, Publishers, Inc., 1963), pp. 148–154, and Edward LeRoy Long, Jr., *A Survey of Christian Ethics* (Oxford University Press, Inc., 1967), pp. 108–110.

77. Bennett, *Christian Ethics and Social Policy,* pp. 83–85.

78. Bennett, *Christians and the State,* Ch. 11.

79. John C. Bennett, *Christianity and Communism Today* (Association Press, 1960).

80. Bennett, *Christians and the State,* p. 162.

81. Bennett, "A Changed Liberal—But Still a Liberal," *loc. cit.,* p. 179.

82. John C. Bennett, *Foreign Policy in Christian Perspective* (Charles Scribner's Sons, 1966): "I am unwilling to give up the general position that no type of power should be allowed to go unchecked, if it is possible to prevent it. The balance of nuclear power has helped to preserve a precarious peace for some years." (p. 110.)

83. Bennett, *Social Salvation,* p. 86.

84. Bennett, *Christian Realism,* p. 97. Cf. the entire passage, Ch. 4.

❖ ❖ ❖ *Robert Fullerton Beach is Librarian and Associate Professor of Union Theological Seminary. He has a B.A. from Wesleyan University and the B.S. and M.S. degrees in library science from Columbia. He has served in the libraries of Yale, Berea, Garrett Biblical Institute, and Union and has taught in the summer sessions of the Columbia University School of Library Service. Active in professional and community affairs, he has published several articles, including "The Library in the Life of the Seminary"* in Union Seminary Quarterly Review *and "Protestant Theological Seminaries and Their Libraries"* in Library Trends.

The compiler who would set forth a listing of John Bennett's writings quickly discovers a staggering wealth of materials—too many writings to be exhaustively included in this presentation. Professor Beach's categorization of the more important groups in Bennett's writings indicates the concerns that shine forth from the written word of the man honored by this volume.

12

A SELECT BIBLIOGRAPHY
OF THE WRITINGS
OF JOHN COLEMAN BENNETT

✧ ✧ ✧ *Compiled by Robert F. Beach*

SINCE PRACTICAL LIMITATIONS have placed restrictions on the categories of publications to be included in this bibliography, it will perhaps be helpful to mention here the groups of materials specifically excluded, by format. Needless to say, certain decisions to exclude materials were difficult, and it is interesting to note that over one hundred items fall within the excluded groups.

Categories excluded are: bibliographies and bibliographical articles, book reviews, excerpted articles already cited in fuller version, group or shared articles (including editorials) by three or more authors, interviews, "Letters to the Editor," mimeographed publications, newspaper articles, official statements (reports of bodies, etc.) of which Dr. Bennett is a signer or cosigner, poetry, translations into foreign languages, undergraduate publications.

Moreover, all regularly written "Columns" in periodicals have been excluded. These include, among others, "Editorial Notes," in *Christianity and Crisis* (1945–1956); "The Philosopher's Chair," in *The Intercollegian and Far Horizons* (1929–1932), "Today," in *The Intercollegian* (1932–1934); and the "President's Column," in *The Tower* (1964 to date).

It is a pleasure to acknowledge the assistance of a number of persons in the development of this bibliography. I am grateful to Miss Barbara Ann Griffis, Ecumenical Librarian at Union, for her help in tracking down and verifying certain entries. Credit is due to Mr. Jay Stillson Judah, Librarian of the Pacific School of Religion, and Rev. Calvin H. Schmitt, Librarian of McCormick Theological Seminary. I want to thank Mrs. John C. Bennett and Miss Mae

Gautier, Dr. Bennett's secretary, for skillful and discreet connivance in the project.

Of greatest assistance were the substantial bibliographies in two recent doctoral dissertations about Dr. Bennett:

> Bucher, Glenn R., *Christian Particularity and Moral Consensus in the Social Ethics of John Coleman Bennett.* Boston University, 1968.
> Smith, David H., *Welfare and Consensus: An Interpretation of the Christian Social Ethics of John Coleman Bennett.* Princeton University, 1967.

I am grateful to Dr. Bucher and Dr. Smith for their willingness to permit me to draw upon their extensive listings.

Finally, special credit is due Mrs. Robert F. Beach for skill and patience in preliminary checking and in typing the final manuscript.

R. F. B.

I. BOOKS AND BROCHURES

(Arranged chronologically. Composite works of which Dr. Bennett is editor are marked with an asterisk.)

Christianity and Class Consciousness. Fellowship Leaflet No. 2. New York, Fellowship of Reconciliation, undated. Later published in *The World Tomorrow*, Vol. XV, No. 2 (Feb., 1932), pp. 47–49.

Social Salvation: A Religious Approach to the Problems of Social Change. Charles Scribner's Sons, 1935; reissued with a new preface, in an edition dated 1946.

Christianity and Our World. Association Press, 1936, Hazen Books on Religion; London: SCM Press, Ltd., 1937.

The Religious Foundation for Social Education and Action. Board of Christian Education, Presbyterian Church in the U.S.A., 1937.

Christianity and Social Salvation. Board of Christian Education, Presbyterian Church in the U.S.A., 1938.

Christian Realism. Charles Scribner's Sons, 1941.

Christian Concerns. A Farewell Sermon Preached at the First Congregational Church of Berkeley, Calif., on June 20, 1943. Printed by the Congregation.

Christian Ethics and Social Policy. The Richard Lectures in the University of Virginia, 1945. Charles Scribner's Sons, 1946.

Man's Disorder and God's Design.* Outline of Preparation for the First General Assembly of the World Council of Churches. London: SCM Press, Ltd., 1947. Also published in slightly altered form as follows: New York, New York, Issued by the American Committee for the World Council of Churches, for the Study Department of the World Council of Churches, Pref. 1946.

Christianity and Communism. Association Press, 1948. Amended and republished as *Christianity and Communism Today,* 1960; further additions in 1962.

Communism and the West: The Basic Conflicts. Church Peace Union, and World Alliance for International Friendship Through Religion, 1953. Also appeared as "The Church Between East and West," *Christian Faith and Social Action, A Symposium,* by John A. Hutchison and others. Charles Scribner's Sons, 1953. Pp. 75–91.

Christian Social Action. London: Lutterworth Press, 1954. A British edition of *Christian Ethics and Social Policy.*

The Christian as Citizen. Association Press, 1955; London: Lutterworth Press, 1955, World Christian Books, No. 5.

Christians and the State. Charles Scribner's Sons, 1958.

Some Presuppositions of the Cold War. "A Supplementary Background Paper, Preparatory Study, Commission II." Fifth World Order Study Conference, Nov. 18–21, 1958, Cleveland, Ohio. 1958.

Theological and Moral Considerations in International Affairs. "A Background Paper, Preparatory Study, Commission I." Fifth World Order Study Conference, Nov. 18-21, 1958, Cleveland, Ohio, 1958. Appeared later as "Ethics and Foreign Policy," *Union Seminary Quarterly Review,* Vol. XIV, No. 2 (Jan., 1959), pp. 3–17.

The Religious Concern with Politics. National Conference of Christians and Jews, 1960.

Nuclear Weapons and the Conflict of Conscience.* Charles Scribner's Sons, 1962. Foreword, pp. 7–12; and "Moral Urgencies in the Nuclear Context," pp. 93–121.

Christian Faith and Political Choice. Toronto: The Ryerson Press, 1963. Contains the first three chapters of *When Christians Make Political Decisions.* The Chancellor Dunning Trust Lectures, delivered at Queen's University in Kingston, Ontario, 1963.

Christian Ethics and the National Conscience. The Sixth Annual

Alexander Graham Bell Lecture on "Man's Communication to Man," Boston, 1964.

Moral Tensions in International Affairs. Council on Religion and International Affairs, 1964.

When Christians Make Political Decisions. Association Press, 1964, A Reflection Book.

*Christian Social Ethics in a Changing World: An Ecumenical Theological Inquiry.** Association Press, 1966; London: SCM Press, Ltd., 1966. Working papers prepared under the sponsorship of the Department on Church and Society, World Council of Churches, for the World Conference on Church and Society, Geneva, 1966. Foreword, pp. 17–19; and Epilogue, pp. 369–381.

Foreign Policy in Christian Perspective. Charles Scribner's Sons, 1966.

II. FOREWORDS: CONTRIBUTIONS TO SYMPOSIA AND OTHER COMPOSITE WORKS

(Arranged chronologically; alphabetically within the year)

"The World Needs the Church," *The Younger Churchmen Look at the Church,* ed. by Ralph H. Read. The Macmillan Company, 1935. Pp. 15–32.

"The Social Interpretation of Christianity," *The Church Through Half a Century: Essays in Honor of William Adams Brown,* ed. by Samuel M. Cavert and Henry P. Van Dusen. Charles Scribner's Sons, 1936. Pp. 111–131.

"The Causes of Social Evil," *Christian Faith and the Common Life,* ed. by Nils H. Ehrenstrom *et al.* Willett, Clark & Company, 1938. Pp. 173–195. London: George Allen & Unwin, Ltd., 1938. The official Oxford Conference Book, Vol. IV.

"Man and Society," *New Directions for Campus Christian Action.* Report of the National Assembly of Student Christian Associations, at Oxford, Ohio, Dec. 27, 1937, to Jan. 2, 1938. National Intercollegiate Christian Council, 1938. Pp. 25–30.

"New Emphases in Christian Social Teaching," *The Church Faces the World,* ed. by Samuel McCrea Cavert. Round Table Press, 1939. Pp. 1–18. This article appeared in *Religion in Life,* Vol. VII, No. 4 (Autumn, 1938), pp. 525–535.

"Christianity and World Tensions . . . in North America," *Students and the World Mission of Christianity.* Report of the North Amer-

ican Student Consultation on the World Mission of Christianity
. . . Dec. 27, 1939, to Jan. 1, 1940, at the University of Toronto,
Canada. New York: Student Volunteer Movement for Foreign
Mission, 1940. Pp. 57–63.

"The Christian Conception of Man," *Liberal Theology: An Appraisal; Essays in Honor of Eugene William Lyman,* ed., by David
E. Roberts and Henry P. Van Dusen. Charles Scribner's Sons,
1942. Pp. 191–204.

"Peace Terms Must Not Be a Vehicle for Vengeance," *A Righteous
Faith for a Just and Durable Peace.* Federal Council of Churches
of Christ in America, Commission on a Just and Durable Peace,
1942. Pp. 45–52.

"A Touchstone of Democracy," *A Touchstone of Democracy: The
Japanese in America.* Council for Social Action of the Congregational Christian Churches, 1942. Pp. 7–11.

"Christian Concerns," *The Massanetta Echoes.* Massanetta Springs
Conferences, Vol. I. Summer, 1943. Pp. 50–52.

"The Hardest Problem for Christian Ethics," *Christianity and the
Contemporary Scene,* ed. by Randolph C. Miller and H. H.
Shires. Morehouse-Gorham Company, Inc., 1943. Pp. 119–131.

"The Christian as Soldier," *Christians Face War.* Published for the
National Intercollegiate Christian Council by the Association
Press, 1944. Pp. 25–30.

"The Christian Basis for Enduring Peace," *Approaches to World
Peace,* ed. by Lyman Bryson *et al.* Harper & Brothers, 1944. Pp.
740–754.

"Christianity and Secularism," *Contemporary Thinking About Jesus,*
ed. by Thomas S. Kepler. Abingdon-Cokesbury Press, 1944. Pp.
314–320. A reprint of the first fifteen pages of *Christianity and
Our World.* Association Press, 1936.

"Exponent of Social Christianity," *This Ministry: The Contribution
of Henry Sloane Coffin,* ed. by Reinhold Niebuhr. Charles Scribner's Sons, 1945. Pp. 83–94.

"The Protestant Churches and World Order," *World Order: Its
Intellectual and Cultural Foundations,* ed. by F. Ernest Johnson.
Harper & Brothers, 1945. Pp. 124–136.

"The Forms of Ecumenical Christianity," *Toward World-wide Christianity,* ed. by O. Frederick Nolde. Harper & Brothers, 1946. Pp.
59–77. The Interseminary Series, Vol. IV.

"The Limitations of the Church," *The Gospel, the Church, and the*

World, ed. by Kenneth S. Latourette. Harper & Brothers, 1946. Pp. 134–157. An "edited version" of the article entitled "Limitations of the Church—Inherent and Accidental," *Christendom,* Vol. XI, No. 1 (Winter, 1946), pp. 2–12.

"The Involvement of the Church," *Man's Disorder and God's Design.* Amsterdam Assembly Series. London: SCM Press, Ltd., 1948. Vol. III, *The Church and the Disorder of Society.* Pp. 91–102.

"Basic Christian Convictions," *Orientation in Religious Education,* ed. by Philip H. Lotz. Abingdon-Cokesbury Press, 1950. Pp. 26–36.

"Supplement to 'The Christian Basis for Enduring Peace,' " *Perspectives on a Troubled Decade: Science, Philosophy, and Religion, 1939–1949,* ed. by Lyman Bryson *et al.* Harper & Brothers, 1950. Pp. 695–701.

"Christian Ethics" (with Waldo Beach), *Protestant Thought in the Twentieth Century: Whence and Whither?* ed. by Arnold S. Nash. The Macmillan Company, 1951. Pp. 125–144.

"The Church's Responsibility for Social Welfare," "A Christian View of the State," "Church and State in the United States," three addresses, *The Church, the State and Human Welfare.* The Thirty-fourth Annual Convocation, Howard University, School of Religion, Nov. 14–16, 1950. Washington, D.C., 1951.

"The Church Between East and West," *Christian Faith and Social Action, A Symposium,* by John A. Hutchison and others. Charles Scribner's Sons, 1953. Pp. 75–91. Also appeared as a separate pamphlet entitled *Communism and the West: The Basic Conflicts.* Church Peace Union, and World Alliance for International Friendship Through Religion, 1953.

"A Protestant Conception of Religious Authority," *The Protestant Credo,* ed. by Vergilius Ferm. Philosophical Library, Inc., 1953. Pp. 127–138. Originally appeared as "A Protestant Conception of Religious Authority," *Union Seminary Quarterly Review,* Vol. VII, No. 1 (Nov., 1951), pp. 3–10.

"A Theological Conception of Goals for Economic Life," *Goals of Economic Life,* ed. by A. Dudley Ward. Harper & Brothers, 1953. Pp. 397–429.

"Christian Ethics and Forms of Economic Power," *Christian Values and Economic Life.* Harper & Brothers, 1954. Pp. 235–257. See also pp. xi–xv and 201–234 for additional contributions.

"Christian Ethics in Economic Life," *Christian Values and Economic Life.* Harper & Brothers, 1954. Pp. 201–234. See also pp. xi–xv and 235–257 for additional contributions.

"An Approach to the Christian Faith," *Our Faith and Ourselves Today.* National Student Council of the Y.M.C.A. and Y.W.C.A., 1955. Pp. 19–42.

"The Prophetic Side of Christianity," *Best Sermons, 1955 Edition,* ed. by G. Paul Butler. McGraw-Hill Book Company, Inc., 1955. Pp. 277–285.

"The Issues: A Debate," *The Kingdom Without God: Road's End for the Social Gospel,* ed. by Gerald Heard *et al.* Foundation for Social Research Studies, Vol. V, No. 1 (Spring, 1956). Pp. 19–52.

"Reinhold Niebuhr's Social Ethics," *Reinhold Niebuhr: His Religious, Social, and Political Thought,* ed. by Charles W. Kegley and Robert W. Bretall. The Macmillan Company, 1956. Pp. 45–77.

"What Can We Hope for in Society?" *What the Christian Hopes for in Society,* ed. by Wayne H. Cowan. Association Press, 1957. Pp. 19–36. This article appeared under the title "What May [sic] We Hope for in Society?" in *Christianity and Crisis,* Vol. XII. No. 23 (Jan. 5, 1953), pp. 179–183; and in *The Congregational Quarterly,* Vol. XXI, No. 2 (April, 1953), pp. 104–113.

"The Demand for Freedom and Justice in the Contemporary World Revolution," *Religion and Culture: Essays in Honor of Paul Tillich,* ed. by Walter Leibrecht. Harper & Brothers, 1959. Pp. 321–334. This essay also appeared under the title "The Christian Response to Social Revolution," *The Ecumenical Review,* Vol. IX, No. 1 (Oct., 1956), pp. 1–15.

"The Present Conflict Between Ideologies," *The Student Seeks an Answer,* ed. by John A. Clark. Colby College Press, 1960. Pp. 51–70.

"A Protestant Looks at American Catholicism," and "Reply to Mr. Lowell," *Facing Protestant–Roman Catholic Tensions,* ed. by Wayne H. Cowan. Association Press, 1960. Pp. 21–38, 40–42.

"Ethics and Calculation," *The Moral Dilemma of Nuclear Weapons: Essays from* Worldview. Church Peace Union, 1961. Pp. 44–46. This essay appeared as "The Ethics of Calculation," *Worldview,* Vol. II, No. 11 (Nov., 1959), pp. 7–8.

"How My Mind Has Changed," *How My Mind Has Changed,* ed.

by Harold E. Fey. Meridian Books, 1961. Pp. 11–24. This article appeared originally in *The Christian Century,* Vol. LXXVI, No. 51 (Dec. 23, 1959), pp. 1500–1502.

"What Hopes and What Misgivings . . . ?" *One Fold, One Shepherd: A Christian Exchange.* The America Press, 1961. Pp. 14–16.

"Christian Ethics and Foreign Policy," *Representative American Speeches, 1961–1962,* ed. by Lester Thonssen. The H. W. Wilson Company, 1962. Pp. 132–147.

"Church and State," *New Frontiers of Christianity,* ed. by Ralph C. Raughley, Jr. Association Press, 1962. Pp. 174–200.

"The Church as Prophetic Critic," *The Christian Century Reader* . . . , ed. by Harold E. Fey and Margaret Frakes. Association Press, 1962. Pp. 47–53.

"Comment," *The Ethic of Power: The Interplay of Religion, Philosophy, and Politics,* ed. by Harold D. Lasswell and Harland Cleveland. Harper & Brothers, 1962. Pp. 139–141.

"Reinhold Niebuhr's Contribution to Christian Social Ethics," *Reinhold Niebuhr: A Prophetic Voice in Our Time,* ed. by Harold R. Landon. The Seabury Press, Inc., 1962. Pp. 57–79, followed by "Discussion," pp. 80–95. A shortened version appeared in *The Expository Times,* Vol. LXXV, No. 8 (May, 1964), pp. 237–240.

"Religious Ethics and Foreign Policy," *A Humane Society,* ed. by Stuart E. Rosenberg. Toronto: University of Toronto Press, 1962. Pp. 114–126.

"Christianity and Secularist Humanism," *Christianity on the March,* ed. by Henry P. Van Dusen. Harper & Row, Publishers, Inc., 1963. Pp. 127–147.

"The View of an American Theologian," *The Road to Peace.* London: SCM Press, Ltd., 1965. Pp. 32–41. Also published by Fortress Press, Facet Books, Social Ethics Series, No. 10.

"Foreword," *Washington and Vietnam: An Examination of the Moral and Political Issues,* by Dorothy Dunbar Bromley. Oceana Publications, 1966. Pp. vii–viii.

"The Issue of Peace: The Voice of Religion," *Representative American Speeches, 1965–1966,* ed. by Lester Thonssen. The H. W. Wilson Company, 1966. Pp. 142–155. (See the following entry for another appearance of the same article.)

"The Issue of Peace: The Voice of Religion," *Religion and Peace,* ed. by Homer A. Jack. The Bobbs-Merrill Company, Inc., 1966. Pp. 36–47. (See the preceding entry for another appearance of the same article.)

"A Protestant Looks at American Catholicism," *Witness to a Generation,* ed. by Wayne H. Cowan. The Bobbs-Merrill Company, Inc., 1966. Pp. 49–58.

"A Response," *The Documents of Vatican II,* ed. by Walter M. Abbott. Herder & Herder, Inc., and Association Press, 1966. Pp. 652–655.

"A Roman Catholic for President?" *Witness to a Generation,* ed. by Wayne H. Cowan. The Bobbs-Merrill Company, Inc., 1966. Pp. 62–65. This article appeared also in *Christianity and Crisis,* Vol. XX, No. 3 (March 7, 1960), pp. 17–19.

"Capitalism, Ethics, and Morality," *The Future of Capitalism.* The Macmillan Company, 1967. Pp. 157–170. This article appeared also as "Capitalism and Ethics," *Catholic Mind,* Vol. LXV, No. 1213 (May, 1967), pp. 42–52.

"Democracy," pp. 86–87; "Freedom," pp. 133–134; "Niebuhr, Reinhold," pp. 232–233; and "State," pp. 331–333: *Dictionary of Christian Ethics,* ed. by John Macquarrie. The Westminster Press, 1967.

"In Defense of God," *Radical Theology: Phase Two; Essays in a Continuing Discussion,* ed. by C. W. Christian and Glenn R. Wittig. J. B. Lippincott Company, 1967. Pp. 141–151. This article appeared in *Look,* Vol. XXX, No. 8 (April 19, 1966), pp. 69–70, 72, 75–76.

"John Knox at Union," *Christian History and Interpretation: Studies Presented to John Knox,* ed. by W. R. Farmer, C. F. D. Moule, R. R. Niebuhr. London: Cambridge University Press, 1967. Pp. xiii–xix.

"Principles and the Context," *Storm Over Ethics,* by John C. Bennett *et al.* United Church Press, 1967. Pp. 1–24. A revision of the presidential address delivered in 1961 to the American Society of Christian Social Ethics.

"Foreword," *Bonhoeffer in a World Come of Age,* comp. by Peter Vorkink. Fortress Press, 1968. Pp. v–vi.

III. PERIODICAL ARTICLES, INCLUDING EDITORIALS

(Arranged chronologically; alphabetically within the year)

1926

"Religious Doubt," *Mansfield College Magazine,* Vol. XII, No. 10 (June, 1926), pp. 256–265.

1927

"The Form of the Curriculum," *Alumni Bulletin of the Union Theological Seminary,* Vol. II, No. 4 (April–May, 1927), pp. 166–168.

1930

"Can Armistice Sunday Be Saved?" *The Christian Century,* Vol. XLVII, No. 48 (Nov. 26, 1930), pp. 1444–1445.
"The Myth of Equal Opportunity," *The Christian Century,* Vol. XLVII, No. 44 (Oct. 29, 1930), pp. 1308–1309.
"Seeing the Real Europe," *The Intercollegian,* Vol. XLVII, No. 8 (May, 1930), pp. 225–226, 238–239.

1931

"Building a Philosophy of Life," *The Chapel Bell,* Vol. XII, No. 1 (Sept., 1931), p. 1. Theological Seminary, Auburn, New York.
"Can Christianity and Socialism Make Terms?" *The Christian Century,* Vol. XLVIII, No. 10 (March 11, 1931), pp. 338–339.
"The Collegiate Back Yard," *The Intercollegian,* Vol. XLVIII, No. 5 (Feb., 1931), pp. 151–152.
"Currents of Religious Thought in America," *The Student World,* Vol. XXIV, No. 1 (First Quarter, 1931), pp. 6–24.

1932

"Christianity and Class Consciousness," *The World Tomorrow,* Vol. XV, No. 2 (Feb., 1932), pp. 47–49. Originally appeared in Fellowship Leaflet No. 2. New York, Fellowship of Reconciliation.
"The Church—What It Might Be and What It Is in Part," *The Chapel Bell,* Vol. XII, No. 7 (March, 1932), p. 2.
"Religion: Opiate or Stimulant?" *The World Tomorrow,* Vol. XV, No. 6 (June, 1932), pp. 178–180.

1933

"After Liberalism—What?" *The Christian Century,* Vol. L, No. 45 (Nov. 8, 1933), pp. 1403–1406.
"That Fellowship Questionnaire," *The World Tomorrow,* Vol. XVI, No. 29 (Dec. 21, 1933), pp. 690–692.
"The World That Waits for the Class of '37," *The Intercollegian,* Vol. LI, No. 1 (Oct., 1933), pp. 5–7.

1934

"The Church and the Coming Conflict," *The Presbyterian Tribune,* Vol. L, No. 4 (Oct. 4, 1934), pp. 7–9.

1935

"The Fight Against War in Time of Peace," *The Student World,* Vol. XXVIII, No. 1 (First Quarter, 1935), pp. 19–24.

"Moral Landmarks in a Time of Confusion," *Christendom,* Vol. I, No. 1 (Autumn, 1935), pp. 67–78.

"The Relevance of the Ethic of Jesus for Modern Society," *Religion in Life,* Vol. IV, No. 1 (Winter, 1935), pp. 74–83.

"The Task of Theology," *The Chapel Bell,* Vol. XIII, No. 3 (Dec., 1935), pp. 8–15.

1936

"Christianity—A Statement of Faith," *The Intercollegian and Far Horizons,* Vol. LIV, No. 1 (Oct., 1936), pp. 7–8, 10.

"Is a Godless World Incredible?" *The Intercollegian and Far Horizons,* Vol. LIII, No. 5 (March, 1936), pp. 127–128, 146.

1937

"Can Oxford Speak to Our Condition?" *The Student World,* Vol. XXX, No. 2 (Second Quarter, 1937), pp. 169–178.

"The Christian Churches," *The Intercollegian and Far Horizons,* Vol. LIV, No. 7 (May, 1937), pp 163–164, 168.

"The Contribution of Reinhold Niebuhr," *Religion in Life,* Vol. VI, No 2 (Spring, 1937), pp. 268–283.

"The Oxford Conference," *The Chapel Bell,* Vol. XVI, No 3 (Sept., 1937), pp. 1–2.

"Personal Salvation and Social Conditions," *Social Progress,* Vol. XXVIII, No. 7 (March, 1937), pp. 6–11.

1938

"Idealism Left Behind by Events," *The Intercollegian and Far Horizons,* Vol. LV, No. 5 (March, 1938), pp. 99–100.

"New Emphases in Christian Social Teaching," *Religion in Life,* Vol. VII, No. 4 (Autumn, 1938), pp. 525–535.

"The Problem of Evil," *Journal of Religion,* Vol. XVIII, No. 3 (Oct., 1938), pp. 401–421.

1939

"A Changed Liberal—But Still a Liberal," *The Christian Century*, Vol. LVI, No. 6 (Feb. 8, 1939), pp. 179–181.

"Christians and the International Crisis," *Christendom*, Vol. IV, No. 2 (Spring, 1939), pp. 174–182.

"I Believe," *The Intercollegian and Far Horizons*, Vol. LVII, No. 2 (Nov., 1939), pp. 31–33, 54. Reprinted from an article entitled "My Beliefs," *The Presbyterian Tribune*, Vol. LIV, No. 23 (Aug. 17, 1939), pp. 7–9.

"Neutrality: The Christian's Dilemma," *The Christian Century*, Vol. LVI, No. 44 (Nov. 1, 1939), pp. 1329–1331.

1940

"Can the Protestant Minister Be Good Enough?" *The Garrett Tower*, Vol. XVI, No. 1 (Nov., 1940), pp. 1–2, 4.

"Christianity and Democracy," *Christendom*, Vol. V, No. 2 (Spring, 1940), pp. 162–171.

"The Christian's Ethical Decision," *Religion in Life*, Vol. IX, No. 3 (Summer, 1940), pp. 393–401.

"Church Unity and the Small Community," *The Commonwealth Review*, Vol. XXII, No. 2 (May, 1940), pp. 74–79.

"God's Will and Our Decisions," *The Student World*, Vol. XXXIII, No. 1 (First Quarter, 1940), pp. 32–37.

"If America Is Drawn Into the War, Can You, as a Christian, Participate in It or Support It?" *The Christian Century*, Vol. LVII, No. 49 (Dec. 4, 1940), pp. 1506–1508.

"Religion and the Empirical Method," *Journal of Religion*, Vol. XX, No. 2 (April, 1940), pp. 173–175.

1941

"American Students Have Been Misled," *The Intercollegian*, Vol. LVIII, No. 3 (Jan., 1941), pp. 57–58.

"Barth's Letter to the British Christians: A Comment," *Christianity and Crisis*, Vol. I, No. 19 (Nov. 3, 1941), pp. 6–7.

"The Christian Ethic and Political Strategy," *Christianity and Crisis*, Vol. I, No. 2 (Feb. 24, 1941), pp. 3–6.

"Christianity and Its Alternatives," *Christendom*, Vol. VI, No. 3 (Summer, 1941), pp. 352–363.

"The Church and 'Free Enterprise,'" *Advance*, Vol. CXXXIII, No. 5 (May, 1941), p. 212.

"The Outlook for Theology," *Journal of Religion*, Vol. XXI, No. 4 (Oct., 1941), pp. 341–353.

1942

"The Archbishop of Canterbury," *The Seminar Quarterly*, Vol. XII, No. 1 (Nov., 1942), pp. 16–20.

"The Christian as Soldier," *The Intercollegian*, Vol. LIX, No. 5 (March, 1942), pp. 99–100.

"A Christian Perspective of the War," *The Friend*, Vol. CXII, No. 3 (March, 1942), pp. 29–31.

"The Churches and the War," *Christianity and Crisis*, Vol. II, No. 15 (Sept. 21, 1942), pp. 1–2.

"Dealing with Japanese Evacuees," *Christianity and Crisis*, Vol. II, No. 18 (Nov. 2, 1942), p. 6.

"A False Christian Nationalism," *Christianity and Crisis*, Vol. II, No. 4 (March 23, 1942), pp. 6–7.

"In Such a Time," *Christendom*, Vol. VII, No. 2 (Spring, 1942), pp. 162–168.

"Revolution or Counter-Revolution?" *The Christian Century*, Vol. LIX, No. 7 (Feb. 18, 1942), pp. 209–211.

"William Temple," *Christianity and Crisis*, Vol. II, No. 9 (June 1, 1942), pp. 1–2.

1943

"American Christians and the War," *The Student World*, Vol. XXXVI, No. 1 (First Quarter, 1943), pp. 81–89.

"America's Temptation," *Christian Advocate*, Vol. CXVIII, No. 42 (Oct. 21, 1943), pp. 5, 22, 26.

"Being a Christian in Time of War," *The Church School*, Vol. II, No. 3 (March, 1943), pp. 129–130, 189.

"The Choice Before Our Nation," *Christianity and Crisis*, Vol. III, No. 5 (April 5, 1943), pp. 1–2.

"Christianity and Race," *The Church School*, Vol. II, No. 8 (Aug., 1943), pp. 433–448.

"Comment on 'A Letter to American Christians' by Karl Barth," *Christendom*, Vol. VIII, No. 4 (Autumn, 1943), pp. 460–462.

"An Ecumenical Consensus," *Christianity and Crisis*, Vol. III, No. 13 (July 26, 1943), pp. 4–6.

"Enduring Bases of Christian Action," *Social Action*, Vol. IX, No. 6 (June 15, 1943), pp. 5–34.

"Inaugural Address," *Alumni Bulletin of the Union Theological Seminary*, Vol. XIX, No. 1 (Dec., 1943), pp. 2–6.

"Injustice to Japanese Christianity," *Christianity and Crisis*, Vol. III, No. 21 (Dec. 13, 1943), pp. 7–8.

"An International Christian Round Table," *Christianity and Crisis*, Vol. III, No. 13 (July 26, 1943), pp. 1–2.

"New but Lasting Values in Social Action," *Social Action*, Vol. IX, No. 6 (June 15, 1943), pp. 8–22.

"The New Hope and the New Unity," *Christianity and Crisis*, Vol. III, No. 20 (Nov. 29, 1943), pp. 1–2.

"The Person of Christ," *Religion in Life*, Vol. XII, No. 4 (Autumn, 1943), pp. 503–513.

"The Spiritual Basis of Democracy," *Advance*, Vol. CXXXV, No. 5 (May 1, 1943), pp. 194–195.

"Sumner Welles Is Right," *Christianity and Crisis*, Vol. III, No. 18 (Nov. 1, 1943), p. 6.

"William Temple," *The Anglican Theological Review*, Vol. XXV, No. 3 (July, 1943), pp. 257–271.

1944

"An Approach to Christian Faith in God," *The Woman's Press*, Vol. XXXVIII, No. 7 (July–Aug., 1944), pp. 316–317.

"Comments on the Sixth and Seventh Statements, Pattern for Peace . . . ," *World Affairs*, Vol. CVII, No. 1 (March, 1944), pp. 42–44.

"Establish World Organization Now," *Christianity and Crisis*, Vol. IV, No. 10 (June 12, 1944), p. 1.

"Faith," *The Missionary Herald at Home and Abroad*, Vol. CXL, No. 1 (Feb., 1944), pp. 3–5.

"An Opportunity Neglected," *Christianity and Crisis*, Vol. IV, No. 14 (Aug. 7, 1944), pp. 1–2.

"Peace-Time Conscription," *Christianity and Crisis*, Vol. IV, No. 21 (Dec. 11, 1944), p. 1.

"Results of an Ecumenical Study," *Christendom*, Vol. IX, No. 2 (Spring, 1944), pp. 142–152.

"Russia and the Christians of the West," *The Student World*, Vol. XXXVII, No. 3 (1944), pp. 179–182.

"The Test of Domestic Policy," *Christianity and Crisis*, Vol. IV, No. 6 (April 17, 1944), p. 1.

"William Adams Brown," *The Presbyterian Tribune*, Vol. LIX, No. 4 (Jan., 1944), pp. 12–13.

"William Adams Brown," *The Union Review*, Vol. V, No. 1 (March, 1944), pp. 3–4. Originally in *The Presbyterian Tribune*, Vol. LIX, No. 4 (Jan., 1944), pp. 12–13.

1945

"America and Russia," *Christianity and Crisis*, Vol. V, No. 21 (Dec. 10, 1945), pp. 1–2.

"American Criticism of Britain," *Christianity and Crisis*, Vol. IV, No. 24 (Jan. 22, 1945), pp. 6–7.

"The Charter," *Christianity and Crisis*, Vol. V, No. 14 (Aug. 6, 1945), pp. 1–2.

"The Christian's Cause," *Christianity and Crisis*, Vol. V, No. 20 (Nov. 26, 1945), pp. 4–6.

"The Christian's Dual Citizenship," *Christianity and Crisis*, Vol. V, No. 1 (April 2, 1945), p. 1.

"The Church and Politics," *The Presbyterian Tribune*, Vol. LX, No. 8 (May, 1945), pp. 15–17.

"The Church and the War," *Motive*, Vol. V, No. 6 (March, 1945), pp. 5–7.

"Ecumenical Theology: Comments on Professor Pauck's Paper," *Journal of Religion*, Vol. XXV, No. 4 (Oct., 1945), pp. 274–275.

"Realistic Theology and Social Action," *Christianity and Society*, Vol. X, No. 3 (Summer, 1945), pp. 11–15.

"The United Nations Organization: What It Is and What It Is Not," *The Pilgrim, Adult Bible Class Quarterly*, Vol. VIII, No. 4 (Oct.–Dec., 1945), pp. 11–13.

"The World Council Fosters World Thinking," *Messenger*, Vol. X, No. 3 (Feb. 6, 1945), pp. 14–16. Slightly modified version of the article "The World Council of Churches . . . The Council's Research and Study Work," *The United Church Observer*, Vol. VI, No. 21 (Jan. 1, 1945), p. 5.

"The World Council of Churches . . . The Council's Research and Study Work," *The United Church Observer*, Vol. VI, No. 21 (Jan. 1, 1945), p. 5.

1946

"The Christian's Cause," *Motive*, Vol. VI, No. 6 (March, 1946), pp. 5–6, 42. Originally appeared in *Christianity and Crisis*, Vol. V, No. 20 (Nov. 26, 1945), pp. 4–6.

"Limitations of the Church—Inherent and Accidental," *Christendom*, Vol. XI, No. 1 (Winter, 1946), pp. 2–12.

"The Meaning of Redemption in Personal and Social Life Today," *The Journal of Religious Thought*, Vol. III, No. 1 (Autumn–Winter, 1946), pp. 54–62.

"The Protestant–Catholic Issue," *Christianity and Crisis*, Vol. VI, No. 9 (May 27, 1946), pp. 1–2.

"The Russian-Communist Drive for Power," *Christianity and Crisis*, Vol. VI, No. 20 (Nov. 25, 1946), pp. 1–2.

"Socialist Without Being Totalitarian," *Social Action*, Vol. XII, No. 2 (Feb. 15, 1946), p. 3.

"Some Impressions from Geneva," *Christianity and Crisis*, Vol. VI, No. 17 (Oct. 14, 1946), pp. 3–5.

"The Theological Revival and Preaching," *The Minister's Quarterly*, Vol. II, No. 2 (May, 1946), pp. 3–6.

"World Order as a Christian Concern," *The Student World*, Vol. XXXIX, No. 4 (Fourth Quarter, 1946), pp. 329–344.

1947

"America's Decision," *Christianity and Crisis*, Vol. VII, No. 18 (Oct. 27, 1947), pp. 1–2.

"Amsterdam, 1948," *Christendom*, Vol. XII, No. 2 (Spring, 1947), pp. 199–203.

"Bennett on Europe," *The Intercollegian*, Vol. LXIV, No. 6 (Feb., 1947), pp. 7–8.

"A Defense of Niemoller," *The Witness*, Vol. XXX, No. 12 (March 6, 1947), pp. 9–10.

"The Ecumenical Institute," *Christendom*, Vol. XII, No. 1 (Winter, 1947), pp. 10–16.

"Evangelism," *Christianity and Crisis*, Vol. VII, No. 1 (Feb. 3, 1947), pp. 1–2.

"Labor Legislation," *Christianity and Crisis*, Vol. VII, No. 8 (May 12, 1947), pp. 1–2.

"Politics and Christian Ethics," *The Student Movement*, Vol. XLIX, No. 4 (March–April, 1947), pp. 8–11.

"Prophet, Not Without Honor," *Messenger*, Vol. XII, No. 9 (April 29, 1947), pp. 8–11.

"Report from Geneva," *The Chapel Bell*, Vol. XXV, No. 1 (Winter, 1947), pp. 8–10.

"The World Council of Churches—Recent Developments," *Union*

Seminary Quarterly Review, Vol. II, No. 3 (March, 1947), pp. 3–8.

"The World Council of Churches: The 1948 Assembly," *The American Friend,* Vol. LIV, No. 20, old series; XXXV, No. 20, new series (Oct. 2, 1947), pp. 387–388.

1948

"The American Churches in the Ecumenical Situation," *The Ecumenical Review,* Vol. I, No. 1 (Autumn, 1948), pp. 57–64.

"Amsterdam and the Social Crisis," *The Christian Century,* Vol. LXV, No. 23 (June 9, 1948), pp. 569–571.

"And Now the World Council," *Advance,* Vol. CXL, No. 5 (May, 1948), pp. 4–5.

"Anti-American Attitudes and the American Christian's Response," *Christendom,* Vol. XIII, No. 1 (Winter, 1948), pp. 1–9.

"Are Americans Too Critical of America?" *Christianity and Crisis,* Vol. VIII, No. 17 (Oct. 18, 1948), pp. 129–130.

"Capitalism and Communism at Amsterdam," *The Christian Century,* Vol. XLV, No. 50 (Dec. 15, 1948), pp. 1362–1364.

"Christianity and Communism," *The Presbyterian Tribune,* Vol. LXIII, No. 8 (May, 1948), pp. 9–10.

"The Church and the Social Disorder," *Christendom,* Vol. XIII, No. 4 (Autumn, 1948), pp. 480–485.

"East and West in Amsterdam," *Christianity and Crisis,* Vol. VIII, No. 16 (Oct. 4, 1948), pp. 122–123.

"East and West in Amsterdam," *Union Seminary Quarterly Review,* Vol. IV, No. 1 (Nov., 1948), pp. 15–17. Same article as the preceding one.

"Implications of the New Conception of 'Separation,' " *Christianity and Crisis,* Vol. VIII, No. 12 (July 5, 1948), pp. 89–90.

"Introduction to the Thought of Reinhold Niebuhr," *Christian Frontiers,* Vol. II, No. 10 (April, 1948), pp. 257–260.

"Modern Protestantism and Democracy," *The Review of Religion,* Vol. XII, No. 2 (Jan., 1948), pp. 166–178.

"Our Mistaken Approach to Communism," *Christianity and Crisis,* Vol. VIII, No. 8 (May 10, 1948), pp. 57–58.

"Preparation for Amsterdam," *Religion in Life,* Vol. XVII, No. 2 (Spring, 1948), pp. 211–217.

"A Radical Vision of Social Justice," *The Anglican Theological Review,* Vol. XXX, No. 2 (April, 1948), pp. 121–123.

"The Report on Social Disorder," *The Living Church*, Vol. X, No. 1 (Oct. 17, 1948), p. 15.

"The Social Significance of the Amsterdam Assembly," *Social Action*, Vol. XIV, No. 10 (Dec. 15, 1948), pp. 22–31.

"Unity and Rebirth at Amsterdam," *Messenger*, Vol. XIII, Nos. 17–18 (Aug. 24, 1948), pp. 5–6.

"What Results Can We Expect?" *The Living Church*, Vol. CXVI, No. 26 (June 27, 1948), pp. 20–21.

1949

"After the Easter Parade," *The Christian Century*, Vol. LXVI, No. 16 (April 20, 1949), pp. 496–497.

"America's Other Face," *Christianity and Crisis*, Vol. IX, No. 8 (May 16, 1949), pp. 57–58.

"The Atomic Bomb and the Future," *Christianity and Crisis*, Vol. IX, No. 17 (Oct. 17, 1949), pp. 129–130.

"For Justice and Freedom in the Social Order," *The Missionary Herald at Home and Abroad*, Vol. CXLV, No. 2 (Feb., 1949), pp. 50–53.

"Major Issues Confronting the Church Today in the Political and Economic Disorder of Society," *Current Religious Thought*, Vol. IX, No. 7 (Sept., 1949), pp. 1–5.

"The Responsible Society," *The Congregational Quarterly*, Vol. XXVII, No. 4 (Oct., 1949), pp. 321–327.

"Roman Catholics and Communism," *Christianity and Crisis*, Vol. IX, No. 3 (March 7, 1949), pp. 17–18.

"Those Who Decide to Stay," *Christianity and Crisis*, Vol. VIII, No. 23 (Jan. 10, 1949), pp. 177–178.

1950

"The Christian Answer to Communism," *Theology Today*, Vol. VII, No. 3 (Oct., 1950), pp. 352–357.

"Christian Faith and Social Action," *Christian Community*, Vol. II, No. 2 (Feb., 1950), pp. 1–3.

"Comment on Vernon Holloway's Paper 'Power Politics and the Christian Conscience,'" *Social Action*, Vol. XVI, No. 2 (Feb. 15, 1950), pp. 40–42.

"Communism in Asia," *The Presbyterian Tribune*, Vol. LXVI, No. 2 (Nov., 1950), pp. 10–12.

"Current Movements and Christianity—Communism: Ally, Competitor, or Both," *The Witness*, Vol. XXXIII, No. 8 (March 2,

1950), pp. 10–12.

"The Present Hysteria," *Christianity and Crisis,* Vol. X, No. 16 (Oct. 2, 1950), pp. 121–122.

"The Problem of Asiatic Communism," *Christianity and Crisis,* Vol. X, No. 14 (Aug. 7, 1950), pp. 109–112.

"The Self-defeating Attitude of America's 'Reactionaries,'" *Christianity and Crisis,* Vol. X, No. 8 (May 15, 1950), pp. 57–58.

"A Step Toward Church Union," *Christianity and Crisis,* Vol. IX, No. 23 (Jan. 9, 1950), pp. 177–178.

"What to Do About Communism . . . ," *Advance,* Vol. CXLII, No. 5 (May, 1950), pp. 15–16.

1951

"American Policy from Asia," *British Weekly,* Vol. CXXIX, No. 3360 (April 5, 1951), pp. 1–2. Also *Christianity and Crisis,* Vol. XI, No. 3 (March 5, 1951), pp. 18–20, under the title "Viewing American Policy from Asia"; and *World Call,* Vol. XXXIII, No. 7 (July–Aug., 1951), pp. 15–16, under the title "Asia Views American Policy."

"Asia Views American Policy," *World Call,* Vol. XXXIII, No. 7 (July–Aug., 1951), pp. 15–16. Also *Christianity and Crisis,* Vol. XI, No. 3 (March 5, 1951), pp. 18–20, under the title "Viewing American Policy from Asia"; and *British Weekly,* Vol. CXXIX, No. 3360 (April 5, 1951), pp. 1–2, under the title "American Policy from Asia."

"Asiatics and Communism," *Current Religious Thought,* Vol. XI, No. 5 (May, 1951), p. 18.

"The Christian Answer to Communism," *Social Progress,* Vol. XLI, No. 5 (Jan., 1951), pp. 6–9. Also *Theology Today,* Vol. VII, No. 3 (Oct., 1950), pp. 352–357.

"The Christian Confronts Communism," *The Intercollegian,* Vol. LXIX, No. 4 (Dec., 1951), pp. 6–8.

"The Christian Faith and the Communist Faith," *Michigan Christian Advocate,* Vol. LXXVIII, No. 43 (Oct. 25, 1951), pp. 10–11.

"A Christian View of the State," *The Journal of Religious Thought,* Vol. VIII, No. 2 (Spring–Summer, 1951), pp. 105–113.

"Christianity and Communism," *Michigan Christian Advocate,* Vol. LXXVIII, No. 41 (Oct. 11, 1951), pp. 6–7.

"Christians and Communism in Asia," *International Review of Missions,* Vol. XL (July, 1951), pp. 296–304.

"Communism in Asia," *Michigan Christian Advocate,* Vol. LXXVIII, No. 42 (Oct. 18, 1951), pp. 8–9.

"Direct Christian Evangelism Must Be a Major Emphasis of the Next Period in Christian Missions," *Advance,* Vol. CXLIII, No. 4 (April 2, 1951), pp. 9–10.

"Has India an Alternative?" *The Christian Century,* Vol. LXVIII, No. 9 (Feb. 28, 1951), pp. 265–266.

"The Impact of Communism in Asia," *Messenger,* Vol. XVI, No. 24 (Dec. 18, 1951), pp. 11–13.

"The MacArthur Controversy," *Christianity and Crisis,* Vol. XI, No. 8 (May 14, 1951), pp. 57–58.

"The MacArthur Controversy," *Messenger,* Vol. XVI, No. 12 (June 5, 1951), pp. 4–6. Also, slightly shortened, *Christianity and Crisis,* Vol. XI, No. 8 (May 14, 1951), pp. 57–58.

"The Next Period in Christian Missions," *Advance,* Vol. CXLIII, No. 4 (April 2, 1951), pp. 9–10.

"The Next Period in Christian Missions," *Union Seminary Quarterly Review,* Vol. VI, No. 4 (June, 1951), pp. 12–14. Also *Advance,* Vol. CXLIII, No. 4 (April 2, 1951), pp. 9–10.

"Our Korean Policy in Perspective," *Christianity and Crisis,* Vol. XI, No. 13 (July 23, 1951), pp. 97–98.

"Patience and Concern," *The Y.W.C.A. Magazine,* Vol. XLV, No. 9 (Dec., 1951), pp. 10–11, 28.

"A Protestant Conception of Religious Authority," *Union Seminary Quarterly Review,* Vol. VII, No. 1 (Nov., 1951), pp. 3–10.

"Turn Communists to Christianity," *The Christian Century,* Vol. LXVIII, No. 16 (April 18, 1951), pp. 494–496.

"The Vatican Appointment," *Christianity and Crisis,* Vol. XI, No. 20 (Nov. 26, 1951), pp. 153–154.

"Viewing American Policy from Asia," *Christianity and Crisis,* Vol. XI, No. 3 (March 5, 1951), pp. 18–20. Also *World Call,* Vol. XXXIII, No. 7 (July–Aug., 1951), pp. 15–16, under the title "Asia Views American Policy"; and *British Weekly,* Vol. CXXIX, No. 3360 (April 5, 1951), pp. 1–2, under the title "American Policy from Asia."

1952

"Can We Ever Support Communism?" *The Christian Century,* Vol. XLIX, No. 24 (June 11, 1952), pp. 696–698.

"Christianity and the State," *The Seminarian,* Vol. XLIII, No. 9 (May 7, 1952), pp. 10–11, 13.

"Europe Versus Asia," *Christianity and Crisis*, Vol. XII, No. 16
   (Sept. 29, 1952), pp. 121–122.
"The Future of McCarthyism," *Christianity and Crisis*, Vol. XII,
   No. 21 (Dec. 8, 1952), pp. 161–162.
"The Indian Elections," *Christianity and Crisis*, Vol. XII, No. 4
   (March 17, 1952), pp. 25–26.
"Mr. Dulles' Proposals," *Christianity and Crisis*, Vol. XII, No. 10
   (June 9, 1952), pp. 73–74.
"Protestant Strategy in the World Struggle," *British Weekly*, Vol.
   CXXXI, No. 3403 (Jan. 31, 1952), pp. 1–2.
"Riverside Church Joins Our Fellowship," *Advance*, Vol. CXLIV,
   No. 13 (June 23, 1952), p. 15.
"A Tribute to Truman," *Christianity and Society*, Vol. XVII, No. 3
   (Summer, 1952), pp. 4–5.
"Two Goals in Foreign Policy," *Christianity and Crisis*, Vol. XII,
   No. 8 (May 12, 1952), pp. 57–58.
"Whither the National Council?" *Christianity and Crisis*, Vol. XI,
   No. 23 (Jan. 7, 1952), pp. 177–178.

1953

"Christians and Communism in Asia," *Cross Currents*, Vol. III, No.
   3 (Spring, 1953), pp. 208–215. Also *International Review of
   Missions*, Vol. XL (July, 1951), pp. 296–304.
"A Christmas Message," *Christianity and Crisis*, Vol. XIII, No. 22
   (Dec. 28, 1953), pp. 171–172.
"The Danger in Our Intransigence," *Christianity and Crisis*, Vol.
   XIII, No. 10 (June 8, 1953), pp. 73 74.
"Dear Dr. Bennett: Dear Mr. Opitz," *Faith and Freedom*, Vol. IV,
   No. 8 (April, 1953), pp. 3–6.
"Dear Dr. Bennett: Dear Mr. Opitz" (Part Two), *Faith and Free-
   dom*, Vol. IV, No. 9 (May, 1953), pp. 10–15.
"Focus for Christian Action," *Christianity and Society*, Vol. XVIII,
   No. 4 (Autumn, 1953), pp. 16 20, 31.
"Is It the End of Point Four?" *Christianity and Crisis*, Vol. XIII,
   No. 18 (Nov. 2, 1953), pp. 137–138.
"John Foster Dulles," *Christianity and Society*, Vol. XVIII, No. 1
   (Winter, 1953), pp. 4–5.
"The Protestant Clergy and Communism," *Christianity and Crisis*,
   Vol. XIII, No. 14 (Aug. 3, 1953), pp. 107–110.
"A Responsible Society," *The Christian Advocate*, Vol. CXXVIII,
   No. 48 (Nov. 26, 1953), pp. 6–7, 29–30.

"What May We Hope for in Society?" *Christianity and Crisis,* Vol. XII, No. 23 (Jan. 5, 1953), pp. 179–183.

"What May We Hope for in Society?" *The Congregational Quarterly,* Vol. XXXI, No. 2 (April, 1953), pp. 104–113. Also *Christianity and Crisis,* Vol. XII, No. 23 (Jan. 5, 1953), pp. 179–183.

1954

"Billy Graham at Union," *Union Seminary Quarterly Review,* Vol. IX, No. 4 (May, 1954), pp. 9–14.

"Christianity in Its Political Setting," *Religion in Life,* Vol. XXIV, No. 1 (Winter, 1954–1955), pp. 5–16. Also under the title "Is There a Special Affinity Between Christianity and Democracy?" *The Congregational Quarterly,* Vol. XXXIII, No. 2 (April, 1955), pp. 105–115.

"The Church and Foreign Policy," *Christianity and Society,* Vol. XIX, No. 1 (Winter, 1954), pp. 4–5.

"The Church as Prophetic Critic," *The Christian Century,* Vol. LXXI, No. 1 (Jan. 6, 1954), pp. 9–11.

"The Churches and the United Nations," *Christianity and Crisis,* Vol. XIV, No. 20 (Nov. 29, 1954), pp. 153–154.

"A Clear and Noble Decision," *Christianity and Society,* Vol. XIX, No. 2 (Spring, 1954), pp. 3–4.

"A Conflict Within the National Council of Churches," *Christianity and Society,* Vol. XIX, No. 1 (Winter, 1954), p. 8.

"Eisenhower and the Security Program," *Christianity and Society,* Vol. XX, No. 1 (Winter, 1954–1955), p. 6.

"Eisenhower's New Leadership," *Christianity and Society,* Vol. XIX, No. 4 (Fall, 1954), pp. 5–6.

"Evanston on the Economic Order," *Christianity and Society,* Vol. XIX, No. 3 (Summer, 1954), pp. 3–5.

"Evanston on 'The Responsible Society,'" *Union Seminary Quarterly Review,* Vol. X, No. 1 (Nov., 1954), pp. 9–13.

"Impressions of Evanston," *Christianity and Crisis,* Vol. XIV, No. 15 (Sept. 20, 1954), pp. 113–114.

"A New Dimension of Moral Perplexity," *Christianity and Crisis,* Vol. XIV, No. 7 (May 3, 1954), pp. 49–50.

"No Marshall Plan for Asia," *Christianity and Society,* Vol. XX, No. 1 (Winter, 1954–1955), pp. 6–12.

"Our Policy Toward India," *Christianity and Society,* Vol. XIX, No. 2 (Spring, 1954), pp. 4–5.

"Reconsideration of the Security Program," *Christianity and Society,*

Vol. XIX, No. 4 (Fall, 1954), p. 6.

"The Responsible Society," *Social Action*, Vol. XXI, No. 3 (Nov., 1954), pp. 5–8.

" 'The Responsible Society' at Evanston," *Christianity and Crisis*, Vol. XIV, No. 12 (July 12, 1954), pp. 90–92.

1955

"Are There Tests of Revelation?" *Theology Today*, Vol. XII, No. 1 (April, 1955), pp. 68–84.

"The Christian Citizen and Politics," *Wesley Quarterly*, Vol. XIV, No. 3 (July–Sept., 1955), pp. 4–6.

"Concern: A Christian Responsibility," *Social Progress*, Vol. XLVI, No. 3 (Nov., 1955), pp. 5–10, 22–23.

"Federal Initiative and Mrs. Hobby," *Christianity and Society*, Vol. XX, No. 3 (Summer, 1955), p. 6.

"The 'GAW' and the American Economy," *Christianity and Society*, Vol. XX, No. 3 (Summer, 1955), pp. 5–6.

"Introduction" to a Symposium on the National Council of Churches Statement on Assumptions for Economic Life, *Christianity and Society*, Vol. XX, No. 1 (Winter, 1955), p. 13.

"Is There a Special Affinity Between Christianity and Democracy?" *The Congregational Quarterly*, Vol. XXXIII, No. 2 (April, 1955), pp. 105–115. Also under the title "Christianity in Its Political Setting," *Religion in Life*, Vol. XXIV, No. 1 (Winter, 1954–1955), pp. 5–16.

"The Next Moral Dilemma," *Christianity and Crisis*, Vol. XV, No. 17 (Oct. 17, 1955), pp. 129–130.

"Our Distorted View of Asia," *Christianity and Crisis*, Vol. XV, No. 6 (April 18, 1955), pp. 41–42.

1956

"Abundance and the Church," *Christianity and Crisis*, Vol. XVI, No. 8 (May 14, 1956), pp. 58–59.

"Approaches to Communism," *Christianity and Crisis*, Vol. XVI, No. 10 (June 11, 1956), pp. 74–75.

"Capital Punishment," *Christianity and Crisis*, Vol. XVI, No. 7 (April 30, 1956), pp. 50–51.

"The Christian Response to Social Revolution," *The Ecumenical Review*, Vol. IX, No. 1 (Oct., 1956), pp. 1–15.

"Conscience and the H-Bomb," *Christianity and Crisis*, Vol. XVI, No. 20 (Nov. 26, 1956), pp. 157–158.

"The Draft and Christian Vocation," *The Christian Century,* Vol. LXXIII, No. 34 (Aug. 22, 1956), pp. 970–972.

"The Draft and Christian Vocation," *The Chaplain,* Vol. XIII, No. 6 (Dec., 1956), pp. 9–16. Also *The Christian Century,* Vol. LXXIII, No. 34 (Aug. 22, 1956), pp. 970–972.

"An Editor Replies," *Christianity and Crisis,* Vol. XVI, No. 5 (April 2, 1956), p. 38.

"Four Wrongs and the Future," *Christianity and Crisis,* Vol. XVI, No. 22 (Dec. 24, 1956), pp. 173–174.

"Graham and Segregation," *Christianity and Crisis,* Vol. XVI, No. 18 (Oct. 29, 1956), pp. 142–143.

"Karl Barth in Translation," *Christianity and Crisis,* Vol. XVI, No. 16 (Oct. 1, 1956), pp. 122–123.

"Morality and Moralism," *Union Seminary Quarterly Review,* Vol. XI, No. 4 (May, 1956), pp. 39–41.

"Nehru's Contribution," *Christianity and Crisis,* Vol. XVI, No. 22 (Dec. 24, 1956), p. 175.

"A New Mandate in a Changed World," *Christianity and Crisis,* Vol. XVI, No. 19 (Nov. 22, 1956), pp. 149–150.

"Notes on Christian Responsibility and National Interest," *Christianity and Crisis,* Vol. XVI, No. 13 (July 23, 1956), pp. 100–101.

"Our Concern for Civil Liberties," *Advance,* Vol. CXLVIII, No. 6 (March 21, 1956), pp. 13–14, 28.

"The Resourceful Mr. Pew," *Christianity and Crisis,* Vol. XVI, No. 10 (June 11, 1956), p. 75.

"Threats of Persecution," *Christianity and Society,* Vol. XXI, No. 1 (Winter, 1956), p. 6.

"Toward a New Emphasis in Asian Policy," *Christianity and Crisis,* Vol. XVI, No. 1 (Feb. 6, 1956), pp. 1–2.

1957

"Beyond the 'Cold War'?" *Christianity and Crisis,* Vol. XVII, No. 11 (June 24, 1957), pp. 81–82.

"Can It Never End?" *Christianity and Crisis,* Vol. XVII, No. 7 (April 29, 1957), p. 50.

"The Case of Hildy Ellis," *Christianity and Crisis,* Vol. XVII, No. 9 (May 27, 1957), pp. 66–67.

"Catholics in Public Office," *Commonweal,* Vol. LXV, No. 19 (Feb. 8, 1957), pp. 489–490.

"A Church Speaks Its Mind," *Christianity and Crisis,* Vol. XVII,

No. 10 (June 10, 1957), p. 74.

"Comments" (on an article by William F. Kennedy, "The Christian Conscience and Economic Growth"), *Social Order,* Vol. VII, No. 4 (April, 1957), pp. 155–157.

"Developments in the Middle East," *Christianity and Crisis,* Vol. XVII, No. 4 (March 18, 1957), p. 26.

"Dr. Schweitzer and Dr. Libby," *Christianity and Crisis,* Vol. XVII, No. 9 (May 27, 1957), pp. 65–66.

"The Faculty Re-examines Its Work," *Union Seminary Quarterly Review,* Vol. XII, No. 2 (Jan., 1957), pp. 25–29.

"Justice and Mercy," *Christianity and Crisis,* Vol. XVII, No. 18 (Oct. 28, 1957), p. 139.

"A Matter for Regret," *Christianity and Crisis,* Vol. XVI, No. 24 (Jan. 24, 1957), p. 190.

"The Mutual Welfare of Foreign Aid," *Christianity and Crisis,* Vol. XVII, No. 7 (April 29, 1957), p. 51.

"An Old Rut and a New Fear," *Christianity and Crisis,* Vol. XVII, No. 20 (Nov. 25, 1957), p. 154.

"Overcoming Rationalizations," *Christianity and Crisis,* Vol. XVII, No. 1 (Feb. 4, 1957), pp. 2–3.

"Progress in Nashville," *Christianity and Crisis,* Vol. XVII, No. 15 (Sept. 16, 1957), p. 115.

"Protestant–Catholic Relations," *Christianity and Crisis,* Vol. XVII, No. 4 (March 18, 1957), p. 27.

"A Reply to Dean Pearson," *The Christian Century,* Vol. LXXIV, No. 7 (Jan. 2, 1957), p. 14.

"The School Bus Issue," *Christianity and Crisis,* Vol. XVII, No. 7 (April 29, 1957), pp. 49–50.

"The School Bus Issue," *Commonweal,* Vol. LXVI, No. 9 (May 31, 1957), pp. 234–235. Also *Christianity and Crisis,* Vol. XVII, No. 7 (April 29, 1957), pp. 49–50.

"Toward a Christian Humanism," *The Christian Century,* Vol. LXXIV, No. 10 (March 6, 1957), pp. 292–294.

"Victory for Civil Rights," *Christianity and Crisis,* Vol. XVII, No. 15 (Sept. 16, 1957), pp. 114–115.

1958

"The A. E. C. Admits an Error," *Christianity and Crisis,* Vol. XVIII, No. 5 (March 31, 1958), p. 39.

"An Anniversary and an Arrest," *Christianity and Crisis,* Vol. XVIII, No. 9 (May 26, 1958), p. 70.

"Another Disastrous Policy," *Christianity and Crisis,* Vol. XVIII, No. 16 (Sept. 29, 1958), pp. 126–127.

"A Condition for Coexistence," *Christianity and Crisis,* Vol. XVIII, No. 7 (April 28, 1958), pp. 53–54.

"The Depth of the Difference," *Christianity and Crisis,* Vol. XVIII, No. 18 (Oct. 27, 1958), pp. 146–147.

"Faith and Responsibility," *The Christian Century,* Vol. LXXV, No. 49 (Dec. 3, 1958), pp. 1394–1397.

"France and DeGaulle," *Christianity and Crisis,* Vol. XVIII, No. 11 (June 23, 1958), pp. 86–87.

"Horror and Grace," *Christianity and Crisis,* Vol. XVIII, No. 13 (July 21, 1958), p. 103.

"It's Time to Go Beyond Neo-Orthodoxy," *Advance,* Vol. CL, No. 9 (May 9, 1958), pp. 4–5, 23–24.

"The Little Rock Story: Chapter II," *Christianity and Crisis,* Vol. XVIII, No. 12 (July 7, 1958), p. 95.

"Ministers in the South," *Christianity and Crisis,* Vol. XVIII, No. 20 (Nov. 24, 1958), p. 162.

"Needed: Enterprise, Public and Private," *Christianity and Crisis,* Vol. XVIII, No. 6 (April 14, 1958), pp. 45–46.

"New Assumptions for American Policy," *Christianity and Crisis,* Vol. XVIII, No. 1 (Feb. 3, 1958), pp. 1–2.

" 'No' Is Not Sufficient," *Christianity and Crisis,* Vol. XVIII, No. 22 (Dec. 22, 1958), pp. 178–179.

"Official Complacency and Nuclear Tests," *Christianity and Crisis,* Vol. XVIII, No. 10 (June 9, 1958), pp. 77–78.

"Pius XII," *Christianity and Crisis,* Vol. XVIII, No. 19 (Nov. 10, 1958), pp. 154–155.

"A Protestant View of Roman Catholic Power—I," *Christianity and Crisis,* Vol. XVIII, No. 14 (Aug. 4, 1958), pp. 114–116.

"A Protestant View of Roman Catholic Power—II," *Christianity and Crisis,* Vol. XVIII, No. 15 (Sept. 15, 1958), pp. 120–123. This article completes the one cited immediately above.

"Raising the Curtain," *Christianity and Crisis,* Vol. XVIII, No. 2 (Feb. 17, 1958), p. 10.

"Russia and the Hungarian Executions," *Christianity and Crisis,* Vol. XVIII, No. 12 (July 7, 1958), p. 93.

"We Live in a Series of Vicious Circles," *Advance,* Vol. CL, No. 14 (Aug. 15, 1958), pp. 16–18, 27.

"When Christmas Becomes Divisive," *Christianity and Crisis,* Vol. XVIII, No. 20 (Nov. 24, 1958), pp. 162–163.

"The World in Which We Live," *The Congregational Quarterly,* Vol. XXXVI, No. 3 (Oct., 1958), pp. 206–215.

1959

"The Bishop in Berlin," *Christianity and Crisis,* Vol. XVIII, No. 23 (Jan. 5, 1959), p. 187.

"Catholic Bishops on Communism," *Christianity and Crisis,* Vol. XIX, No. 21 (Dec. 14, 1959), p. 179.

"Congressman Judd and Mr. Mikoyan," *Christianity and Crisis,* Vol. XVIII, No. 24 (Jan. 19, 1959), pp. 193–194.

"The Debate About the Khrushchev Visit," *Christianity and Crisis,* Vol. XIX, No. 16 (Oct. 5, 1959), pp. 133–134.

"Duke University and Desegregation," *Christianity and Crisis,* Vol. XIX, No. 7 (April 27, 1959), pp. 54–55.

"Ethics and Foreign Policy," *Union Seminary Quarterly Review,* Vol. XIV, No. 2 (Jan., 1959), pp. 3–17. Also under the title *Theological and Moral Considerations in International Affairs,* a background paper for the World Order Study Conference, Cleveland, Nov. 18–21, 1958.

"The Ethics of Calculation," *Worldview,* Vol. II, No. 11 (Nov., 1959), pp. 7–8.

"The Great Conflict of Opinion," *Christianity and Crisis,* Vol. XIX, No. 8 (May 11, 1959), pp. 61–62.

"How My Mind Has Changed," *The Christian Century,* Vol. LXXVI, No. 51 (Dec. 23, 1959), pp. 1500–1502.

"The Labor Reform Act of 1959," *Christianity and Crisis,* Vol. XIX, No. 15 (Sept. 21, 1959), pp. 123–124.

"A Matter of Propaganda," *Christianity and Crisis,* Vol. XIX, No. 6 (April 13, 1959), p. 47.

"Mr. Dulles' Illness," *Christianity and Crisis,* Vol. XIX, No. 4 (March 16, 1959), pp. 26–27.

"A New Statement of Faith," *Christianity and Crisis,* Vol. XIX, No. 14 (Aug. 3, 1959), pp. 114–115.

"Not by Dread Alone," *Christianity and Crisis,* Vol. XIX, No. 1 (Feb. 2, 1959), pp. 3–4.

"Preventing Nuclear War," *Social Action,* Vol. XXVI, No. 4 (Dec., 1959), pp. 4–9.

"Protestant Ethics and Population Control," *Daedalus,* Vol. LXXXVIII, No. 3 (Summer, 1959), pp. 454–459.

"Protestant Ethics and Population Control," *United Church Herald,* Vol. II, No. 16 (Sept. 3, 1959), pp. 4–6. Same article as the preceding one.

"Protestant–Roman Catholic Dialogue," *Christianity and Crisis,* Vol. XIX, No. 10 (June 8, 1959), pp. 77–78.

"The Punishment of Publicity," *Christianity and Crisis,* Vol. XIX, No. 20 (Nov. 30, 1959), p. 170.

"Results of the Visit," *Christianity and Crisis,* Vol. XIX, No. 17 (Oct. 19, 1959), pp. 147–148.

"Rockefeller and Nuclear Tests," *Christianity and Crisis,* Vol. XIX, No. 19 (Nov. 16, 1959), p. 161.

"Should the Church Participate in Politics?" *United Church Herald,* Vol. II, No. 10 (May 7, 1959), pp. 4–5.

"TV's 'Sunday Best,' " *Christianity and Crisis,* Vol. XIX, No. 11 (June 22, 1959), pp. 90–91.

"Two Revivals," *Christianity and Crisis,* Vol. XIX, No. 22 (Dec. 28, 1959), pp. 192–193.

"Universal Religious Freedom," *Christianity and Crisis,* Vol. XIX, No. 18 (Nov. 2, 1959), p. 155.

"The Voice of the Pulpit," *Christianity and Crisis,* Vol. XIX, No. 12 (July 6, 1959), p. 98.

"The World We Live In," *The New Christian Advocate,* Vol. III, No. 2 (Feb., 1959), pp. 17–21. Also, with slight differences, as "The World in Which We Live," *The Congregational Quarterly,* Vol. XXXVI, No. 3 (Oct., 1958), pp. 206–215.

1960

"Aid for the Aged," *Christianity and Crisis,* Vol. XX, No. 9 (May 30, 1960), pp. 74–75.

"Balancing the Risks in Nuclear Testing," *Christianity and Crisis,* Vol. XX, No. 6 (April 18, 1960), pp. 45–46.

"The Candidacy of Mr. Nixon, *Christianity and Crisis,* Vol. XIX, No. 24 (Jan. 25, 1960), pp. 209–210.

"Chessman and Capital Punishment," *Christianity and Crisis,* Vol. XX, No. 6 (April 18, 1960), p. 47.

"The Church and the South African Tragedy," *Christianity and Crisis,* Vol. XX, No. 7 (May 2, 1960), pp. 53–54.

"The Dangers of Religious Solidarity," *Christianity and Crisis,* Vol. XX, No. 7 (May 2, 1960), p. 54.

"Family Planning and Public Policy: The Moral Question," *Worldview,* Vol. III, No. 1 (Jan., 1960), pp. 9–10.

"In an Age of Science, a New Accent on Religion," *Saturday Review,* Vol. XLIII, No. 10 (March 5, 1960), p. 20.

"In Memoriam . . . Charles Erwin Mathews . . . A Chapel Address," *Union Seminary Quarterly Review*, Vol. XV, No. 3 (March, 1960), pp. 180–182.

"The Kingdom of God," *Christianity and Crisis*, Vol. XX, No. 10 (June 13, 1960), pp. 85–88.

"The Laity and Christian Vocation," *Christianity and Crisis*, Vol. XX, No. 21 (Dec. 12, 1960), p. 179.

"Lincoln's Religious Insights," *Christianity and Crisis*, Vol. XX, No. 1 (Feb. 8, 1960), pp. 2–3.

"The Moral Question," *Worldview*, Vol. III, No. 1 (Jan., 1960), pp. 9–10.

"Mr. Stevenson Speaks to the Nation," *Christianity and Crisis*, Vol. XIX, No. 23 (Jan. 11, 1960), pp. 201–202.

"The Proposal for Church Unity," *Christianity and Crisis*, Vol. XX, No. 22 (Dec. 26, 1960), pp. 189–190.

"A Protestant Looks at the Study Document," *Religious Education*, Vol. LV, No. 4 (July–Aug., 1960), pp. 269–273.

"A Protestant View of Roman Catholic Power," *Theology Digest*, Vol. VIII, No. 1 (Winter, 1960), pp. 35–36.

"A Roman Catholic for President?" *Christianity and Crisis*, Vol. XX, No. 3 (March 7, 1960), pp. 17–19.

"The Roman Catholic 'Issue' Again," *Christianity and Crisis*, Vol. XX, No. 15 (Sept. 19, 1960), pp. 125–126. Also *The Intercollegian*, Vol. LXXVIII, No. 3 (Nov., 1960), pp. 8–9.

"Some Objections to Coexistence," *The Christian Century*, Vol. LXXVII, No. 14 (April 6, 1960), pp. 408–409.

"Triumph for American Democracy," *Christianity and Crisis*, Vol. XX, No. 20 (Nov. 28, 1960), pp 170–171.

"U.N. and the Congo," *Christianity and Crisis*, Vol. XX, No. 14 (Aug. 8, 1960), pp. 119–120.

1961

"Aid to Parochial Schools: Two Considerations," *Christianity and Crisis*, Vol. XXI, No. 7 (May 1, 1961), pp. 61–62.

"Berlin: Restraint and Discrimination in a Crisis," *Christianity and Crisis*, Vol. XXI, No. 15 (Sept. 18, 1961), pp. 149–150.

"Christ and Non-Christians," *Christianity and Crisis*, Vol. XXI, No. 8 (May 15, 1961), pp. 73–76.

"A Conservative Nation in a Revolutionary World," *Christianity and Crisis*, Vol. XXI, No. 10 (June 12, 1961), pp. 101–102.

"Cultural Pluralism: The Religious Dimension," *Social Order*, Vol.

XI, No. 2 (Feb., 1961), pp. 54–64.

"Delayed Action," *Christianity and Crisis,* Vol. XXI, No. 3 (March 6, 1961), pp. 22–23.

"Medical Care for the Aged," *Christianity and Crisis,* Vol. XXI, No. 12 (July 10, 1961), pp. 121–122.

"Morality or Strategy?" *Saturday Review,* Vol. XLIV, No. 47 (Nov. 25, 1961), p. 27.

"The Most Exploited Americans," *Christianity and Crisis,* Vol. XX, No. 23 (Jan. 9, 1961), pp. 203–204.

"A Neutral Laos," *Christianity and Crisis,* Vol. XXI, No. 6 (April 17, 1961), pp. 54–55.

"The New Cabinet," *Christianity and Crisis,* Vol. XX, No. 23 (Jan. 9, 1961), pp. 201–202.

"New Pressures from the Right," *Christianity and Crisis,* Vol. XXI, No. 6 (April 17, 1961), pp. 53–54.

"The Nuclear Dilemma—A Discussion," *Christianity and Crisis,* Vol. XXI, No. 19 (Nov. 13, 1961), pp. 200–202. Continued in Vol. XXI, No. 21 (Dec. 11, 1961), pp. 223–224.

"Our Hopes for the New Administration," *Christianity and Crisis,* Vol. XXI, No. 1 (Feb. 6, 1961), pp. 1–3.

"Postscript on Unity," *Christianity and Crisis,* Vol. XX, No. 23 (Jan. 9, 1961), p. 202.

"Religion and the Cold War," *Christianity and Crisis,* Vol. XXI, No. 3 (March 6, 1961), p. 22.

"Social Issues at New Delhi," *Theology and Life,* Vol. IV, No. 3 (Aug., 1961), pp. 219–227.

"Social Issues at New Delhi," *Christianity and Crisis,* Vol. XXI, No. 18 (Oct. 30, 1961), pp. 190–194. Adapted from *Theology and Life,* Vol. IV, No. 3 (Aug., 1961), pp. 219–227.

"The U.N. and Our Many-sided Crisis," *Christianity and Crisis,* Vol. XXI, No. 17 (Oct. 16, 1961), pp. 169–170.

"A Welcome Protest," *Christianity and Crisis,* Vol. XXI, No. 13 (July 24, 1961), pp. 130–131.

1962

"Absolutism in the Supreme Court," *Christianity and Crisis,* Vol. XXII, No. 14 (Aug. 6, 1962), pp. 135–136.

"Another Choice for the Church," *Christianity and Crisis,* Vol. XXII, No. 18 (Oct. 29, 1962), p. 182.

"The Case of Professor Hick," *Christianity and Crisis,* Vol. XXII, No. 10 (June 11, 1962), p. 99.

"Christian Ethics and Foreign Policy," *Catholic Mind,* Vol. LX, No. 1161 (March, 1962), pp. 13–25.

"Christian Ethics and Political Decision: How Relevant Are Universal Principles to Concrete Situations?" *Worldview,* Vol. V, No. 2 (Feb., 1962), pp. 3–7.

"Christian Ethics and Political Ethics (with Emphasis on Foreign Policy)," *The Alumni Bulletin,* Bangor Theological Seminary, Vol. XXXVII, No. 2 (April, 1962), pp. 1–8.

"Christian Realism," *Christianity and Crisis,* Vol. XXII, No. 6 (April 16, 1962), pp. 51–52.

"The Churches Counterattack," *Christianity and Crisis,* Vol. XXII, No. 5 (April 2, 1962), pp. 43–44.

"Cuba and the Monroe Doctrine," *Christianity and Crisis,* Vol. XXII, No. 17 (Oct 15, 1962), pp. 173–174.

"Cuban Reprieve," *Christianity and Crisis,* Vol. XXII, No. 19 (Nov. 12, 1962), p. 194.

"The Debate on Education and Religion," *Christianity and Crisis,* Vol. XXII, No. 9 (May 28, 1962), p. 79.

"The Debate on the Nuclear Dilemma," *Theology Today,* Vol. XVIII, No. 4 (Jan., 1962), pp. 412–421.

"Ethics and Tactics in a Crisis," *Christianity and Crisis,* Vol. XXII, No. 21 (Dec. 10, 1962), pp. 222–223.

"Ethics, the Bomb and Herman Kahn," *The Christian Century,* Vol. LXXIX, No. 13 (March 28, 1962), pp. 383–385.

"Karl Barth Crosses the Atlantic," *Christianity and Crisis,* Vol. XXII, No. 7 (April 30, 1962), pp. 61–62.

"A Look at New Delhi," *Christianity and Crisis,* Vol. XXI, No. 23 (Jan. 8, 1962), pp. 233–235.

"New Decisions on Nuclear Testing," *Christianity and Crisis,* Vol. XXII, No. 15 (Sept. 17, 1962), pp. 145–146.

"New Delhi Faces Three Social Issues," *Christianity and Crisis,* Vol. XXI, No. 24 (Jan. 22, 1962), pp. 249–251.

"The Nuclear Test Debate," *Christianity and Crisis,* Vol. XXII, No. 3 (March 5, 1962), pp. 21–22.

"Nuclear Weapons and Moral Urgencies," *The Intercollegian,* Vol. LXXX, No. 3 (Dec., 1962), pp. 15–17; Vol. LXXX, No. 4 (Jan.–Feb., 1963), pp. 16–17, 23; Vol. LXXX, No. 5 (March, 1963), pp. 12–15.

"A Prayer for These Days," *Social Action,* Vol. XXVIII, No. 6 (Feb., 1962), p. 31.

"The President's Decision on Nuclear Testing," *Christianity and*

Crisis, Vol. XXII, No. 5 (April 2, 1962), pp. 41–42.

"Report from New Delhi," *Union Seminary Quarterly Review,* Vol. XVII, No. 2 (Jan., 1962), pp. 129–136.

"The Significance of the U.N.," *Christianity and Crisis,* Vol. XXII, No. 7 (April 30, 1962), pp. 63–65.

1963

"Across the Canadian Border," *Christianity and Crisis,* Vol. XXIII, No. 3 (March 4, 1963), pp. 21–22.

"The Case for a Theological Judaism," *Christianity and Crisis,* Vol. XXII, No. 24 (Jan. 21, 1963), p. 250.

"Change and Continuity in the Theological Climate at Union Seminary," *Union Seminary Quarterly Review,* Vol. XVIII, No. 4 (May, 1963), pp. 357–367.

"Changes in the Communist World: What Do They Mean for Us?" *Social Action,* Vol. XXX (Dec., 1963), pp. 14–29.

"Christian Ethics and International Affairs," *Christianity and Crisis,* Vol. XXIII, No. 14 (Aug. 5, 1963), pp. 147–151.

"Church and State—and the Christian College," *Liberal Education,* Vol. XLIX, No. 2 (May, 1963), pp. 251–257. Also as "State Aid and the Church-related College," *Christianity and Crisis,* Vol. XXIII, No. 6 (April 15, 1963), pp. 56–59.

"The Churches and Civil Rights," *Christianity and Crisis,* Vol. XXIII, No. 15 (Sept. 16, 1963), pp. 153–154.

"Concern for Theology" (Protestantism in American Society, II), *Commonweal,* LXXVIII, No. 16 (July 12, 1963), pp. 418–420.

"Cuban Ransom," *Christianity and Crisis,* XXII, No. 24 (Jan. 21, 1963), p. 251.

"Ethics and Military Power in International Relations," *Religious Education,* Vol. LVIII, No. 2 (March–April, 1963), pp. 83–91.

"The Ethics of Poverty," *Social Progress,* Vol. LIV, No. 2 (Nov., 1963), pp. 10–17.

"The Extension of the State's Role in Economic Life—The Conflict of Economic Systems," *Social Action,* Vol. XXIX, No. 7 (March, 1963), pp. 5–17.

"Latin American Policy Questions," *Christianity and Crisis,* Vol. XXIII, No. 5 (April 1, 1963), p. 43.

"Lyndon Johnson: Anxiety Allayed," *Christianity and Crisis,* Vol. XXIII, No. 22 (Dec. 23, 1963), pp. 233–234.

"New Lead in Foreign Policy," *Christianity and Crisis,* Vol. XXIII, No. 12 (July 8, 1963), pp. 123–124.

"Nuclear Weapons and Deterrence," *United Church Herald,* Vol. VI, No. 11 (May 30, 1963), pp. 8–10.

"Pacem in Terris: Two Views," *Christianity and Crisis,* Vol. XXIII, No. 8 (May 13, 1963), pp. 81–82.

"Poverty in America," *Christianity and Crisis,* Vol. XXIII, No. 7 (April 29, 1963), p. 65.

"President Kennedy at Mid-Term," *Christianity and Crisis,* Vol. XXII, No. 23 (January 7, 1963), pp. 237–239.

"A Protestant View of Authority in the Church," *Theology Digest,* Vol. XI, No. 4 (Winter, 1963), pp. 209–219.

"The Republicans' Problem," *Christianity and Crisis,* Vol. XXIII, No. 14 (Aug. 5, 1963), pp. 141–142.

"State Aid and the Church-related College," *Christianity and Crisis,* Vol. XXIII, No. 6 (April 15, 1963), pp. 56–59.

"Toward a Fresh Discussion of Sex Ethics," *Christianity and Crisis,* Vol. XXIII, No. 17 (Oct. 14, 1963), p. 173.

1964

"Churchmanship and Controversy," *Christianity and Crisis,* Vol. XXIV, No. 22 (Dec. 28, 1964), pp. 258–259.

"The Council and the Jews," *Christianity and Crisis,* Vol. XXIV, No. 12 (July 6, 1964), pp. 134–135.

"The Danger of Secularization," *Christianity and Crisis,* Vol. XXIV, No. 10 (June 8, 1964), pp. 110–111.

"The Goldwater Nomination," *Christianity and Crisis,* Vol. XXIV, No. 14 (Aug. 3, 1964), pp. 157–158.

"Goldwater's Victory," *Christianity and Crisis,* Vol. XXIV, No. 11 (June 22, 1964), p. 122.

"The Inaugural Address," *Union Seminary Quarterly Review,* Vol. XIX, No. 4, Pt. ii (May, 1964), pp. 397–408.

"The Johnson–Humphrey Team," *Christianity and Crisis,* Vol. XXIV, No. 17 (Oct. 19, 1964), pp. 193–194.

"Liberalization vs. Liberation," *Christianity and Crisis,* Vol. XXIII, No. 23 (Jan. 6, 1964), pp. 245–246.

"Love and the Law," *Christianity and Crisis,* Vol. XXIV, No. 3 (March 2, 1964), pp. 22–23.

"The Place of Theology in Ecumenical Discussion of Social Ethics," *Bulletin,* Division of Studies, World Council of Churches, Vol. X, No. 1 (Spring, 1964), pp. 9–12.

"The Problem of Violence," *Christianity and Crisis,* Vol. XXIV, No. 11 (June 22, 1964), pp. 122–123.

"Questions About Vietnam," *Christianity and Crisis,* Vol. XXIV, No. 13 (July 20, 1964), pp. 141–142.

"Questions on the Jenkins Case," *Christianity and Crisis,* Vol. XXIV, No. 19 (Nov. 16, 1964), p. 223.

"The Reformation of the Church," *Union Seminary Quarterly Review,* Vol. XIX, No. 2 (Jan., 1964), pp. 99–105.

"Rejection and Election," *Christianity and Crisis,* Vol. XXIV, No. 19 (Nov. 16, 1964), p. 221.

"Senator Fulbright Speaks Out," *Christianity and Crisis,* Vol. XXIV, No. 6 (April 13, 1964), pp. 57–58.

"Theologian of Our Time . . . : Reinhold Niebuhr," *The Expository Times,* Vol. LXXV, No. 8 (May, 1964), pp. 237–240.

1965

"Beyond Frozen Positions in the Cold War," *Christianity and Crisis,* Vol. XXIV, No. 23 (Jan. 11, 1965), pp. 269–270.

"Changes in the Communist World," *Concern,* Vol. VII, No. 15 (Sept. 1, 1965), pp. 4–7.

"The Church and Power Conflicts," *Christianity and Crisis,* Vol. XXV, No. 4 (March 22, 1965), pp. 47–51.

"Education for Continual Reformation," *The Garrett Tower,* Vol. XLI, No. 1 (Dec., 1965), pp. 11–16.

"Have Negotiations Lost Their High Priority?" *Christianity and Crisis,* Vol. XXV, No. 20 (Nov. 29, 1965), pp. 249–250.

"The Indo-Pakistani War," *Christianity and Crisis,* Vol. XXV, No. 16 (Oct. 4, 1965), pp. 197–198.

"It Cannot Last Long," *The Union Seminary Tower,* Vol. XII, No. 2 (Fall, 1965), p. 2.

"It Cannot Last Long," *The Presbyterian Outlook,* Vol. CXLVII, No. 43 (Nov. 29, 1965), pp. 6–7. Same as preceding article, but in shortened form.

"The New Stage of the War," *Christianity and Crisis,* Vol. XXV, No. 15 (Sept. 20, 1965), pp. 182–183.

"Pope Paul's Visit," *Christianity and Crisis,* Vol. XXV, No. 18 (Nov. 1, 1965), pp. 221–222.

"A Protestant Views Religious Liberty," *The Catholic World,* Vol. CCI, No. 1206 (Sept., 1965), pp. 362–368. Also *American Lutheran,* Vol. XLVIII, No. 9 (Sept., 1965), pp. 10–13, 24.

"Publish or Perish," *Christianity and Crisis,* Vol. XXV, No. 5 (April 5, 1965), p. 63.

"Some Old Records," *Christianity and Crisis,* Vol. XXV, No. 17

(Oct. 18, 1965), pp. 210–211.

"The United States and China," *Christianity and Crisis*, Vol. XXV, No. 6 (April 19, 1965), pp. 74, 76.

"Where Are We Headed in Vietnam?" *Christianity and Crisis*, Vol. XXV, No. 3 (March 8, 1965), pp. 29–30. Also *British Weekly*, Vol. CXLIX, No. 4080 (April 8, 1965), p. 8.

1966

"Ambassador Goldberg's Speech," *Christianity and Crisis*, Vol. XXVI, No. 17 (Oct. 17, 1966), pp. 222–223.

"Changes in the Communist World," *Wind and Chaff*, Vol. III, No. 3 (March, 1966), pp. 6–7. Also *Concern*, Vol. VII, No. 15 (Sept. 1, 1965), pp. 4–7.

"China: 'Containment but Not Isolation,' " *Christianity and Crisis*, Vol. XXVI, No. 6 (April 18, 1966), pp. 69–70.

"Christian Realism and Vietnam," *Christian Advocate*, Vol. XI, No. 6 (March 24, 1966), pp. 7–8. (See also three following citations for additional appearances of the same article.)

"Christian Realism in Vietnam," *America*, Vol. CXIV, No. 18 (April 30, 1966), pp. 616–617.

"Christian Realism and Vietnam," *Messenger*, Vol. CXV, No. 11 (May 26, 1966), pp. 6–8.

"Christian Realism and Vietnam," *Social Progress*, Vol. LVI, No. 5 (May–June, 1966), pp. 32–36.

"The Church and the Secular," *The Princeton Seminary Bulletin*, Vol. LX, No. 1 (Oct., 1966), pp. 4–10.

"The Church and the Secular," *Christianity and Crisis*, Vol. XXVI, No. 22 (Dec. 26, 1966), pp. 294–297. Same article as the preceding one.

"The Church in a Revolutionary Age," *Social Action*, Vol. XXXII, Nos. 5–6 (Jan.–Feb., 1966), pp. 16–20. (Note that this is a joint issue of *Social Action*, with *Social Progress*, Vol. LVI, No. 3 [Jan.–Feb., 1966], pp. 16–20.)

"A Critical Look at Pacifism," *The United Church Observer*, Vol. IX, No. 16 (Oct., 1966), pp. 15–19.

"From Supporter of War in 1941 to Critic in 1966," *Christianity and Crisis*, Vol. XXVI, No. 2 (Feb. 21, 1966), pp. 13–14.

"The Geneva Conference 1966," *Christianity and Crisis*, Vol. XXVI, No. 12 (July 11, 1966), pp. 153–154.

"In Defense of God," *Look*, Vol. XXX, No. 8 (April 19, 1966), pp. 69–70, 72, 75–76.

"The Issue of Peace; The Voice of Religion," *Worldview*, Vol. IX, No. 4 (April, 1966), pp. 4–9.

"It Is Difficult to Be an American," *Christianity and Crisis*, Vol. XXVI, No. 13 (July 25, 1966), pp. 165–166.

"Labor's Anti-Communism," *Christianity and Crisis*, Vol. XXVI, No. 12 (July 11, 1966), p. 155.

"New Look at an Old Subject: Pacifism," *Presbyterian Survey*, Vol. LVI, No. 10 (Oct., 1966), pp. 10–13.

"On Vatican II" (guest editorial), *Social Action*, Vol. XXXII, No. 9 (May, 1966), pp. 3–5.

"A Protestant View of Religious Liberty and Relative Church–State Issues," *The Minister's Quarterly*, Vol. XXII, No. 2 (Summer, 1966), pp. 1–7.

"The State of the Union Message," *Christianity and Crisis*, Vol. XXVI, No. 1 (Feb. 7, 1966), pp. 1–2.

"U Thant and Vietnam," *Christianity and Crisis*, Vol. XXVI, No. 22 (Dec. 26, 1966), pp. 289–290.

"A Wise Choice," *Christianity and Crisis*, Vol. XXVI, No. 3 (March 7, 1966), pp. 34–35.

1967

"The Abortion Debate," *Christianity and Crisis*, Vol. XXVII, No. 4 (March 20, 1967), pp. 47–48.

"Capitalism and Ethics," *Catholic Mind*, Vol. LXV, No. 1213 (May, 1967), pp. 42–52.

"Christians Look at Revolution," *The Christian Century*, Vol. LXXXIV, No. 5 (Feb. 1, 1967), pp. 137–138.

"Cold War and Beyond," *Social Action*, Vol. XXXIII, No. 7 (March, 1967), pp. 41–44.

"Critique of Paul Ramsey," *Christianity and Crisis*, Vol. XXVII, No. 18 (Oct. 30, 1967), pp. 247–250.

"Discussion: The Seminary in Ten Years," *Union Seminary Quarterly Review*, Vol. XXII, No. 4 (May, 1967), pp. 329–333.

"Further Thoughts on the Middle East," *Christianity and Crisis*, Vol. XXVII, No. 11 (June 26, 1967), p. 142.

"John Courtney Murray, S.J.," *Christianity and Crisis*, Vol. XXVII, No. 15 (Sept. 18, 1967), pp. 198–199.

"McCarthy Candidacy," *Christianity and Crisis*, Vol. XXVII, No. 21 (Dec. 11, 1967), pp. 286–287.

"Message to Young Ministers," *Pulpit Digest*, Vol. XLVIII, No. 349 (Nov., 1967), pp. 9–12.

"Our Choice in Vietnam," *Christianity and Crisis,* Vol. XXVII, No. 3 (March 6, 1967), pp. 32–33.

"Pacifism: A New Look at an Old Subject," *Leader,* Vol. X, No. 4 (April, 1967), pp. 17–20. Reprinted from *Presbyterian Survey,* Vol. LVI, No. 10 (Oct., 1966), pp. 10–13.

"The Place of Civil Disobedience," *Christianity and Crisis,* Vol. XXVII, No. 2 (Dec. 25, 1967), pp. 299–302.

"Private Wealth and Public Poverty," *Social Service Outlook,* Vol. II, No. 3 (March, 1967), p. 3.

"The Protestant Ethic and Capitalism," *Christianity and Crisis,* Vol. XXVII, No. 5 (April 3, 1967), pp. 64–68.

"Response to Rabbi Brickner," *Christianity and Crisis,* Vol. XXVII, No. 15 (Sept. 18, 1967), pp. 204–205.

"Theological Education and Social Revolution," *Theological Education,* Vol. III, No. 2 (Winter, 1967), pp. 283–290.

"Three for, Two on the Edge: Not Good Enough," *Reflection,* Vol. LXIV, No. 2 (Jan., 1967), pp. 6–7.

"Vietnam's 'Cussers and Doubters,'" *Christianity and Crisis,* Vol. XXVII, No. 14 (Aug. 7, 1967), pp. 182–184.

"What Is Theological Education?" *United Church Herald,* Vol. X, No. 4 (April, 1967), pp. 6M–8M.

"What We Should Do Together," *Religious Education,* Vol. LXII, No. 2 (March–April, 1967), pp. 127–133.

"Why Care About World Affairs?" *International Journal of Religious Education,* Vol. XLIII, No. 6 (Feb., 1967), pp. 4–5, 48.

1968

"The Boston Four," *Christianity and Crisis,* Vol. XXVIII, No. 12 (July 8, 1968), pp. 149–150.

"Changes in the Communist World," *Face to Face,* Vol. I, No. 3 (Nov., 1968), pp. 1–4.

"The Columbia Revolution," *Christianity and Crisis,* Vol. XXVIII, No. 11 (June 24, 1968), pp. 138–139.

"The Contribution of Reinhold Niebuhr," *Union Seminary Quarterly Review,* Vol. XXIV, No. 1 (Fall, 1968), pp. 3–16.

"The Czech Invasion," *Christianity and Crisis,* Vol. XXVIII, No. 15 (Sept. 16, 1968), pp. 194–195.

"The Disastrous Encyclical," *Christianity and Crisis,* Vol. XXVIII, No. 16 (Sept. 30, 1968), pp. 214–215.

"The End of the Bombing," *Christianity and Crisis,* Vol. XXVIII, No. 20 (Nov. 25, 1968), pp. 278–279.

"An Immense Event," *Christianity and Crisis*, Vol. XXVIII, No. 15 (Sept. 16, 1968), pp. 207–208.

"An Improbable Theological Conference," *Christianity and Crisis*, Vol. XXVIII, No. 7 (April 29, 1968), pp. 93–95.

"In the Name of America," *Christianity and Crisis*, Vol. XXVIII, No. 3 (March 4, 1968), pp. 27–28.

"The Kerner Report," *Christianity and Crisis*, Vol. XXVIII, No. 5 (April 1, 1968), pp. 54–55.

"Martin Luther King, Jr., 1929–1968" (with John David Maguire), *Christianity and Crisis*, Vol. XXVIII, No. 6 (April 15, 1968), pp. 69–70.

"The President's Surprise," *Christianity and Crisis*, Vol. XXVIII, No. 6 (April 15, 1968), pp. 70–71.

"Ray Gibbons," *Social Action*, Vol. XXXV, No. 4 (Dec., 1968), pp. 6–8.

"Robert F. Kennedy, 1925–1968," *Christianity and Crisis*, Vol. XXVIII, No. 11 (June 24, 1968), p. 137.

"Two Russian Voices," *Christianity and Crisis*, Vol. XXVIII, No. 18 (Oct. 28, 1968), pp. 245–246.

1969

"The Administrator's Dilemma," *Christianity and Crisis*, Vol. XXIX, No. 9 (May 26, 1969), pp. 143–144.

"End the War Now," *Christianity and Crisis*, Vol. XXIX, No. 18 (Oct. 27, 1969), pp. 261, 263.

"A Missing Dimension," *Christianity and Crisis*, Vol. XXIX, No. 16 (Sept. 29, 1969), pp. 241–242.

"Norman Thomas, 1884–1968," *Christianity and Crisis*, Vol. XXVIII, No. 24 (Jan. 20, 1969), pp. 338–339.

"Partnership in Education. . . . Seminary," *Affirmation*, Vol. I, No. 4 (May, 1969), pp. 17–25.

"The Period of Crossed Fingers," *Christianity and Crisis*, Vol. XXIX, No. 3 (March 3, 1969), pp. 33–34.

"The Politics of Dissent," *Social Action*, Vol. XXXV, No. 5 (Jan., 1969), pp. 5–15.

"Priorities in Theological Education," *Christianity and Crisis*, Vol. XXIX, No. 6 (April 14, 1969), pp. 87–90.

"The Senate Revolt on the ABM," *Christianity and Crisis*, Vol. XXIX, No. 14 (Aug. 14, 1969), pp. 209–210.

"Situation Ethics," *City of God; a Journal of Theology and Urban Life*, Vol. II, No. 1 (Aug., 1969), pp. 2–5.